The Architect in Practice

Seventh Edition

David Chappell
BA (Hons Arch), MA, PhD, ARIBA
and
Christopher J. Willis
FRICS, FCIArb

OXFORD

BLACKWELL SCIENTIFIC PUBLICATIONS

LONDON EDINBURGH BOSTON

MELBOURNE PARIS BERLIN VIENNA

Copyright © David Chappell &
Christopher J. Willis 1992

Blackwell Scientific Publications
Editorial Offices:
Osney Mead, Oxford OX2 0EL
25 John Street, London WC1N 2BL
23 Ainslie Place, Edinburgh EH3 6AJ
3 Cambridge Center, Cambridge,
Massachusetts 02142, USA
54 University Street, Carlton
Victoria 3053, Australia

Other Editorial Offices:
Librairie Arnette SA
2, rue Casimir-Delavigne
75006 Paris
France

Blackwell Wissenschafts-Verlag
Meinekestrasse 4
D-1000 Berlin 15
Germany

Blackwell MZV
Feldgasse 13
A-1238 Wien
Austria

First edition published by Crosby Lockwood
& Son Ltd 1952
Second Edition 1956
Third Edition 1964
Fourth Edition 1970
Fifth Edition published by Crosby Lockwood
Staples 1974
Sixth Edition published by
Granada Publishing Ltd 1985
Reprinted by Collins Professional and
Technical Books 1985
Seventh Edition published by
Blackwell Scientific Publications 1992

Set by DP Photosetting, Aylesbury, Bucks
Printed and bound in Great Britain by
Hartnolls Ltd, Bodmin, Cornwall

DISTRIBUTORS

Marston Book Services Ltd
PO Box 87
Oxford OX2 0DT
(Orders: Tel: 0865 791155
Fax: 0865 791927
Telex: 837515)

USA
Blackwell Scientific Publications, Inc.
3 Cambridge Center
Cambridge, MA 02142
(Orders: Tel: 800 759-6102
617 225-0401)

Canada
Oxford University Press
70 Wynford Drive
Don Mills
Ontario M3C 1J9
(Orders: Tel: 416 441-2941)

Australia
Blackwell Scientific Publications
(Australia) Pty Ltd
54 University Street
Carlton, Victoria 3053
(Orders: Tel: 03 347-0300)

British Library
Cataloguing in Publication Data

A catalogue record for this book
is available from the British Library.

ISBN 0-632-02267-1

Library of Congress
Cataloging in Publication Data

Chappell, David.
The architect in practice/David Chappell
and Christopher J. Willis. — 7th ed.
p.   cm.
Updated ed. of: The architect in
practice/Arthur J. WIllis and W.N.B.
George. 5th ed. 1974.
Includes index.
ISBN 0-632-02267-1
1. Architectural practice—United States.
I. Willis, Christopher James.   II. Willis,
Arthur James. Architect in practice.
III. Title.
NA1996.C47   1992
720'.68—dc20
92-714
CIP

The Inspiration

From a pseudonymous letter of a quantity surveyor to
the *Builder*, 9 March 1951

'I have a great admiration for an architect who does his
job well, because he has one of the most difficult jobs in
the world. He must be an artist but at the same time in his
administration of a building contract be a business man,
and in interpreting it even something of a lawyer.'

The Dedication

To Arthur Willis and Bruce George

and

To the architectural profession

in the hope that the book may encourage that co-
operation of which its joint authorship is a symbol

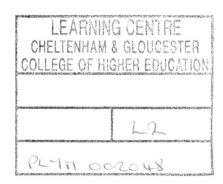

Contents

Preface to the Seventh Edition

The Architect in Practice was first published nearly forty years ago in 1952. It was written by two men, one a quantity surveyor and one an architect, both of whom had a flair for writing and who, after working together for some years, came to the conclusion that a textbook on architectural practice was needed. During those forty years, through six editions, it has remained a leading textbook used in the education of architects world-wide.

When the present authors were invited by the publishers to write this Seventh Edition they were very conscious that they were following in the footsteps of two very distinguished members of their respective professions. They were also very much aware of the changes in practice since the first edition was published shortly after the end of the Second World War at a time when practice picked up the working of the profession little changed from the beginning of the century. Since then there have been many changes reflected in succeeding editions of the book which however continued in the same successful format. The decision that had to be made was whether to continue in the same format or to start again.

After much heart-searching and after taking soundings in the profession and from the schools of architecture throughout the United Kingdom the latter option was chosen. Readers will therefore find the layout to be considerably changed from previous editions. We hope that this will make it more easily accessible to practitioners and students alike. While the format is different the message and philosophy is the same: here is a book which tries to present to the reader some of the elementary duties that architects owe to their clients and contractors alike and to endorse the adage that of the many responsibilities that are borne by the architect, the greatest is the duty of care.

Not only has practice changed; in many ways it has become more complicated. For instance there is now a plethora of forms of building contract to choose from, and it is not possible to write in any detail on such a wide subject: it warrants a textbook on its own. The most helpful thing that we can do is to point the reader to relevant sources for this and other allied subjects.

One of the joys of the original book was that it was so readable. Where else could one find such a riveting account of how to organize a foundation-stone-laying ceremony? Sadly this account has been left out of this edition and readers faced with organizing such a ceremony today must look to past editions. We have however retained in many cases the words of wisdom and the spirit of the original authors which we feel are as relevant and well said today as they ever were.

Finally we hope that our efforts will assist future generations of architects in the way that Arthur Willis and Bruce George assisted our generation.

January 1992   D.M.C.
                                                                C.J.W.

Acknowledgements

We are grateful to Allan Ashworth MSc, ARICS for his agreement to the use in this book of parts of the text of *Practice and Procedure for the Quantity Surveyor*. We are also grateful to the following for particular assistance in commenting on portions of the text as indicated:

    Caroline M. Dalziel LLB, Solicitor for Company Law in Chapter 4

    Steve Drury DipTP, MRTPI for Planning Legislation and Practice in Chapter 8

    Clive A. Marshall FIAS, MCIOB for Building Regulations in Chapter 9

We are also pleased to acknowledge the assistance that we have received from those that responded to our enquiries in the profession and schools of architecture: particularly Peter Allen MA, BAHons, RIBA, ACIArb, FBID of Manchester Polytechnic, John Bennetts DipArch, RIBA, FFAS of Thames Polytechnic, Stanley Cox MBE, RIBA of the Welsh School of Architecture, Eric Hyde MSc, RIBA, FRPS, formerly of Liverpool Polytechnic, Brian McGhee Architect BA (Hons Arch) of Kingston Polytechnic and Roderick Males MA, RIBA formerly of Manchester University.

We are very grateful to the Royal Institute of British Architects and The Royal Institution of Chartered Surveyors for permission to reproduce their standard forms.

List of Abbreviations and Acronyms

AA	Architectural Association
AC	Appeal case
ACA	Association of Consultant Architects
ACAS	Advisory, Conciliation and Arbitration Service
ACE	Association of Consulting Engineers
All ER	*All England Law Reports*
ARCUK	Architects' Registration Council of the United Kingdom
ASI	Architects and Surveyors Institute
BBA	British Board of Agrément
BCIS	Building Cost Information Service
BEC	Building Employers Confederation
BLR	Building Law Reports
BPF	British Property Federation
BRE	Building Research Establishment
BSI	British Standards Institution
BSRIA	Building Services Research and Information Association
CAD	Computer-aided design
CAS	Clients Advisory Service (RIBA)
CAWS	Common Arrangement of Work Sections
CCPI	Co-ordinating Committee for Project Information
CIArb	Chartered Institute of Arbitrators
CIB	Chartered Institute of Building
CILL	*Construction Industry Law Letter*
CIRIA	Construction Industry Research and Information Association
CITB	Construction Industry Training Board
CLD	*Construction Law Digest*
ConLR	*Construction Law Reports*
ConstLJ	*Construction Law Journal*
CPD	Continuing professional development
CPI	Co-ordinated project information
EC	European Community
FCEC	Federation of Civil Engineering Contractors
HMSO	Her Majesty's Stationery Office
IAAS	Incorporated Association of Architects and Surveyors
ICE	Institution of Civil Engineers
IEE	Institution of Electrical Engineers

IFC	Intermediate Form of Contract
ILA	Institute of Landscape Architects
IMechE	Institution of Mechanical Engineers
IStructE	Institution of Structural Engineers
MW	Minor Works Form of Contract
NBS	National Building Specification
NJCBI	National Joint Committee for the Building Industry
NJCC	National Joint Consultative Committee of Architects, Quantity Surveyors and Builders
NSC/A	Standard Form of Nominated Sub-contract Agreement
NSC/C	Conditions
NSC/N	Nomination
NSC/T	Tender
NSC/W	Warranty
PAYE	Pay as you earn
PSA	Property Services Agency
QA	Quality assurance
RIAI	Royal Institute of Architects in Ireland
RIAS	Royal Incorporation of Architects in Scotland
RIBA	Royal Institute of British Architects
RICS	The Royal Institution of Chartered Surveyors
RSUA	Royal Society of Ulster Architects
RTPI	Royal Town Planning Institute
SMM	Standard Method of Measurement for Building Works
WLR	*Weekly Law Reports*

Introduction

Architecture is undoubtedly one of the professions that can be enjoyed. It offers a wealth of interest in a variety of fields which few other professions can match, and provides an emotional satisfaction which only the other arts can stimulate. It exacts a high price for this enjoyment, however, and in order to derive the fullest pleasure from it architects must devote themselves completely to its study and practice. The more proficient they become and the greater mastery they can acquire the more complete will be their enjoyment. In common with other professions architects owe a duty of care to their clients but they have a greater responsibility than most in that the buildings and environments that they create may well have a profound effect on the population at large.

Ability to design and skill in draughtsmanship or in using computer-aided design equipment will not alone make an architect. The purpose of this book is to present to architectural students, and perhaps the less experienced practitioners, some indication of the practice and procedure with which they must be acquainted if they are to follow their profession with success. They must find clients to employ them, they must be able to manage an office and be responsible for a good deal of administrative work in connection with building contracts, and they must know something of finance, law, the general structure of the building industry and the organization and requirements of those authorities who exercise so much control over their day-to-day work. Let the readers therefore leave their drawing board, forget their tee-squares, set squares and scales, move away from their CAD equipment and settle down to their desk or armchair to study an aspect of their work which they may find requires some self-discipline but is nevertheless essential to make them efficient architects.

The architect's work is here looked at mainly from the angle of the private practitioner dealing with the JCT forms of contract, though references are made where appropriate to public service practice and to the Government forms of contract. Architects in private practice are often commissioned to act for public authorities and they must therefore be able to adapt to the differing conditions which this type of work involves.

The chapters have been arranged in the sequence which the progress of a building contract makes natural. Part 1 opens with an introduction to the building industry and is followed by some basic principles of practice, sources of information, legal and administrative matters. Part 2 follows the running of a building project, the chapters being based on the work stages of the RIBA Plan of Work. Part 3 ends the book with what can best be described as management matters, covering finance, insurance, obtaining work and employing staff. Each chapter ends with notes of law cases referred to, some forms and precedents and a selected bibliography.

Part 1

Background to Practice

Chapter 1

The Construction Industry

1.1 *People*

1.1.1 The employer

The employer is also sometimes known as the *building owner*. The building industry team comprises the designers and the constructors both working at the behest of the employer, perhaps the most important member. It is therefore appropriate that this first chapter should open with an introduction to the person responsible for commissioning the design in the first place and ultimately for the construction.

Employers appear in many guises. They are the clients of the professionals; they are the employers under the building contract and they are the ultimate owners of the building until such time as they dispose of it. It is the building owner who in the long run pays the bill and in that respect calls the tune, which is something which must never be forgotten.

Architects must have clients before they can practise. Unlike the painter, the author or the poet, they are not at liberty to choose their own subject. They may of course be their own clients as, for instance, when they design their own houses; but otherwise they are dependent on a commission from somebody else. This applies whether architects are principals or assistants in private practice or are salaried officials in government or local government, in which case their clients will be the council or committee they serve.

Relationships with the client are of prime importance: an architect must not only embark on a process of design (which is a personal thing) but must also attempt to interpret the client's needs and provide an article that is wanted.

An architect acts as the client's agent in spending sums of money, which may be substantial: on the skill and efficiency of the architect may depend the amount of the bill which the client will eventually have to meet. It is essential, therefore, that client and architect should feel complete confidence in each other particularly as the architect has also certain responsibilities towards the contractor. The old adage that a good building requires a good client as well as a good architect is as true today as it ever was.

How then does a client choose the architect? It may be in one of several ways. The client may have approached the Client's Advisory Service of the RIBA and have been provided with a short list of suitable architects, from which a choice can be made. Possibly the client has seen a building or photograph of a building which is liked and finds out the name of the architect. Possibly the architect is recommended by a mutual acquaintance. Perhaps the architect has specialized in designing a particular building type. Finally it may be through success in an open competition for a particular building or project, or it may be by an entry in a directory or by commissioning external public relations consultants (who themselves must not infringe the Code of Professional Conduct) (*see* Chapter 17).

1.1.2 The architect

Architects are the designers of the building project and have the difficult task of translating their client's ideas into an acceptable design and then into working drawings. It should be noted that the profession of architect is, subject to an Act of Parliament,[1] a registered profession. For business purposes no one can call him or herself an architect in the United Kingdom unless they are on the register maintained by the Architects' Registration Council of the United Kingdom (ARCUK). Only those qualified in accordance with these regulations can be admitted to the register.

As the name implies, the architect should be the master-builder – the leader of the building industry team referred to above (the word 'architect' is derived from the Greek root *arch* meaning 'chief' and the word *tekton* meaning 'carpenter or builder'). Architects are qualified to design and administer the erection of buildings, and must possess both theoretical and practical knowledge. Their work is a science as well as an art, for they must produce a structure as well as create form, and must combine aesthetic effect with practical considerations. They must visualize the interior as well as the exterior of the building and must ensure that the accommodation is properly related to the requirements of owners and occupiers, and that the form and construction are appropriate to the function of the building and its setting.

Like playwrights, architects are dependent on other people to interpret their designs, and their involvement during the erection of a building is as important to its ultimate success as are the directions given by the producer and stage manager for a play.

Architects must have a good, practical knowledge of building and allied trades and must have at least a working knowledge of the more specialized aspects of building, such as mechanical and electrical engineering services. Finally they must endeavour to be creative and can never afford to rest on their laurels.

1.1.3 The quantity surveyor

The work and services provided by the quantity surveyor today may be described as the financial management of the project, whether it be on behalf of the building owner or the contractor. The term 'quantity surveyor' does not now reflect the services which are provided, since these have been extended during the past 30 years to cover what might be more appropriately termed *project cost management*.

The work of the quantity surveyor can therefore be summarized briefly as follows (shown diagrammatically in Figure 1.1):

- Preliminary cost advice and approximate estimating.
- Cost planning including investment appraisal, life-cycle costing and value analysis.
- Contractual procurement and tendering procedures.
- Assisting in the preparation of contract documentation.
- Evaluation of tenders received.
- Cash flow forecasting, financial reporting and interim payments.
- Final accounting and involvement in the settlement of contractual disputes.
- Cost advice during use by the client.

Traditionally, certainly during the early part of the century, quantity surveyors were employed as preparers of bills of quantities for building projects. Their role was constrained to a limited but important part of the development process. This role was quickly extended to include the preparation of valuations for interim certificates and the agreement of final accounts with the contractor.

During the 1960s the quantity surveyor's role was enlarged to include design cost planning in an attempt to provide the building owner with some form of value for money and cost-effectiveness (see Chapter 9, section 9.3). In more recent times greater emphasis has

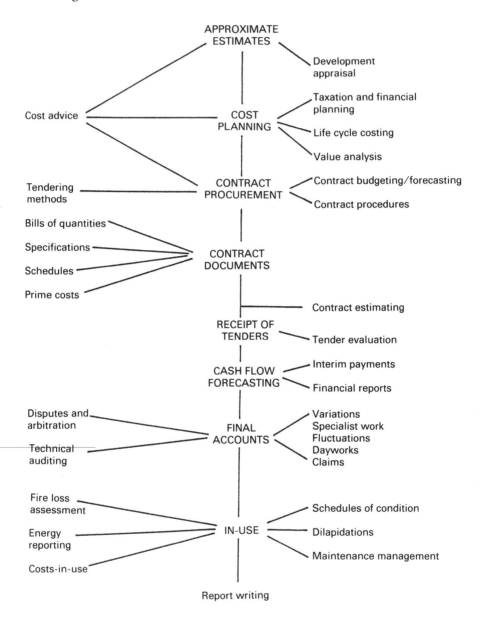

Figure 1.1   The work of the quantity surveyor.

been placed on the need to examine construction costs in terms of their life cycle rather than solely in terms of initial costs.

It is now advantageous for the quantity surveyor to become fully involved at the outset of a project's development. Although lip-service has been paid to this in the past, the designer has often completed this stage of the development process relying only on a very limited input from the quantity surveyor. It is during this stage that the type and size of the project are largely determined and these two factors alone commit a considerable proportion of the total cost. Quantity surveyors can therefore provide a proper and sizeable contribution during the process of strategic planning. They thus can become familiar with the special needs of the building owner and can properly evaluate the options which are under consideration.

1.1.4 Other consultants

The other members of the design team who will be involved can include the following:

- Structural engineers.
- Services engineers.
- Landscape consultants.
- Specialist consultants.

Structural engineers

The structural engineers' function is to advise on structural design from foundations to roof including advice on ground conditions on projects where such services are required. The structural stability of the building will be their responsibility which will include advice, specification, design and supervision of the works in progress. They should be an early appointment as their advice will greatly influence the outcome of the ultimate design which in many cases cannot be furthered without the basic structural information being available. Some structural engineers will offer drainage and other infrastructure advice and designs or this may be provided by an engineer specializing solely in this type of work.

Services engineers

Services both mechanical and electrical today form a major part of many projects. Services engineers provide advice, specification and schematic or detailed drawings and are often responsible for obtaining tenders from specialist firms. Again they should be an early appointment and should be closely involved in ensuring the proper integration of services into the design. Failure to achieve such integration is a frequent cause of delay and disruption on building sites leading to acrimony, costs and at the worst litigation.

Landscape consultants

With the current emphasis on environmental aspects of building projects it is not unusual for architects specializing in landscape work or specialist consultants to be involved in the design and supervision of what are traditionally known as the external works. Ground formations, planting and arboreal work are the finishing touches which can make or break the visual effect of a new or refurbished building.

Specialist consultants

On certain projects there is a need for other specialist consultants. These can include:

- *Acoustic engineers* where concert halls, theatres and the like are involved.
- *Theatre consultants* for all types of theatre work.
- *Curtain walling engineers* for special cladding work.
- *Interior or furniture designers* where the architect feels that this is outside his or her scope of expertise or where the employer wishes to use a special interior designer.

The list of such specialist consultants is not endless but as the years go by more and more such specialists tend to appear. They all need to be paid and this is something that must always be borne in mind when preparing fee budgets for a building owner who will need to be convinced of the necessity for their employment.

1.1.5 The clerk of works

The clerk of works is normally employed as the employer's inspector on the building site.[2] Clerks of works are responsible for checking and approving that the materials and workmanship conform to the specification outlined in the contract documents. They may be authorized to issue instructions to the contractor but under JCT forms of contract their powers are more limited.

While architects are required to give adequate inspection to ensure that a building is erected in accordance with the provisions of the contract, their terms of appointment rarely require them to make constant inspections. There is, however, often a need for such constant attention: hence the employment of a clerk of works. An architect has to act impartially between the building owner and the contractor, but the clerk of works is only responsible to the building owner. The architect must therefore maintain a delicate balance in dealing with the clerk of works and contractor and, whilst preserving the authority of the clerk of works, the risk of unfair dictation to the contractor must be guarded against.

The clerks of works' duties and limitations should be clearly understood, and it is the responsibility of the architect to see that they are properly instructed. Good clerks of works can be of the greatest assistance to the architect, who should make a point of getting to know them well and gaining their confidence at the earliest stage. They are usually men of considerable practical experience who have graduated from a particular trade (the training of a carpenter and joiner is probably the most common background) and the architect should not hesitate to take their advice on practical matters when the occasion demands.

The primary duty of the clerk of works is, as already mentioned, to ensure that the work is carried out in strict accordance with the drawings and specification. Their authority is therefore limited to ensuring that the standard required under the terms of the contract is maintained and they can condemn any work or materials which fall short of this standard. The clerk of works must be on site throughout the hours that the contractor's operatives are there and, further, must endeavour to be everywhere at once! It is a most difficult job to do well, and requires both tact and knowledge. The architect should recognize this and do all that is possible to help.

The clerk of works can also be of considerable assistance by keeping, for instance, a record of any work that is likely to be covered up so that the measuring can be correct. This applies particularly to foundations and other items subject to re-measurement or required for 'as built' record purposes.

Besides these duties there are a variety of other records which the clerk of works should keep. Daywork sheets will be submitted when works may need to be valued on a daywork basis and it will be necessary to certify that the time and materials are correct. Records of operatives on site and what they are doing, visitors, weather records and the like can prove invaluable later on. Altogether a most important person.

1.1.6 The contractor

The building contractor, the second party to the building contract with the employer, is the constructor, whose operations are at the hub of the complex building industry. Contracting firms vary greatly in their size and capabilities. Many are small firms whose work may vary from one or two houses and some jobbing work to individual contracts of perhaps £250 000 in value. However, the bulk in value of building work is in the hands of a comparatively small number of larger firms, often with several branches, and many carrying out work in continental Europe and in other more distant parts of the world. Most firms are limited companies, some are public companies, but some of the very small contractors still operate as partnerships (see also Chapter 4).

Traditionally the contractor was chosen by competitive tender having priced either a specification and drawings or a bill of quantities. Alternatively work was negotiated with a chosen contractor. Today the procurement processes and the contractual arrangements which are entered into are many and varied. The role of architects when working for a contractor is described in Chapter 3 and their relationship with the contractor regarding procurement procedures, programming and construction is covered in Chapters 10, 11 and 12.

1.1.7 Sub-contractors

Sub-contractors are, as their name suggests, firms to whom work is sub-let. When work is sub-let it is delegated; however the contractor is still liable to the employer for any defects in such work. It will be sub-let for one of two reasons. It may be the specific wish of the architect that a certain parcel of work be carried out by a particular firm, in which case they will be 'nominated' or, depending on the contract, sometimes 'named'. Alternatively it will be at the wish of the contractor that work shall be sub-let in which case the sub-contractor will be known as a 'domestic' sub-contractor. These three types of sub-contractor can be defined as follows.

Nominated

At the choice of the architect who, with the employer's agreement, will seek the tenders, evaluate, decide and instruct the main contractor to enter into a sub-contract. The JCT forms of contract give both the main and sub-contractor rights regarding such matters as extensions of time, loss and expense payments, rights to direct payment in the event of default by the main contractor and renomination if there is default on the part of the sub-contractor.

Named

The choice of the contractor from a list of not less than three names provided by the architect whose duties and responsibilities do not extend beyond naming (JCT 80 clause 19.3) and the naming procedures contained in IFC 84 (clause 3.3.1). The sub-contractor then becomes 'domestic' (see below) and neither main nor sub-contractor enjoys any of the contractual rights of nomination under the main form of contract.

Domestic

At the sole choice of the main contractor who will enter into a direct sub-contract unrelated to the main contract. The architect's powers are limited to approving or otherwise the names put forward by the main contractor.

1.2 Organizations

1.2.1 Professional

Members of the building team all have their professional organizations which act as learned societies with library and research facilities for members and in some cases provide recognized educational qualifications as well. In the interests of the general public they are responsible for overseeing the conduct of members and practice generally. They also provide a central source for social activities and for the general dissemination of information by way of journals, lectures etc. The major such bodies are:

- *Architects*
  Royal Institute of British Architects (RIBA)
  Royal Incorporation of Architects in Scotland (RIAS)
  Royal Society of Ulster Architects (RSUA)
  Royal Institute of Architects in Ireland (RIAI)
  Association of Consultant Architects (ACA)
  Incorporated Association of Architects and Surveyors (IAAS)

- *Clerks of works*
  Institute of Clerks of Works of Great Britain Incorporated

- *Engineers*
  Institution of Civil Engineers (ICE)
  Institution of Electrical Engineers (IEE)
  Institution of Mechanical Engineers (IMechE)
  Institution of Structural Engineers (IStructE)

- *Landscape*
  Institute of Landscape Architects (ILA)

- *Planners*
  Royal Town Planning Institute (RTPI)

- *Surveyors*
  Royal Institution of Chartered Surveyors (RICS)
  Architects and Surveyors Institute (ASI).

1.2.2 Contractors

In the same way members of the contracting side of the industry have their organizations who look after their members in a similar way and represent their interests in national and regional negotiations on such matters as wages, working rules and contract conditions. The two major bodies in this respect are:

- *Building contractors*
  Building Employers Confederation (BEC)
- *Civil engineering contractors*
  Federation of Civil Engineering Contractors (FCEC)

1.2.3 Manufacturers' trade associations

There are a number of associations representing manufacturers from whom useful information and advice can be obtained as to the use of material which their members manufacture or use. Amongst these may be mentioned:

- Aluminium Window Association
- Brick Development Association
- British Constructional Steelwork Association Ltd
- British Precast Concrete Foundation Ltd
- British Woodworking Federation

- British Cement Association
- Clay Pipe Development Association Ltd
- Copper Development Association
- Lead Development Association
- Mastic Asphalt Council and Employers' Federation
- Sand and Gravel Association
- Timber Research and Development Association
- Zinc Development Association.

In fact, nearly all manufacturers have some sort of publicity organization for their particular trade.[3]

1.2.4 General organizations

Other organizations exist which further the work of the industry in many ways. A selection of the more important of these are described below.

British Board of Agrément

This is an official body for the assessment of new building products for which certificates are issued. Since its formation the scope has widened to include traditional construction products which have an export potential. The Board works in conjunction with the European Organization for Technical Approvals.

British Standards Institution

This institution has a scope much wider than that of the building industry alone. It is the recognized authority in the UK for the preparation of national standards covering specifications for dimensions, preferred sizes, quality, performance, methods of testing, terms, definitions and symbols, and codes of practice. All publications are listed in the *British Standards Yearbook* which is available from the BSI sales office in London and Milton Keynes. A large number of standards apply to the building industry. Committees responsible for framing the standards have representatives of contractors, architects, engineers and surveyors as well as experts in the manufacture of the material concerned. British Standards are also widely adopted in the Commonwealth countries. Currently BSI are working with the European Committee for Standardization who will in due course be drafting European Standards. British Standards as we know them may well change. For the foreseeable future however British Standards will continue to be applicable.

Building Centre

This organization, which is located at 26 Store Street, London WC1A 7BT, is backed and supported by manufacturers of all types of building product. It maintains a permanent exhibition where samples of a wide variety of materials can be seen. It is an agency from which names and addresses and often leaflets of manufacturers can be obtained, and is particularly useful when only the branded name of a material is known. For those who work some distance from London enquiries can be made by telephone. Similar centres exist in a number of other major cities of the UK.

Building Cost Information Service

Although the BCIS has been largely formulated for quantity surveyors, it is now open to anyone of any discipline who is willing and able to contribute information in accordance with the reciprocal basis of the service. It also distributes up-to-date information on construction economics. The main sections deal with cost analyses, cost indices and trends and market conditions.

Building Research Establishment

The BRE's main establishment is at Garston near Watford and is a branch within the Department of the Environment. It undertakes research on building materials and is prepared to advise on difficulties within its sphere of work. A large proportion of its annual budget is spent on research, with the remainder on information activities. It often prepares the results of research in publications, which are available through HMSO. The BRE also includes the Forest Products Research Station and the Fire Research Station at Borehamwood. It is engaged in research across a wide spectrum of activities associated with building. In addition it undertakes work for the British Board of Agrément.

Construction Industry Research and Information Association

CIRIA also carries out research activities, but has no laboratories of its own. It acts as a focal point for the approval of projects and provision of funds. For this purpose it obtains government grants, but it also relies upon research contracts from industry. Thus it is able to sponsor projects in universities, polytechnics, industrial research centres and in government departments themselves.

Construction Industry Training Board

The CITB was established under the Industrial Training Act in July 1964. This Act is intended to secure an improvement in the quality and efficiency of industrial training, and to make sure that an adequate supply of people are properly trained for all levels of operation within the industry. The CITB is funded by raising a levy on contracting firms based on the number of employees. In return it is able to offer grants to employers who undertake their courses, and co-operates with Colleges of Technology in providing the courses necessary for such training. A wide range of courses is also offered at their training centres at Birmingham, Erith, Glasgow and Bircham Newton in Norfolk.

Joint Contracts Tribunal

This organization is composed of representatives of employers, architects, surveyors, contractors and sub-contractors. The constituent bodies are as follows:

- Royal Institute of British Architects
- Building Employers' Confederation
- Royal Institution of Chartered Surveyors
- Association of County Councils
- Association of Metropolitan Authorities
- Association of District Councils
- Confederation of Associations of Specialist Engineering Contractors
- Federation of Associations of Specialists and Sub-contractors
- Association of Consulting Engineers
- Scottish Building Contracts Committee
- British Property Federation

It is responsible for drafting the various JCT Forms of Building Contract, for their periodic revision and the issue of practice notes for clarification purposes. Its work also includes considering questions raised by and through the representative members on the forms of contract.

National Council of Building Material Producers

This council was constituted to represent the collective interests of its members to government, the Commission of the European Communities, the EDCs, CBI, BSI and other trade and professional organizations. It also seeks to promote increased collaboration between building material producers. It nominates representatives on government and other committees, and seeks to promote both home and overseas trade. The Council is also able to provide advice on legislation, technical matters, contracts and commercial matters appropriate to its interests. It provides an annual report and weekly information in addition to other technical literature.

National Joint Consultative Committee

The NJCC has five constituent members: RIBA, RICS, BEC, ACE and the National Group of Sub-contractors. It provides a medium whereby matters of national importance in which the constituent groups are interested may be discussed, with appropriate action taken.

National Joint Council for the Building Industry

The NJCBI is the body which determines the wages and conditions for the industry on a national basis. It also arranges negotiations between employers and operatives for the settlement of disputes. It operates a national joint training scheme and works on a regional basis. There are regional joint committees and area joint committees as connecting links between the Council and individual members. The Council has done much to stabilize and improve working conditions in the industry.

References

(1) Architects Registration Acts 1931–1969.
(2) *Handbook for Clerk of Works*, Greater London Council, 3rd edn 1983.
(3) *Directory of Official Architecture and Planning*, 1992, Longman.

Chapter 2

Basics

2.1 Architectural education and training

Many years ago, the traditional way of becoming an architect was for a young person to be articled to a practising architect for a number of years. It was customary to pay the architect for the privilege and the architect would give the pupil a small allowance each week. The pupil had to pass the external examinations of the Royal Insitute of British Architects. That system ended early in the 1960s and full-time education became the norm. The *Architects Registration Council of the United Kingdom* (ARCUK) has a statutory responsibility in the setting of standards and recognition of architectural examinations. The checking of standards in schools of architecture is undertaken by visiting boards which are composed of members of the RIBA and ARCUK.

There are currently 36 schools of architecture in the UK whose examinations are recognized by the RIBA as giving exemption from the RIBA's own examinations.[1] The full-time course begins with three years at a recognized school leading to a first degree in architecture which may be BArch or BA(HonsArch) depending upon the school. This gives exemption from the RIBA Part 1 examination, after which the student may have a year's practical training in specific areas of architectural practice which is recorded. With the co-operation of practices, the schools operate a system of checks by members of staff to ensure as far as possible that the student is getting appropriate experience.

There usually follow a further two years of full-time education in a school of architecture, but not necessarily the same school in which the student passed the initial three years. It is always open to a student to apply to another school to complete the course and this can often be beneficial both for the school and for the student. Demand for places at all levels and in all schools is very high. Some students decide after securing their first degrees to look for careers outside the practice of architecture. Interior design, planning and graphics are popular.

At the end of the second period of full-time education successful students will usually be awarded a second degree or a diploma, depending upon the establishment. This will give exemption from the RIBA Part 2 examination. A minimum of one years' practical training is required before the student can present him or herself for the examination in professional practice or the RIBA Part 3 examination, after which the student is entitled to become registered (see 2.4 below) on completing some formalities.[2]

To enter upon an architecture course, a student must have at least three GCSE passes and two A-level passes among which must be included English Language and Mathematics or a similar mathematics-based subject. Students with the bare minimum qualifications are unlikely to be offered a place unless they have other outstanding qualities. BTech diploma or certificate passes and merits are also considered to be acceptable qualifications for entry in most schools.

It has always been possible to qualify as an architect by part-time study at a small number of schools, but only a small proportion of architects qualify by this method. The minimum period is seven years. Students have to have a post in a firm where they can get appropriate guidance and experience and this normally means living near the schools. There have been moves to change this situation and to open up architectural education to those who cannot attend full-time, but who would clearly benefit from contact with a school. The system depends upon individual part-time students having tutors, usually from the schools, to assist them in achieving the necessary standards to pass the external examinations. The whole system is the subject of much debate at the time this book is being written. There are many suggestions, including a four-year full-time course and a return to pupillage.

2.2 *Continuing professional development*

An architect would have to be totally cut off from his fellows not to have come across the concept of continuing professional development (CPD). It is not, of course, confined solely to architects. The other construction professionals such as engineers, surveyors and planners are required to undertake structured courses of study after qualification. Outside the construction industry, doctors and solicitors and others also have an express obligation in this area. Strictly speaking, it can and is argued that CPD is always implied in the obligations of any professional person: in other words, the obligation to keep up to date. CPD is rather more than that and assumes that the professional will not just keep up to date, but will also develop expertise in specific directions.[3]

The RIBA have decided that CPD is to become obligatory for its members on 1 January 1993. It is stated to be 'obligatory' not 'mandatory'. The precise difference is not clear, but there are no sanctions proposed for architects who fail to fulfil the requirements. It seems that the biggest spur will be that architects investigated by the Institute in respect of their competence or concerned in legal proceedings may find their case prejudiced if they have neglected their obligations in this respect. CPD could also be an important factor in quality assurance (QA). A leaflet published by the RIBA to all members in 1991 lists examples of activities which could constitute part of a structured CPD plan:

- Technical and professional conferences, lectures, workshops, seminars and courses.
- Teaching/tutoring/mentoring (for those not in teaching posts).
- Practice (for those in teaching posts).
- Structured home reading: open and distance learning.
- Preparing articles for the technical and professional press.
- Directed studies during educational and sabatical leave.
- Practice and peer review.
- In-house and inter-professional study meetings.
- Practitioner research for publication.
- Recorded on-the-job research.
- Supervised research for further qualification.
- Service on BSI or BBA committees and working groups, on RIBA technical and practice-related committees, and service as an RIBA external examiner and on RIBA visiting boards.

Each architect is expected to have a CPD partner who will monitor progress and suggest further fields of study. This acknowledges that it is difficult for a person to self-monitor effectively. The partner should be chosen with care and should be another architect who has a sound knowledge of the first architect's strengths and weaknesses. It will be tempting for architects to concentrate their CPD activities on those areas which they find of most interest, whereas it is likely that they should be concentrating on just those areas of practice where interest is lacking. For example, most architects are interested in design; that is why they entered the profession in the first place. They will need little encouragement to attend lectures and carry out research in this area. Architects tend to have less interest in the business side of practice or the legal and contractual implications which is perhaps where effort should be concentrated. At least 35 hours must be allocated each year by every member.

2.3 Distance learning

This is one of those terms which is so simple and self-explanatory that people are often misled. It is a term used to differentiate from the kind of learning which takes place geographically in the same place as the tutor, for example in college or university. Correspondence courses are examples of distance learning. Particular emphasis is being put on the concept as part satisfaction of CPD requirements, but there is no substitute for having the tutor alongside the student to explain difficult points as they arise. Thus CPD should be a mixture of distance learning (probably the majority of hours), private study and tutor-centred learning. Two examples of types of distance learning are the video packages produced by the CPD in Construction Group[4] and the Open Learning packages prepared by the RIBA.[5] The RIBA production is in the form of loose-leaf binders, one binder for each topic. Narrative, example, assignments, and suggestions for further reading are a feature.

Learning is a very individual thing. Some persons can only learn if they write or read or discuss with others, some only if they do all those things. Therefore each person will choose the kind of learning which suits him or her best. After qualification, and for some even before qualification, it is a luxury to attend a seminar or a short course. Distance learning packages are an acceptable short-term substitute provided that the student gets the opportunity to take part in face-to-face dialogue with a tutor from time to time.

2.4 Registration and practice in the UK

The Architects (Registration) Act 1931 set up the Architects Registration Council of the United Kingdom (ARCUK) as the body controlling the architectural professional in England, Wales, Scotland and Northern Ireland. The Act was followed by the Architects Registration Acts 1939–1969. Any person wishing to use the title 'architect' for business purposes must be registered with ARCUK. There are only two ways in which a person can become registered:

- By passing an examination which is recognized by ARCUK.

- By a resolution of a constituent body of the Council and recommended for acceptance in accordance with the regulations.

Architects can be removed from the register only in the following instances:

- Conviction of a criminal offence or being found guilty of disgraceful conduct.[6]
- Failure to pay the annual retention fee at the appropriate time.
- Failure to notify ARCUK of a change of address after being requested to do so.

ARCUK has three principal duties:

- To maintain a register of architects and to publish it annually.
- To maintain proper standards of professional conduct.
- To award scholarships to students without means.

An unregistered person who carries on a business with the word 'architect' in the title is liable to a heavy fine together with a continuing daily fine if the offence continues. Strangely, there is no offence if that person carries out all the functions of an architect, but takes some other title such as 'architectural consultant' or 'design consultant'. A person who is a member of the RIBA but not registered may not be styled 'chartered architect' and may not even use the affixes ARIBA or RIBA, because they contain the prohibited word.

The constituent bodies of the Council are (the figures in brackets refer to the representation 1991/1992):

- Royal Institute of British Architects (44).
- Incorporated Association of Architects and Surveyors (1).
- Architects and Surveyors Institute (1).
- Architectural Association (2).
- STAMP section of UCATT (1).
- Council of Provincial Associations (1).
- Unattached Architects (14).
- Royal Society of Ulster Architects (1).
- Secretary of State for Education and Science (1).
- Department of Environment (2).
- Secretary of State for Scotland (1).
- Secretary of State for Northern Ireland (1).
- Royal Institution of Chartered Surveyors (1).
- Institution of Structural Engineers.

- Society of Engineers (1).
- Chartered Institute of Building (1).
- Building Employers Confederation (1).

ARCUK has taken its place as a full member of the Assembly of the Architects Council of Europe.

2.5 *Registration and practice in the EC*

Directive 85/384/EEC covers the registration of architects within the European Community. In the UK, the Architects Registration Acts 1931 and 1938 have been amended to take account of the Directive, and in most other member countries appropriate laws have been enacted or amended, the broad effect of which is to make it possible for architect nationals of member countries to practise in other countries within the Community. Registration under the Directive is confined to persons, not practices. With some exceptions it is also confined to nationals of member countries so that, for example, an Indian architect may be registered in the UK having satisfied the requirements but may not seek to practise in the EC on that basis.

Relatively few architects take advantage of the opportunity to practise in other member countries. For example, in the UK the numbers of persons with EC qualifications registering in 1990 was 68, a fall on the totals for the previous two years (116 in 1988, 74 in 1989.[7] The Architects' Directive specifies in very broad terms the areas which must be covered by architects during studies. It also stipulates a minimum of four years' full-time study at a university or equivalent institution.

The Directive has not had an easy passage and at the time of writing there are still some EC countries which have not fully implemented it. One of the problems is that the education of architects in the various member countries and the roles of the various persons termed 'architects' are not uniform. Much of this diversity derives from construction industry practices in particular countries. In Germany, for example, much construction is carried out on a separate trades basis and architects are expected to carry out the contract site management. In France, by contrast, although a trade-by-trade contracting system is also common, architects play a less practical role and it is common for production drawings to be prepared by contractors. Clearly, architects in the UK must spend some time researching such differences before opting to practise elsewhere in the EC. To describe the construction industries in European countries fully is beyond the scope of this book, but useful information is available in a large number of publications.[8,9,10] The requirements for registration in EC member countries are complex and advice should be sought from ARCUK.

2.6 Code of Professional Conduct

The RIBA, to which most but not all architects belong, publishes a code of conduct which is binding on its members. ARCUK also publishes a code which is similar in general principle, but much shorter.[11] A member of the Institute may be required to answer enquiries regarding his or her professional conduct. The member is liable to reprimand, suspension or expulsion if the member's conduct is found by the Disciplinary Committee of the Institute to be in contravention of the Code or otherwise inconsistent with status as a member or derogatory to professional character.

The object of the Code of Professional Conduct is to promote the standard of professional conduct or self-discipline required of members of the RIBA, in the interests of the public. The Code regulates the actions of members between themselves, to their clients and to the public at large. The Code simply puts into words what most clients would expect of their professional advisors. It is more than just a set of rules for fair dealing; it points out the high standard of behaviour which is expected of a professional person in a position of trust.

A member may engage in any activity, whether as proprietor, director, partner, salaried employee, consultant or in any other capacity provided that the member's conduct complies with the Code. The Code is divided into three 'Principles', each of which is followed by a set of rules and notes which amplify the Principles.

2.6.1 Principle One – RIBA Code

'A member shall faithfully carry out the duties which he undertakes. He shall also have proper regard for the interests both of those who commission and of those who may be expected to use or enjoy the product of his work.'

Members should make sure that they have the resources to carry out commissions, and student members should seek guidance from architects if they intend to undertake commissions themselves.

Before entering into an agreement members must clearly set out the terms, including what services will be provided, responsibilities, any limitation of liability, how fees will be calculated and how the agreement may be terminated. The agreement should be in writing and the RIBA Architects' Appointment should be used (see Chapter 7, section 7.1.2). Members must not sub-let work without the client's permission. This merely states the legal position that, if the client engages an architect to do work, the architect must not pass the work to someone else. Naturally, office staff services will be used, but if the work were to be passed on to another architect's practice to carry out, the architect would be in breach not only of the Code but also of the agreement with the client.

Where members are acting between parties, they must be impartial. So, for example, they must interpret the building contract fairly between client and contractor. If called upon to decide the line of a boundary between neighbours or any other matter where both sides look to them for expert judgement, they must give an honest opinion. This provision does not of course prevent them from representing the client in any such dispute against an opponent. The architect's duty to act fairly will arise only when both sides are relying on his or her judgement.

Members must ensure that any offices which are dealing with architecture are under the control of an architect. This rule prevents architects from opening branch offices under the control of unqualified assistants. 'Unqualified' in this context means unqualified as architects; architects may well have assistants or even partners who are qualified as surveyors or as architectural technicians. The Code precludes them from controlling branch offices.

2.6.2 Principle Two – RIBA Code

'A member shall avoid actions and situations inconsistent with his professional obligations or likely to raise doubts about his integrity.'

Members' other business interests are covered by this principle. If they are such as might lead the client to question the architect's integrity because they are or appear to be related to the subject of the commission, the architect is obliged to disclose them before being engaged by the client. Obvious examples of such situations are cases where the architect already acts for a contractor in some other matter and the client may wish to employ the contractor to carry out building work, or where the architect owns land adjacent to the client's property and over which it will be necessary to agree an easement.

If any such potential conflict of interest arises after the architect has entered into an agreement with the client, the architect must do one of three things:

- withdraw from the situation, or
- remove whatever is causing the conflict of interests, or
- inform the client and anyone else concerned and obtain the agreement of all parties to the architect's continued engagement.

Two examples noted in the Code are as follows:

- Where a member is appointed assessor for a competition, he or she must not subsequently take any part in the work unless the appointment as consultant was previously arranged or if the member is asked to act as arbitrator between the promoters of the competition and the selected architect in any dispute.
- Where the member is under pressure to act in contravention of the Code, he or she must report the facts to the RIBA and anyone else affected.

A member engaged as an expert to advise on some matter cannot thereafter be used as an arbitrator in any related dispute.

Members must not hold themselves out to be, or practise as, independent consulting architects if at the same time they:

- engage in the business of trading in land or buildings, or
- act as a property developer, or
- act as auctioneers or house or estate agents, or
- act as contractors or sub-contractors, or
- manufacture or supply goods to or for the building industry, or
- have partners or co-directors who engage in one of the above.

An exception may be made to this rule if members can demonstrate that the combination will not prevent compliance with the Code as it applies to their circumstances.

Members must not hold themselves out to be independent if they or their employers are contractors. If they practise as both architects and contractors, they cannot pretend to be independent and must inform the client of the right to appoint another architect to act as professional advisor or agent in such matters as quality and financial control. It should be clearly understood that architects who combine architectural and contracting services are offering clients what amounts to package deals (see Chapter 8, section 8.2). Where architects practise in this way, the client has the additional protection that they are bound by the Code, but it is for the client to decide whether to engage an architect who is offering this kind of service, to ask for architectural services only, or to engage an architect who has no related interests.

Members must not take any discounts, commissions or gifts as inducements to show favour to anyone (this is corrupt and a criminal offence). If architects act as contractors, they may take the usual trade discounts customary to the industry. Members must not try improperly to influence the granting of any kind of statutory approval. An example of this might be where an architect sits as a member of an advisory panel to examine planning applications and whose own application comes before the panel. In such a case the architect would be obliged to declare an interest and, usually, take no part in any discussion of that application.

Members must take into account the professional obligations and qualifications of their employees and colleagues. Responsibilities and liabilities must be carefully set out. Among other things, they must:

- Allow their employees appropriate authority and responsibility.
- Give employees suitable public credit for their work.
- Allow employees to engage in spare-time practice provided that, in turn, the employees inform their employers.
- Allow appropriate opportunities for employees to continue their professional development.
- Co-operate in the educational requirements of such students as they may employ.

Members must not have partners or co-directors who are disqualified from registration or expelled from the register or disqualified by reason of expulsion from any other professional body, without the permission of the RIBA.

Members must conform with the rules for clients' accounts then in force.

2.6.3 Principle Three – RIBA Code

'A member shall rely on ability and achievement as the basis for his advancement.'

This portion of the Code is designed to regulate the ways in which members can obtain work. The Code encourages members to play their full parts in bodies, such as amenity societies, concerned with the quality of the environment. They may criticize what they believe to be harmful, shoddy or inappropriate provided that no malice is involved and the criticism does not contravene any rule under Principle Three.

Members must not give discounts or gifts for the introduction of clients or work. If members operate as contractors they may give all the customary trade discounts.

Members may quote a fee for carrying out commissions. However, they must have enough information to know what a project entails and what services will be required. A member must not offer a quotation unless it has been requested. In effect therefore a client can obtain competitive quotations from several architects. Members are not allowed to reduce their fees to take account of quotations which a client may have obtained from other architects. This is to remove the possibility of a 'dutch auction' taking place. Some architects do not care to participate in quoting competitively. Such an attitude in no way reflects on the quality of their service or the fees they charge. It may be that they do not wish to spend time and effort on such an exercise or they may have had unfortunate experiences in connection with fee tendering in the past.

Provided that the client is not seeking competitive quotations, there is nothing to prevent negotiations with the architect after having received the initial quotation. The architect may be prepared to reduce fees to take account of particular factors which were not clear at the time of the first quotation, or may suggest a reduction in the services. The basic position is that a member must not attempt to supplant another architect. Thus an architect may not approach a client offering services knowing that the client has already entered into discussions with another architect.

If the client proposes a fee basis which the architect feels unable to accept because to do so would call into question integrity or professional obligations, the architect is obliged to withdraw from the negotiations and report the facts to the RIBA. Obviously, a member would not take such action lightly before fully explaining the position to the client. The situation might arise in any number of ways. It could be, for example, that the client is attempting to link remuneration to some other financial activity rather than pay an agreed fee for the work. If a member is employed within the client's organization and is relied upon to negotiate an agreement with another independent consulting architect, there is an obligation to respect the obligations of the independent architect under the Code.

If a client approaches a member to undertake a commission knowing it is being handled, or has been handled, by another architect, the member is obliged to notify the original architect of the enquiry. The member's obligation is to make reasonable enquiries to ascertain whether such a situation exists. The object of the procedure is to enable the original architect to take whatever steps may be appropriate. In most cases the original architect will do nothing other than acknowledge the notice.

If the client has omitted to pay the fees of the original architect, the client can expect to receive a bill forthwith. In that situation or if the client's reason for changing architects was because of a dispute, the new architect may well ask for further information on the subject and, at the very least, require a payment on account before beginning any work. In some cases, all that will be required is that the client gives the original architect proper notice of termination of appointment in accordance with the agreement. There is an exception to this rule if the client can show the new architect that to give notice to the original architect would be prejudicial to prospective litigation.

Members may let clients know of their availability together with the extent of their experience by any means, but the information given must be factual, relevant and neither misleading nor unfair to others nor discreditable to the profession. Thus architects may send letters to clients offering services and may put advertisements in newspapers or magazines. Members may employ external public relations consultants to handle that part of the business, but there are safeguards, including a signed declaration to the RIBA, to ensure that the public relations consultants cannot do anything to contravene the Code.

The final part of the Code prevents any member from entering an architectural competition which is not conducted in accordance with the appropriate RIBA regulations.

References

(1) *Schools of Architecture*, Royal Institute of British Architects.
(2) *A Career in Architecture*, Royal Institute of British Architects.
(3) Weightman, Anne (1991) Learning to survive: CPD in action, *Architects' Journal* (13 February) pp.63–64.
(4) Continuing Professional Development in Construction Group, 26 Store Street, London WC1E 7BT.
(5) *Professional Studies in British Architectural Practice*, Open Learning Project, Department of Education and Professional Development, RIBA.
(6) A very useful discussion of ARCUK's powers in relation to 'disgraceful conduct' is to be found in: Parris, John (1979) Does the Code carry the weight of law?, *Building Design* (14/21 December) p.22.
(7) ARCUK Annual Report and Accounts, 1988, 1989, 1990.

(8) Spencer Chapman, N.F. and Grandjean, C. (1991) *The Construction Industry and the European Community*, BSP Professional Books, Oxford.

(9) *RIBA Architectural Practice in Europe*, a series of guides published by the RIBA.

(10) Other series are published by the Construction Industry Research and Information Association, the Centre for Construction Market Information, and the Building Services Research and Information Association. These publications tend to be fairly expensive. A useful manual covering all the EC countries with much statistical information is *Gateway to Europe*, National Economic Development Council.

(11) *Conduct and Discipline*, ARCUK.

Chapter 3

Employment

3.1 Introduction

Twenty years ago, opportunities for employment were fairly clear cut for architects: they were employed either in private practice or in local government. There were a few architects employed in other areas, but they were the minority. Architects in private practice tended to be considered 'real' architects while their fellows in local government were said to lead a sheltered life in which they were not called upon to exercise the full range of architectural responsibilities. Undoubtedly, the kinds of responsibility shouldered by architects in each area of employment are not identical but, if exercised properly, the architects' duties are just as onerous in local government as in the private sector. Indeed, many such public sector offices have effectively been made into self-contained 'private' firms offering their services to a broad spectrum of clients over the last ten years. Moreover, it is generally accepted that a great many opportunities exist for architects outside the usual fields of employment.

In general, it must be said that other areas of employment have always existed, but architects have tended to ignore the variety in favour of the traditional. The uncertain economic situation has forced many architects to seek work totally outside the construction industry where their hard-won skills may be of little value. In other cases, architects have looked more seriously at occupations within the industry which were not popular. In some of these occupations the architect is employed largely in a traditional way. In other cases just one facet of the architectural 'package' is used: for example, design, project management, or drawing ability. One of the great advantages of an architectural education is that because it is so broadly based, the architect has the chance to examine a great many possibilities in some detail.

A brief summary follows. It cannot be comprehensive because the list of possible opportunities is as long as individual ingenuity makes it.

3.2 *Private practice*

This is still considered by most lay people as being the area wherein architects are employed. An architect will opt for private practice for many reasons, as follows.

Because the type of work is likely to be varied

This is the kind of statement which in practice scarcely bears examination. There are certainly practices both large and small which handle an amazing variety of work, but most practices tend to have certain project types in which they profess particular expertise and they tend to get commissions for work for which they have a reputation. Even in a large office handling different project types, the individual architect will often find that he or she is always given a particular kind of work to do.

Because of the particular type of work

There are some private firms which tackle projects which an architect would not encounter elsewhere: very large and prestigious buildings; buildings under the direction of a famous and much sought-after master architect; or highly specialized building types. Although many large organizations have their own architects' departments, the design of a new radio station, railway station or hospital is rarely left to the in-house architects. Therefore an architect seeking to gain experience in such specialized buildings must join those private firms which specialize in them.

This is not really the place to enter into a long discussion about whether a client is better to engage a private firm which specializes in hotels to design a new hotel or whether a firm which has no previous hotel experience would actually produce a refreshingly different solution to an old problem. In theory, every architect can design any building after going through the appropriate processes of briefing, analysis and synthesis but, in practice, time is money and the architect with previous experience of a particular building type will most likely be put to design the next such building commission to come into the office.

The opportunity to become involved

This is very closely related to the next reason.

The opportunity to take responsibility

Certainly, in the small to medium-sized office an architect will be encouraged to take responsibility, provided the architect can demonstrate the appropriate ability. In larger offices there may be more bureaucracy at work but, even there, an architect prepared to work hard and gifted with ordinary competence can enjoy a fulfilling life. With greater than ordinary competence or a real flair in some field, there is no reason why the architect should not rise to the top of the firm in due course. Although the authors have not seen statistics, many years of observation suggest that it is much more likely that an architect will gain promotion by staying a number of years in a private office than if the same architect stayed for the same number of years in a public sector office.

The opportunity to advance to principal status

This is closely linked to the previous reason. An architect who feels involved in the firm's fortunes, who takes on responsibility above that indicated in the job description (if any) and who demonstrates ability is almost certain to rise to the top of any private firm. This is because such a firm owes its existence to satisfied clients who return with new commissions. A private firm cannot afford to carry passengers, because they must be paid for out of the income generated by the rest. A really first-class architect generating more than his or her fair share of fee income for the firm, attracting and keeping clients, eventually *becomes* the firm in that, if such an architect left, the firm would be hard pressed to survive long afterwards. That scenario is more common among small practices, but the principle holds good in any practice. It is possible for an architect employed in a private practice to become the firm or a very sizeable portion of it.

There are many one-person practices in the country and a few very large multi-disciplinary practices employing over 200 staff. Most practices, however, fall into the category of medium to small employing 3–30 persons. Some architects prefer the small office because of its friendly atmosphere. It by no means follows that a small office is friendly and a large office unfriendly. Indeed, a clash of personalities which can be absorbed within a firm employing 50 people would be disastrous in an office of five people. The larger office may offer certain advantages in the form of back-up and benefits which may not be available in a small office. There may be greater freedom in a small office, but there is less flexibility to meet sudden surges in workload. The most notable point about a private office is that there is always the pressure to earn the income to pay the bills. For the architect at the bottom of the hierarchy, the pressure is more noticeable in the smaller firm where the key policy decisions can be readily seen in a fairly crude way. Such pressure gives many people a sense of excitement. We suspect that it is an important if perhaps unrecognized factor in the decision to work in private practice.

3.3 *Local authority*

Many architects are employed in local government or in government departments. After the 1974 reorganization of local government most county councils and district councils appointed an architect as one of the chief officers at the head of a department. The size of department and the precise responsibilities varied with the authority. For some years now, certain local authorities have adopted a policy of making the architects' department a separate entity from the other council departments, economically more accountable than before and often able to take on commissions from other organizations. In some instances, a department has been made completely independent. In such an instance, it becomes a private practice rather like any other except that its birth took place under unusual circumstances. In other instances, the architects' department has ceased to exist altogether, certainly as an identifiable unit. At the time of writing, there is a government proposal to introduce compulsory competitive tendering (CCT) for all professional services provided by local authority. It is feared by some observers that the proposal will spell the end of architects' departments within local authorities if services are judged on cost rather than quality.

The character of local government offices varies greatly and so does the scope of the work. Some operate, as noted above, as large departments under the leadership of a chief officer responsible to the council. In other cases, the department may be part of the surveyor's or engineer's department, or it may be part of the council's building department.

The work of an architect in local government is basically the same as that of the architect in private practice. The council will in effect be the client although the relationship between council and architect will be that of master and servant. The architect will be governed by the council's standing orders. However, in carrying out duties, the architect must always remember the obligation to behave in a thoroughly professional manner particularly when called upon to carry out duties under the contract such as certifying or giving extensions of time. Not only should the council not prevent the architect from acting in this way, the council has a positive duty to ensure that the architect carries out his or her duties fairly.[1]

Architects in local government have certain advantages. If the authority is of reasonable size, they have the authority's other departments, legal, public health, building control, planning and so on available for advice. In the larger authorities, the architects' departments will doubtless contain many specialist sections such as quantity surveyors, mechanical and electrical engineers, structural engineers, landscape architects and interior designers. Architects operating in that kind of office will in effect be in a multidisciplinary environment and hence will be able to call upon any assistance necessary.

It is sometimes said that local government offices do not offer as much scope as private practices. The truth, of course, is not so simple. Many offices have a high reputation and such offices will tackle all the authority's prestige works. Smaller offices may confine themselves to routine tasks or smallish projects, handing out the occasional large project to a private firm on a consultancy basis. Any architect contemplating working in local government must make appropriate enquiries first. Not all architects want to design large, prestigious projects. Many feel more at home working on smaller jobs. A particular feature of working in local government is that architects who put in a number of years' service with the same authority will build up an understanding of the philosophies of the departments who regularly require building work. There is the opportunity to make considerable progress through the development of briefs for particular purposes. Such architects have a unique opportunity to evaluate the performance of existing buildings and to feed back the information into current design.

There are also many opportunities for architects in the planning departments of local authorities, influencing design and planning on a larger scale, perhaps through structure plans or local plans or through involvement in town design, listed buildings, conservation areas and the like. Very often, such architects are also members of the Royal Town Planning Institute.

The opportunities for advancement may be slower and along more rigidly defined lines than in private practice, but the staff will be divided into recognized grades. Each has a maximum and minimum salary and regular annual incremental increases. Promotion tends to be based upon seniority as well as technical and administrative ability. There are well-defined conditions of service which include such matters as holidays, sick leave, superannuation (which is generous) and hours of service.

3.4 *Nationalized industries and the like*

Many would say that these are getting fewer. Examples are British Rail, British Coal and the area health authorities. Nationalization varies in popularity with the government in power. These industries tend to offer specialized experience. Regional architects' departments are often a feature and they are closer in organisational structure to a local government office than to a private practice. They offer a unique opportunity to develop a profound expertise in a particular building type. This can be a very satisfying experience. For example, many architects gain enormous satisfaction from a professional lifetime spent in the rapidly developing world of health care. The principal disadvantage of working in such industries stems from the same root: the difficulty in moving to an office carrying out different kinds of projects unless the particular expertise is required.

In this category, it is also possible to group universities and polytechnics which very often employ their own buildings officers (who may be architects) to deal with minor building works, investigation of defects, maintenance and to liaise with independent consultants. It is possible to gain considerable experience in dealing with a wide variety of building structures in such offices. The buildings can vary from the very old and historic to the brand new.

Ecclesiastical authorities generally entrust new building to private architects. There are limited openings for the post of diocesan surveyor to carry out church inspections and maintenance work. The Church of England has a well-organized system. The Roman Catholic, Methodist and other non-conformist churches have few official posts, most work being undertaken on an *ad hoc* basis as required.

Some housing associations have their own architects' departments, but most work is carried out by independent consultants and increasingly on a design-and-build basis by contractors.

3.5 *Large companies*

Some large companies have their own architects' departments. The work tends to be highly specialized, but this very much depends on the company. The atmosphere is more commercial than in local government, but there are similarities, particularly in the way in which the architect works for the employer rather than in an independent capacity for a client. The career structure and conditions of service are also likely to be better defined than in many private offices. Work within one company can vary: for example, laboratories, warehouses, offices and housing for employees. Many companies have overseas branches and the chance to travel is attractive to some architects.

3.6 Contractors

Some large contractors employ their own architects. The quantity surveyor has always had a place in building contracting and it seems natural that the architect should be involved also. Architects, however, have a poor reputation among building contractors and they are more likely to be employed in a design capacity than in a practical quality control role. The majority of medium-sized contractors carrying out design-and-build work will engage private firms of architects on a project basis, because this is more cost-effective than maintaining an architects' department. Some of the larger contractors, however, do maintain departments of their own, and since they often have the facility to inject major capital sums into CAD and other expensive equipment, they can create a stimulating and exciting environment in which to work.

Although architectural designs emanating from contractors have aroused adverse comment from time to time, there are many good examples. In addition, there is often a good opportunity for quality control and detailed administration. This is particularly the case because changes to the design are very significant to contractors when it is they who pick up the cost not, as is usual, the building owner. There are opportunities for architects who are sufficiently flexible. Indeed, there is no reason why an architect should not rise to director level.

Many architects dislike the idea of working for a contractor because they feel a split duty between the contractor, as their employer, and the ultimate purchaser of the building. In practice, this need not be a problem. The contractor's objective is to construct a building which satisfies the requirements as laid down in the contract and to make a reasonable profit. In addition, the contractor wants the purchaser to be happy with the building. Very few contractors are rogues. Some may be hard business men, but many are just the opposite: hence the large number of bankruptcies in the industry. There are a few things to remember:

- A contractor who has an architect as an employee will not ask him to act contrary to his professional judgement. That is probably why the architect was appointed in the first place.
- An architect employed by a contractor cannot give the contractor's client independent advice.[2] An architect must always make the position clear to the client. It is especially important when it appears that the architect is acting in the capacity of an independent consultant. This can happen, for example, when the contractor undertakes a design-and-build project and the architect is involved in settling the client's brief.

Every architect should spend some time, if possible, working for a contractor. There is much practical experience to be gained together with an indefinable empathy with the contractor's difficulties.

3.7 *Manufacturers*

Product design and development has traditionally had a valuable input from architects. Furniture design is a good example where many architects try their hands. Some classic pieces of furniture are named after the architect who designed them. A less common area of employment is in the field of building components. There is a multitude of products which would and in some cases do benefit enormously from architectural input: electrical fittings, ironmongery, floor, wall and ceiling tiles and panels, glazing units, doors and windows for example. In many instances, a relatively common building component might be improved by an experienced architect. The number of architects who work in this field is small and it is usually an interest which develops.

3.8 *Teaching*

There are good opportunities for architects in schools of architecture in universities and polytechnics if they have an interest in teaching. That is the most important thing. Most schools advertising for staff lay stress on skill in design, but they also expect a prospective lecturer to offer one or two other subjects about which they feel confident to lecture. A lecturing post, therefore, will usually involve a few hours' lecturing every week together with studio, workshop and some administrative responsibilities. There are some who regret the emphasis on design skills and argue that, while design is the distinguishing architectural skill, every school should have some lecturers whose principal skills lie elsewhere, for example in construction, building procurement, professional practice or building sciences. It is probably important that these people are also qualified architects.

There are also openings for lecturers in other construction disciplines such as surveying or building and besides polytechnics, there are many colleges of building where architects can make a valuable contribution.

Starting salaries are often considered to be low compared with salaries for architects of equivalent experience in other fields. This actually varies with the economic climate. As a result, lecturing tends to attract younger members of the profession because, as an architect gains experience outside teaching, he or she cannot afford to take a drop in salary in order to make the move from, say, private practice to teaching. Experience in practice is the great difference between the requirements for a lecturer in architecture and a lecturer in, say, mathematics or history. The budding lecturer should therefore gain as much experience as possible before becoming a full-time teacher. Most posts have opportunities for research and consultancy work.

Architects who do not wish to take up lecturing as a full-time career, but who are interested none the less, can often contribute useful practical input by doing part-time lecturing. The financial rewards tend to be modest, but there is a great deal of satisfaction to be gained.

3.9 *Specialization*

All professionals tend to specialize in one way or another as they gain experience. This is for the perfectly natural reason that they realize that their own profession is not just performing one activity, but a collection of activities to different degrees. There are many opportunities for architects to specialize within the profession: for example, in a particular building type – housing, schools, hospitals, or industrial buildings. Architects may also specialize in the tasks they do. For example, they may do only design, or production drawings, or survey work, or contract administration, or model making, or perspectives. These are to some extent fairly obvious ways in which architects can specialize. There are other less obvious specialisms: investigating defects, expert witnessing, contractual advice are examples.

Few architects can help attaining some degree of specialization as they gain experience, because the range of skills traditionally required of the architect is just too great now that each skill is becoming so complex. To many architects, however, the most satisfying element in their work is the chance to be involved in so many different ways in the production of a building. These architects will always fight to retain a degree of broad architectural activity against which to practise their specialisms.

References

(1) *Perini Corporation* v. *Commonwealth of Australia* (1969) 12 BLR 82.
(2) Principle 2.3, *RIBA Code of Professional Practice.*

Chapter 4

Types of Practice

4.1 Sole principal

A large number of architects carry on practice as sole principals. The latest figures at the time of writing suggest that 51% of all practices are organized in this way.[1] Because a practice is run by a sole principal, of course, does not mean that it is a one-person practice. The sole principal may indeed work entirely alone or may employ a dozen staff of various kinds. The following are factors:

- In times of recession an architect might set up in practice alone as the only way of getting employment. If successful, the architect continues, but if not, he or she will look for opportunities in employment again when the recession is over.
- Many young architects look upon sole practice as an ambition.
- A successful sole practitioner cannot remain alone for very long. The workloads will become too big and some form of partnership becomes necessary.
- Some architects become sole practitioners by purchasing a practice from a retiring architect.
- Sometimes an architect moves from being a member of staff into partnership as a temporary measure for two or three years, before the old sole practitioner retires, before becoming a sole practitioner.
- An architect will very often build up a sizeable private practice as a spare time occupation before taking the plunge and becoming a sole practitioner.

It is probably the most difficult form of practice, but it is potentially very rewarding personally and financially. An architect contemplating this form of practice must have considerable reserves of self-reliance and an iron nerve to face alone all the problems of architectural practice. Most of these problems will have little to do with architecture. They will concern the business.[2] Even though an architect in this situation may have no shortage of friends with whom to talk over important decisions, such as whether expansion should take place, they have nothing riding on the correctness of the decision.

4.2 *Partnership*

At the time of writing, the latest statistics suggest that nearly 40% of architectural practices are carried on in the form of partnerships.[1] Partnership is defined by the Partnership Act 1890 as 'the relationship which subsists between two or more persons carrying on business in common with a view to profit'. It is important to remember that simply sharing accommodation or staff with another on financial terms is not 'carrying on business in common'. If the courts have to decide whether in any particular case a partnership exists, a crucial factor is whether or not the parties share the profits or losses. In general, if they do, it is a partnership.

Partners are jointly and severally liable for the acts of the partnership. Thus, they are liable both as a group and individually and one partner is liable for the act of his or her partner provided only that it was carried out in the course of the partnership business. Normally, in the case of partnership contract debts such as the purchase of a word processor, they are only jointly liable.

Suits for *negligence* are on the increase. A party seeking damages can pursue all the partners or individual partners in turn or any combination of partners until the damages are recovered in full. This can be disastrous both to the partnership and to the individual partner, because the sums of money involved can be quite beyond the means of a private person and bankruptcy may be the outcome. In the case of a simple contract debt, the party requiring payment is only entitled to choose one of the options. Invariably, a party seeking recovery of a debt or of damages against a partnership will take action against all the partners together.

A partner is responsible to the full extent of his or her personal wealth for the acts of the partnership irrespective of a partner's particular partnership share. For example, if partner A has a one third share, partner B has a two thirds share, and partner B is not available to pay the appropriate share of a debt, partner A will be obliged to pay the whole amount. If the firm is worth less than the amount of the debt, partner A will have to make up the difference. If partner B subsequently becomes available, of course, partner A can sue for the appropriate amount to cover partner B's share. If all partners are available to pay, they will normally contribute according to the proportion of their shareholding (see also Chapter 17, section 17.4).

A partnership usually has a written partnership agreement. Although this is not strictly necessary, it can prevent disputes about trivial things from getting out of hand. Written evidence of the agreement is not necessary to indicate the existence of a partnership to third parties (who would not know, in any case, that a written agreement existed). It can be seen from the firm's notepaper, bearing the name of the firm and probably the names of the individual partners. As far as third parties are concerned, it is usually sufficient if the architect either states that he or she is a partner (whether or not this is true) or acts as though that was the case.

The advantages of a partnership are as follows:

- When the business expands beyond a certain point (which will vary depending on the architect concerned), the principal will not have full knowledge of every project nor the ability to give proper supervision. A choice must be made: either to have a very experienced architect at high salary to help with the administration or to have a partner to share the burden, not necessarily on equal terms, but on terms satisfactory to both parties. A partner will have a real interest in the success of the business and an incentive to contribute to the utmost.
- Economy in expenditure can be effected by the pooling of accommodation, equipment, or staff by partners. Whereas one principal might not have enough work to employ three assistants, two jointly might be able to do so. The two partners and staff of three might be accommodated in two rooms, whereas as separate businesses they would need four. Of course, both staff and accommodation can be shared without any partnership existing. Each principal would have his own work, the time of staff being recorded and their salaries allocated accordingly.
- Two or more partners should be able to generate more ideas and attract more work together than the sum of such ideas and work separately.
- There may be more capital available for expansion.
- A partner establishes a goodwill value to a business (more about goodwill later). If an architect is in practice alone, there is virtually no goodwill value because, if such an architect dies or retires, existing clients are little more likely to continue with a totally new architect who may take over the business than they are to go elsewhere. In both cases they are venturing into new territory. A new and younger partner, however, will be able to maintain a continuity of personnel and establish a relationship, even if not primary, with all the firm's clients.

Goodwill is difficult to define. It is the benefit which a practice acquires by virtue of its prestige and the fact that clients return for further commissions. A partnership should not be thought of as stationary. At any time there may be partners leaving or joining and the workload will vary according to the economic climate. All this has a bearing on the goodwill. It used to be the custom for a new partner to have to buy a share in the partnership by bringing in a large capital sum. It was known as 'buying a share of the goodwill'. Figure 4.1 shows one method of calculation.

If a new partner could not afford to put up the initial capital sum, it was sometimes agreed that payment could be made on an instalment basis – a certain fixed sum every year for a given period. As a result, many partners lived in near poverty for years until they paid off the capital sum required and they only attained a comfortable income late in life. It is now becoming common for goodwill to be given a nil value. More emphasis is placed on attracting a person with the right professional attributes into a partnership. The chances of doing this are obviously increased if the incoming partner is not required to contribute a substantial amount to the partnership coffers. The new partner is given an appropriate share in the partnership and the actual

Profits:	Year 1	£40000
	Year 2	£80000
	Year 3	£90000
Total		£210000

Average: $\dfrac{210000}{3}$ =   £70000

Value of goodwill: £70000 × 2* =   £140000

Existing partners' share: A at 60% =   £84000
B at 40% =   £56000

New partner buys, say, 20% share
at cost of $\dfrac{20 \times 140000}{100}$ =   £28,000

A and B might sell 10% each, thus receiving £14000 each.
If the following year's profits were £100000, the partners would share as follows:

A at 50% = £50000
B at 30% = £30000
C at 20% = £20000 (new partner)

* The multiplying factor is somewhat arbitrary, but it is not less than 1 and seldom more than 2.

Figure 4.1 Buying a share of the goodwill.

income which the share will generate will clearly bear a relationship to the total fee income over the year.

The new partner, in return, will be expected to leave a proportion of earnings in the practice to act as working capital. It has to be said that existing partners who may have been obliged to purchase shares in the partnership are not always receptive to this approach, because it denies them the chance to sell their own shares to a new partner. Against this must be weighed the consideration that new partners are the lifeblood of any practice and without them income can decrease and existing partners' shares may decrease in value. In essence, the modern approach is a change from looking at capital gains to looking at increases in annual income.

It is obviously advantageous if partners have similar views regarding the general philosophy of a partnership, but there is merit in healthy differences regarding the methods of attaining desired ends. Partners should have the utmost trust and confidence in one another. This suggests that they should know one another quite well before the final step of partnership is taken. It is, therefore, most common for a firm to take its new partners from its own staff, whose capabilities and suitabilities are known and have been judged over a lengthy period.

If a new partner is introduced to facilitate a continuance of the business, age is a factor which must be taken into consideration. A (aged 50) might take a partner aged, say, 35. In ten or fifteen years' time, A retires and the new partner continues the business, looking for a successor and so on. Life, and partnerships, never work out quite so neatly, but that is the theory.

It is usual that the rights and duties of each partner are set out in the form of a legal agreement drafted by a solicitor experienced in that kind of work. Although the agreement (which will be in the form of a deed) can be as long or as short as the partners wish, it is advisable to include any matter which might be anticipated to cause problems. Typical heads of terms include the following:

- Name of the firm.
- Place of business.
- Date of commencement.
- Value of goodwill.
- Amount of capital provided by each partner.
- Treatment of work in progress.
- Duties of partners.
- Proportions of profits or losses between each partner.
- Amount of cash drawings per partner per month.
- Banking arrangements.

- Termination provisions.
- Partner insurance.
- Professional indemnity insurance and any other professional requirements.
- Partnership perks.
- Arbitration of disputes.

In fixing the amount of drawings, it must be remembered that the firm is assessed for income tax on the basis of its profits. The cash drawings must allow for this and it is good practice for the partners to set aside an appropriate amount to tax every month as they make drawings. The advice of the firm's accountants should be sought on this and other aspects of the agreement. Unless the agreement specifies a period of notice, a partnership agreement may be terminated by any partner simply by giving notice to that effect. All partnerships are terminated by death and by the taking of a new partner or the retirement of an old partner. This is the essential difference between a partnership and forms of corporate body which continue although the persons constituting the membership may change.

Termination of a partnership does not remove liability from any of the partners and it is usual for partnerships to maintain professional indemnity insurance in respect of retired members. Problems can arise if all the partners split up and there is no continuing partnership to carry on insurance premium payments. In these circumstances, some insurers offer special deals (see Chapter 17, section 17.4).

Many practices use the designation *associate* to signify that the particular member of staff has attained a status which is higher than other members of staff, but short of partnership. Very often it is an indication that the person concerned will eventually become a partner. Although it is usual to list the names of associates on the letterhead, it is good practice to separate the associates from the partners by putting the associates at the bottom of the page. This signals to the public that an associate is not a partner. It is an important safeguard as far as the associate is concerned who otherwise could be liable as a partner if a court decided that the associate had held him or herself out as such.

Associates are normally appointed by letter, but some firms like to give the arrangement some additional solemnity by having a deed prepared. Associates do not have any share in the partnership profits, although they may have a share in a bonus scheme like other members of staff. Associates usually have extra benefits such as payment of private telephone charges, a better-than-average car, and a health care package.

The practice of appointing *salaried partners* appears to be dying out. Salaried partners suffer the worst of both worlds. They are often considered to be full partners if there is a question of liability and certainly in the eyes of the public it is likely that such would be the case. However, they normally receive a very small share in the profits on top of their salary. It is a position to be avoided, because they are often undifferentiated from other partners on the letterhead and therefore they are just as likely to be sued. Although the partnership agreement may contain an indemnity for all salaried partners from the full partners, the indemnity will be of no avail if there is a large claim which claims the assets of the firm and the individual partners.

Although it is common for a person to be designated *consultant* on the letterhead, the reality is often that the architect is a retired partner of long standing who is kept on the letterhead to reassure clients that there is a continuity in the partnership. The consultant, more often than not, will be paid a small retainer. A consultant, in these terms, may occasionally be called in by the remaining partners to contribute a recollection of an old project or to deal with some particular small matter which can be kept within precise boundaries.

4.3 *Unlimited liability*

This kind of company finds little favour with architects' practices; only about 2% of firms are set up in this form.[1] The principal advantages are that a director of such a company is free from liability after a period of 12 months has expired from leaving the company and there is no requirement for filing reports with the Registrar of Companies. There are some formalities, however. An unlimited company is one stage removed from the partnership. The members of such a company are liable to contribute in the proportion of their shareholdings if the company's assets are not sufficient to pay debts. There may be a maximum of 50 members.

4.4 *Limited liability*

This is a company where the liability of the members is limited to the nominal value of the shareholding: hence the name. If the company is faced with a debt which is greater than the company's assets, the company can be wound up and the shareholders have no further liability. The situation may sound attractive to architects as an escape from liability and indeed that is probably the chief reason for the growth in limited liability companies in architectural practice to the current level of about 7.5% of all practices.[1] Although there was no legal reason why architects should not form limited liability companies, the idea was frowned upon by both ARCUK and RIBA until 1981. Trading with limited liability is not without its problems, of course, and the Insolvency Act 1986 provides severe penalties for directors who continue to trade whilst insolvent. The court has power to order them to contribute to the company's debts out of personal assets. There are other measures the court may order against culpable directors: for example, after insolvency liquidation, a former director may not be involved in the formation of a company with a similar name for a period of five years.

The principal difference between a limited company and a partnership is that when the shareholders (members) form a company, they are creating a separate legal entity. If the shareholders are also directors, they are employees of the company. Directors are paid a salary by the company and if the year end shows a profit, a dividend may be declared and shareholders share in the dividend according to the amount of their shareholding. In the case of architectural practices formed as limited companies, it is likely that the directors will also be the shareholders holding a similar percentage of the shares as they would have done in the case of a partnership. It is quite possible, however, that some shares may be held by persons not employed by the company or that some directors may not hold shares at all.

The advantages of a limited liability company are as follows:

- Except in rare circumstances, the directors are not personally liable for the debts of the company.
- It is more flexible than the partnership, because trusted members of staff can be promoted to director status on a salary without giving them a part of the company.
- Directors can be removed with far less difficulty than is the case with a partner.
- The company does not dissolve when a director leaves or when shares change hands. Therefore, there are no complex legalities involved. The company simply continues as normal.
- Companies attract capital more easily than do partnerships. This is important if expansion is planned. This is because other firms are used to doing business with companies.

There are disadvantages:

- A company is governed by the Companies Acts 1985 and 1989. It comes into existence only after registration by the Registrar of Companies. From that time, it can act only in accordance with the Acts. If the company carries out transactions before registration, they may be treated as the transactions of a partnership.

- Every company must file accounts with the Registrar, where they are then open to public inspection. Partnership accounts are private to the partners.
- A very important restriction is that a company may only act in accordance with the 'objects clause' which is to be found in the Memorandum of Association. This clause sets out the purpose of the company and what its powers are. A company which attempts to do something which is not included in the clause is said to be acting *ultra vires* (i.e. beyond its powers). Such actions can lead to many problems, for the company itself and for those who trade with it. For this reason, the objects clause should always be drafted with great care by an experienced company lawyer.
- There are certain formalities associated with the running of a company. The Companies Acts require that at least one general meeting of shareholders be held every year.
- The dissolution of a partnership can be a fairly simple, though traumatic, process, but a company must be wound up. This can take a long time.
- No discretion can be exercised over the apportionment of dividends. They must be divided strictly in accordance with the shareholding.
- In general, a director's tax position is not as good as that of a partner's, because a director pays tax on the PAYE system and there is no opportunity to take advantage of some advantageous 'self-employed' tax concessions. This situation, however, is subject to change depending on government policy.
- A client may dislike doing business with architects practising as a limited company (even though the client may also be a limited liability company) because it is considered by some to be unprofessional.

Although the shareholders together wield power over the way a company is run, and they have the power to dismiss a director, they must act within the Companies Acts and the company's objects clause and a single shareholder has no power to bind the others by any of his or her actions. A company can be tailor-made by a solicitor quite inexpensively. It is even cheaper to buy a company 'off the shelf'. Such companies are ready formed. All the paperwork is complete and they generally have a code name. The objects clauses are drafted for various purposes in fairly broad terms and after purchase it is a relatively simple matter to change the name. Some key points in relation to private limited companies are as follows:

- Must have one director (public companies must have two).
- There must be a company secretary who cannot be the same person as a sole director.
- A private company cannot offer shares to the public.
- There is no limit on the number of members, but if the number falls below two for six months, personal liability can be incurred.
- There must be a Memorandum subscribed to by at least two people taking at least one share each.
- The Memorandum must include the following clauses:
  name;
  office where registered (e.g., England, Wales or Scotland);
  objects;
  liability (whether limited);
  capital.
- The name must have a 'Ltd' as the last word.
- The name must appear in full on business correspondence.
- The name cannot be registered if there is another company of the same name on the index, if the name is offensive or if it would be a criminal offence.
- Business correspondence must also include the registered number.
- There must be printed Articles of Association.
- The Articles must be signed by the subscribers.
- The company can use another name provided that the company name also appears on correspondence.
- A register of directors must be kept and the registrar must be notified of changes.
- There must be a qualified independent auditor.
- There must be at least one AGM and unless otherwise unanimously agreed by those entitled to attend, 21 clear days' notice must be given.

4.5 *Public company*

A more recent development has been for some architectural practices to carry on business as public companies and, indeed, a few large practices have already taken this route. It is important, of course, that control of the company remains in the hands of architects, but this is much more difficult to ensure in the case of a public than a private company. The essential difference between private and public companies is that members of the public can buy and sell the shares of the latter. In theory, it is possible for a publicly quoted company to be completely controlled by people who are not architects. Since, however, that would fall foul of ARCUK which insists that an architectural practice should be controlled by architects, such a move would be self-defeating. It is clearly a valuable asset for a company to be able to describe itself as 'architects'. Any kind of agreement to restrict the number of shares on sale to the public (e.g. keeping 51% for architect directors) would be frowned upon by the Council of the Stock Exchange.

Members of the public who buy shares receive a share of the profits each year depending on the dividend announced. Therefore, trading as a public company is a useful way of generating finance for expansion. The regulations with regard to public companies are more stringent than is the case with private companies. In addition, a public company must put the status or the letters 'PLC' after its name. A public company is normally formed after a period as a private limited company. In order to achieve a successful flotation, the prospective shareholders must be convinced that the company has a good chance of giving a worthwhile return on money invested. Some kind of track record is essential. Floating a company is a specialized operation.

4.6 Co-operative

Although some practices operate as co-operatives, the members must have particular views in common. To operate in this way could be said to be making a social statement as much as acting as a business. Control is on the basis of 'one member one vote'. Responsibility and rewards are shared. If it is intended to register under the Industrial and Provident Societies Act a co-operative must have a minimum of seven members. If there are less than seven members, they must practise as a partnership or a limited or unlimited company. If the co-operative faces large debts to the extent that liquidation is necessary, the liability of individual members is confined to the amount of their shareholdings. Generally the members have shares of only nominal value.

4.7 Group practice

This is a comparatively recent development. The idea is that independent firms of architects associate themselves to mutual benefit, but they do not share profits nor do they have joint responsibility to their clients. They may share staff and offices, telephones and other overheads, dividing the expenses on an agreed basis. The firms may well be situated in different localities; indeed this is often an advantage in easing the pressure by sharing the load. If one practice is badly affected by recession, another in the group may be able to share out tasks. It is a very worthwhile form of practice provided that all parties are committed to the same ends. There are five common types of group practice:

- *Group association:* A loose association of firms for the purpose of sharing experience and knowledge. Each firm has a clearly separate identity as far as clients are concerned.

- *Shared facilities:* No real association other than sharing accommodation, equipment and occasionally staff.

- *Single project group practice:* Usually formed for the purpose of carrying out a specific commission, because it is too large for any of the firms to tackle it individually. When the purpose of the association has been accomplished, it automatically comes to an end.

- *Group co-ordinating firm:* Another way of carrying out a large project is for one of the firms involved to act as co-ordinator and the other firms to take responsibility for specific parts of the scheme. Obviously, this kind of arrangement can only work for large projects where the parts can easily be identified. The co-ordinating firm normally takes overall responsibility so far as the client is concerned.

- *Group partnership:* A partnership composed of individual firms which continue to practise separately, but which combine on certain large or complex projects on a regular basis.

The distribution of liabilities can be extremely complex in any kind of group practice. It needs very little imagination to see that some forms are more risky than others. Whenever group practice is contemplated, it is essential to take proper legal advice, not from the family solicitor, but from someone experienced and knowledgeable in the pitfalls to be avoided.

4.8 *Developer/architect/builder*

Subject to the provisions of the codes of conduct (Conduct and Discipline and, if the architect is a member of the RIBA, Code of

Professional Conduct: see Chapter 2, section 2.6) an architect can practise in any combination of the above. An architect may even act as an estate agent. This is a comparatively recent development. It is to be welcomed as giving the architect greater flexibility, but an architect choosing to practise simultaneously in two or more of these activities must take great care that his or her professional integrity is preserved. It is important that a client properly understands that, for example, such an architect cannot act as a builder for a development and at the same time give truly independent advice on that same development as an architect.

References

(1) RIBA (1989) *Census of Private Architectural Practices 1988*, RIBA Market Research Unit.
(2) Sharp, D. (1991) *The Business of Architectural Practice*, 2nd edn, BSP Professional Books, Oxford.

Chapter 5

Sources of Information

5.1 Basic library

Every practice needs a basic library. The extent to which an architect must refer to and rely upon technical information cannot be overemphasized. The size and complexity of the library will depend on the size and needs of the practice.

Various kinds of information need to be on hand. First there will be technical books on such matters as design, building construction, and contract law. Some of these will be retained from student days; others will be acquired as the practice develops – sometimes new, sometimes second-hand. Textbooks, particularly those dealing with the law, have a habit of becoming out of date very quickly and, despite the inevitably high costs, have to be replaced as it is essential that all references are kept up to date. Such books should be kept on a library shelf and if the practice cannot run to the luxury of a specialist librarian then a system should be devised whereby a record is kept of who has taken the book for reference and when, as it is very easy for these books to be mislaid causing unnecessary frustration to a prospective user who cannot find what is wanted when it is wanted.

The second type of information that needs to be held is technical information on products. Some will be in the form of well-prepared and fully illustrated catalogues, preferably in strong, clearly marked loose-leaf binders. This permits revised sheets being inserted and the superseded sheets removed and, if not wanted as a record for an old job, destroyed. Other information will be in pamphlet form which can be stored in folders kept in open-ended boxes for ease of retrieval. Again, it is essential that all information is up to date; some practices go so far as to acquire new information every time it is wanted. There is a great temptation to take information which is two or three months old and assume, often quite wrongly, that it is still current; some material will almost certainly have been withdrawn and new introduced with concommitant numbering alterations.

A third category of information that needs to be available is government and statutory publications. Examples of this type of information include technical circulars from government ministries on such matters as health and education, design criteria and technical requirements. A particular requirement in an architect's office is an up-to-date set of the current Building Regulations and a summary of all building British Standards (*BS Handbook No. 3*) and in many cases the full Standard as well.

5.2 *Classification and proprietary systems*

5.2.1 Classification

The great increase in technical and trade information in recent years has tended to swamp *ad hoc* systems of classification devised by individuals for their own use. Currently the most common system of classification is the SfB system, although this may in time give way to Common Arrangement (Chapter 11, section 11.1) It originated in Sweden; the letters SfB stand for *Samarbetskommittén för Byggnadsfrågor* (the name of the Swedish committee concerned). Using this system it is possible to give any book, catalogue, official bulletin or pamphlet used by architects a classification according to its contents. The classifying symbols are easily remembered, and frequent use will enable the architect quickly to find the material wanted.

The SfB system classifies information in four main tables:

- Table 0 – Built environment.
- Table 1 – Elements.
- Table 2/3 – Construction form and materials.
- Table 4 – Activities and requirements.

Tables 1 and 2/3 include most technical and trade literature while Tables 0 and 4 include most technical references, text books, official publications and regulations. Much technical and trade literature has an SfB classification already printed on it, and this greatly facilitates the incorporation of such material into the library.

5.2.2 Proprietary systems

The need to keep a library up to date is all important and great care has to be taken with cataloguing incoming information, including allocating an SfB reference if one is not provided. It is also necessary to keep the office index up to date, as it is of little use having information stored on a shelf or elsewhere without having the facility to find out firstly whether what is being sought is available and second, if it is, where it can be found.

All this can be very time-consuming and there are a number of commercial undertakings which provide an information service for architects' offices. They obtain the trade and other information, provide files and shelving to keep it in, give a regular up-dating service to the library and, in some cases, an information advisory service by telephone or post. However, remember that these firms have to operate at a profit. Some charge a fee to the firms whose trade literature they circulate, while others charge a fee to the offices receiving the service as well. In each case the trade literature supplied will not be all-embracing, as there will be firms who will rely on advertising their products directly to the profession and the industry.

5.3 *Selected job records and feedback*

It will be found very useful to keep a record of all notes and data about a job in a separate file, with a simple history sheet in front to summarize what stage it has reached. The various stages of the work (e.g. sketch plans, applications, approvals) should be listed and the dates on which action was taken inserted against them; references and file numbers should be added as appropriate. This will not only save a considerable amount of hunting through files, but will also make it that much easier if it becomes necessary to hand the job over to someone else. A specimen job history sheet is shown in Figure 5.1.

When the job is complete all the office information (files, drawings, bills of quantities etc.) becomes history but, for some years at least, important history. Careful decisions will need to be made as to what is destroyed and what is kept. The negatives of the drawings will be stored either in special storage envelopes (see Chapter 15, section 15.5.2) or, as is becoming more common these days, on microfiche. The files will be parcelled up, labelled and catalogued before storing.

Much time and effort is put into every job and as much use as possible should be made of the information which arises, hopefully to save similar efforts next time. For instance the possibility of standard detailing for another occasion may arise, specification information may be able to be re-used, never forgetting the need to check and amend if necessary. The quantity surveyor will usually have made a cost analysis of the tender and will have provided the architect with a copy so that cost information arising from the job can be utilized (after

JOB HISTORY SHEET

Job .... Job no ....

Address ....

Client ....

Address .... Tel. no ....

Sponsoring authorities .... (Officer ....)

.... (Officer ....)

Local authority ....

Adjoining owner(s) ....

....

Party wall surveyors ....

Date of instructions ....

Final design approved .... Estimated cost ....

Production drawings commenced .... completed ....

Application for planning consent ....

  Approval received .... Reference ....

Application for Building Regs. approval ....

  Approval received .... Reference ....

Application for Approval of Means of Escape ....

  Approval received .... Reference ....

Quantity surveyors .... Tel. no ....

Consultants .... Tel. no ....

.... Tel. no ....

.... Tel. no ....

Bills of quantities commenced .... Completed ....

Tenders invited .... Tenders received ....

Successful contractor .... Tel. no ....

Address ....

Contract amount .... Date of contract ....

Nominated sub-contractors and suppliers

....

....

....

....

Agent foreman .... Tel. no ....

Clerk of Works .... Tel. no ....

Starting date .... Completion date ....

Defects liability period commences .... Expires ....

Final account certified .... Amount ....

Figure 5.1   A specimen job history sheet.

suitable updating) if a similar project is being considered. Finally the needs of the lawyers should not be overlooked. If an architect is unfortunate enough to be involved in a job which has ended up in arbitration or the courts the information he or she holds may be vital to their client's case. It is an established truism that the side that presents the best records is the side most likely to win.

5.4 Legal/administrative

5.4.1 Textbooks

Every practice should have a comprehensive set of textbooks dealing with the law and also with what might be described as the business side of architectural practice. Architects are expected to be neither lawyers nor tycoons, but they are expected to have a fairly detailed understanding of the law as it affects them and to be able to understand and apply basic business techniques. An architect must be able to advise the client on choosing the appropriate form of contract and must understand the principles behind such matters as extensions of time, liquidated damages, variations, determination and planning law. It is also conceivable that the client may need some initial advice on easements, boundaries, rights of light and basic obligations during the progress of the building contract. In some of these areas all that is required of the architect is to know enough to appreciate when it is appropriate to consult, or advise the client to consult, specialized legal, management or other practitioners.

The criticism most often levied at architects is in this area of business and law. It should be obvious that the person administering the contract should be at least competent in these necessary skills. In practice, it appears to be something merely left to be picked up as the architect does the job. Although everyone needs practical experience, it is only useful as a way of tempering theoretical knowledge. Without the theory first, there is nothing to temper and the architect simply amasses a motley collection of information, often inaccurate and incomplete. The groundwork should have been laid in the schools of architecture. Schools vary in the time they devote to these topics but in any event they only provide a skeleton which the student or young architect must flesh out by private reading.

There are two kinds of textbook: the simple and the complex. Serious legal textbooks will not only state the law, but also give copious references together with a discussion of difficult points. This kind of book is fine for the lawyer. It is also useful to have on the shelf as a reference for the architect who takes a keen interest in such things. For most architects, however, an altogether simpler approach is welcomed and, generally, all that is necessary. The same thing can be said about management textbooks. Every office should have a standard text, but also numerous easy-to-read guides.

Standard forms of building contract loom large in the average architect's working life and architects should be knowledgeable in this particular field; after all, they are the professionals which most forms assume will administer the contract. Guidance and explanatory texts dealing with all the standard forms should be on every practice shelf. Never forget that architects who cause their clients to suffer loss through ignorance in administering a contract may be liable for professional negligence. Thus architects who made several errors when certifying, including deducting liquidated damages in the certificate and deducting them before the contract completion date had been reached, narrowly escaped suffering the consequences of these errors. In passing, the court considered that the architects in question were 'doing their incompetent best'.[1]

Specific topics which should be covered by appropriate textbooks are:

- *Law*
  A simple general exposition[2]
  A construction law book[3]
  A good book on contract law[4]
  Some books on specific topics such as planning law,[5], design
     liability[6] or warranties.[7]

- *Standard forms of building contract*
  One or two general texts[8]
  Texts dealing with specific contracts, such as JCT 80[9], IFC 84[10],
     MW 80.[11]

- *Management*
  One or two standard management texts.[12]
  Some texts with special relevance to managing a practice, managing
     contracts, etc.[13]

5.4.2 Acts of Parliament

Acts of Parliament do not normally make easy, let alone engrossing, reading. Indeed, it sometimes taxes the courts to decide upon the true meaning. Nevertheless, there are some Acts which a practice must have on its shelves.[14] Care must be taken to keep the Acts regularly updated. Statutory Instruments and Regulations are regularly issued under powers conferred by Acts of Parliament and it may be the Regulations which are most important so far as the busy architect is concerned.[15] It is essential that, in the absence of a librarian, someone in the practice is given the responsibility of making sure that the Acts, Instruments and Regulations are up to date.

5.4.3 Selected law reports

The English legal system depends in large measure on the doctrine of judicial precedent. That means broadly that, in general, a court must follow the decision of previous courts in similar circumstances. To be precise, a court must follow the *ratio decidendi* (the reason for the decision). There may be many other things which a judge will say in the course of giving judgment, but it is only the *ratio* which is binding. The other statements may have persuasive force on another court, perhaps depending on the judge uttering them. The idea behind the doctrine is to impart some degree of certainty into the law. However, there is considerable scope for a court to depart from a previous decision if it is considered that aspects of the earlier case are significantly different from the case being tried. When a court decides not to follow a previous decision, it is said to 'distinguish' the earlier case. The courts may do this to avoid injustice in a particular case.

The general rule is that every court binds a lower court by its decisions. The hierarchy of the courts is shown in simplified fashion in Figure 5.2. A decision of the House of Lords is binding on all other courts, but it has the right to depart from its own decisions in future cases for very good reasons. It occasionally does so. The Court of Appeal binds itself and all courts below. Most construction cases are dealt with and disposed of, if not appealed, by the Official Referees. They are specialist judges who deal with cases which have a high technical content. Their work is not confined to construction cases, but the construction industry is the major user of their services.

In order for this system to work, it is essential that reports of the judgments in decided cases are easily available. Law reports have been available for about 700 years in various forms. It is perhaps a peculiarly English trait that, in spite of the importance, there is no official system of law reporting. Reporting depends on private enterprise. The nearest thing to an official set of reports is *The Law Reports* published by the Incorporated Council of Law Reporting since 1965. There are many other series, such as the *All England Law Reports, Lloyds' Law Reports,*

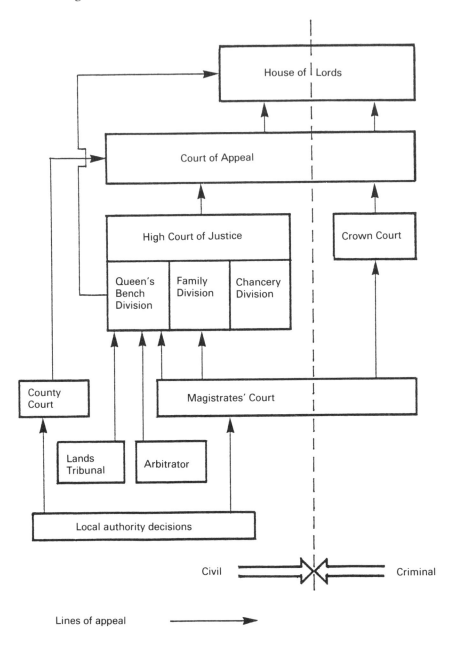

Figure 5.2   Court hierarchy.

and the *Times Law Reports*. Not all decisions are reported and, until comparatively recently, many decisions of importance to the construction industry went unreported.

It is unrealistic to expect architects to read every law report or even to read all the reports relating to construction. However, architects should be aware of legal decisions which might affect them and they should know where to lay their hands on the full report of the judgment. Architects should, of course, be wary of attempting to identify the *ratio* in each case. Courts often appear to have grave difficulty in this regard when examining the judgments of higher courts which they are expected to follow. Nevertheless, the reports can provide valuable insights in certain circumstances.

There are now a number of series of reports which are concerned only with construction cases, as follows. No one series covers all the cases.

- *Building Law Reports* (BLR): Fully indexed series, giving the full judgments; each case is prefaced by a brief résumé of the key facts and decisions together with a useful commentary on some of the features of the case in question. Published by Longmans (hardback).

- *Construction Law Reports* (ConLR): Fully indexed series, giving the full judgments; each case is prefaced by a brief résumé of the key facts and decisions. Concentrates, although not exclusively, on the judgments of the Official Referees Courts. Published by Butterworths (hardback).

- *Construction Law Journal* (Const LJ): Fully indexed series, generally giving full judgments; each case is prefaced by a brief résumé of the key facts and decisions. Each issue also contains articles on some aspect of construction law and contracts and book reviews. Published by Sweet & Maxwell (paperback).

- *Construction Law Digest* (CLD): Fully indexed series, providing digests of construction cases of interest, highlighting key points, together with details of standard contract amendments, Acts of Parliament, etc. Each issue has a penetrating insight into key issues of construction law. Published by BSP Professional Books (paperback with hardback yearly binder).

- *Construction Industry Law Letter* (CILL): Fully indexed series, giving brief reports on cases of interest together with short commentary. Also contains occasional articles on construction law topics, details of Acts of Parliament, standard contract amendments, etc. Published by Legal Studies & Services (Publishing) Ltd (paperback with hardback binder).

CLD or CILL are probably the most useful for a busy architect, but the practice should back up these 'immediate' quick reports with one or more of the other series in order to be able to refer to the full judgment of a particular case.

References to law reports (there are some references given in the notes to other parts of this book) are given by means of a standardized abbreviation system. The abbreviations referring to the reports noted above are given immediately after the titles in each case, but in addition it is necessary to include further information to enable location of the precise report. Usually that is achieved by giving the volume number and the page number. Therefore, '32 BLR 51' refers to volume 32 of *Building Law Reports*, page 51. (CLD and CILL have slightly different systems.)

5.4.4 Professional publications

Professional journals offer a quick way of keeping up to date with construction law and standard contract amendments. Many of them offer a regular series of updates on these matters. The *Architects' Journal*, *Chartered Quantity Surveyor*, *Building* and the *Practice* insert to the *RIBA Journal* are all valuable in this respect. A specialist construction law journal entitled *Constructional Law* is filled with useful articles.

References

(1) *Lubenham Fidelities & Investment Co. v. South Pembrokeshire District Council* (1986) 6 Con LR 85.
(2) Padfield, C.F. (1987) *Law Made Simple*, 6th edn, Heinemann.
(3) May, A. (1991) *Keating on Building Contracts*, 5th edn, Sweet & Maxwell.
    Walker-Smith, D. & Povey, P. (1991) *The Standard Forms of Building Contract*, with Supplement 6, Charles Knight.
    Bickford-Smith, S., Anderson, A.J., Freeth, E. & Powell-Smith, V. (1980) *Emden's Building Contracts and Practice*, 8th edn, Butterworth.
(4) Furmston, M.P. (1991) *Cheshire, Fifoot and Furmston's Law of Contract*, 12th edn, Butterworth, London.
(5) Heap, D. (1987) *An Outline of Planning Law*, 9th edn, Sweet & Maxwell.
(6) Cornes, D.L. (1989) *Design Liability in the Construction Industry*, 3rd edn, BSP Professional Books, Oxford.

(7) Paterson, Frances A. (1991) *Collateral Warranties Explained*, RIBA Publications Ltd, London.

(8) Chappell, D. (1991)*Which Form of Building Contract*, Longman.
Chappell, D. (1991) *Understanding JCT Building Contracts*, 2nd edn, E. & F.N. Spon.
Powell-Smith, V. & Chappell, D. (1989) *Building Contracts Compared and Tabulated*, 2nd edn, Legal Studies & Services (Publishing) Ltd.

(9) Parris, J. (1985) *Standard Form of Building Contract*, 2nd edn, BSP Professional Books, Oxford.

(10) Jones, N.F. & Bergman, D. (1991) *A Commentary on the JCT Intermediate Form of Building Contract*, 2nd edn, BSP Professional Books, Oxford.

(11) Chappell, D. & Powell-Smith, V. (1990) *The JCT Minor Works Form of Contract (MW 80) - A Practical Guide*, Legal Studies & Services (Publishing) Ltd.

(12) Drucker, P.F. (1968) *The Practice of Management*, Pan.
Drucker, P.F. (1968) *The Effective Executive*, Pan.
Peter, L. (1971) *The Peter Principle*, Pan Books.
Townsend, R. (1985) *Up the Organisation*, Penguin.

(13) Cox, S. & Hamilton, A. (1991) *Architect's Handbook of Practice Management*, 5th edn, RIBA Publications Ltd, London.
Beaven, L., Cox, S., Dry, D. & Males, R. (1988) *Architect's Job Book* 5th edn, RIBA Publications Ltd.
Chappell, D. (1990) *Contractual Correspondence for Architects*, 2nd edn, Legal Studies & Services (Publishing) Ltd.
Sharp, D. (1991) *The Business of Architectural Practice*, 2nd edn, BSP Professional Books, Oxford.
Barrett, P. & Males, R. (Eds) (1991) *Practice Management*, E. & F.N. Spon.

(14) Arbitration Acts 1950, 1979.
Building Act 1984.
Companies Acts 1985, 1989.
Consumer Protection Act 1987.
Copyright, Designs and Patents Act 1988.
Defective Premises Act 1972.
Health and Safety at Work Act 1974.
Insolvency Act 1986.
Latent Damage Act 1986.
Limitation Act 1980.
Misrepresentation Act 1967.
Occupiers Liability Acts 1957, 1984.
Partnership Act 1890.
Sale of Goods Act 1979.
Supply of Goods and Services Act 1982.
Trade Descriptions Act 1968.
Unfair Contracts Terms Act 1977.

(15) A good example is the Building Regulations 1985.

Part 2

Running a Job

Chapter 6

Stage A: Architects' Services

6.1 Enquiries

Marketing is dealt with in Chapter 19. The results of marketing should be enquiries from prospective clients. Enquiries can take many forms. Ideally, they come in the form of a letter, stating requirements and courteously requesting details of fees and conditions of engagement. The reality is almost never like that. Established architects will usually have clients with whom they do business on a continuing basis. In such cases, the enquiry is likely to be quite informal, during a meeting about some other matter or by telephone. Many new clients make their first approach by telephone; very few call personally at the architect's office in the first instance.

The way in which a client makes an enquiry can often tell the architect a great deal about the kind of client he or she is. It is always wise to respond to any kind of approach from a new client by arranging a meeting. At the meeting, the client can assess the architect and the architect can decide whether he or she wishes to work with that client. As in every other field, personalities have a major part to play in the equation. Clients are dealt with in Chapter 1, section 1.1.1. A client may sometimes be a friend or relative, but more generally, a complete stranger. Some may have built before; others will be building for the first time. By its nature, the production of a building may take a very long time from inception to completion. It is important to start the relationship on a firm foundation or it will not survive.

6.2 Extent of services

There is some confusion regarding the services provided by the architect. Some clients firmly believe that the architect's fee for a commission will include anything and everything the client may require, provided only that it has some relationship to the job. Other clients believe that the architect will prepare a set of plans, but anything else the client may need will cost extra. Both views are wrong, but there is a grain of truth in each belief, which is why it is often difficult to explain the architect's services satisfactorily.

The question of fees is dealt with in Chapter 7, section 7.1, but it is worth remembering at this point that architects sell their services just like anyone else. If, for example, an architect is asked to prepare a sketch scheme to satisfy the client's requirements, that is what will be done. It is totally unreasonable to expect preparation of working drawings, invitation of tenders and inspection of work in progress at no additional cost. Moreover, the client may not like the sketch scheme produced by the architect, but provided that it satisfies the requirements given by the client, the architect is entitled to the fee.

In practice, most architects are prepared to carry out considerable reworking of their schemes until the client is entirely happy. This is very worthy and in the best traditions of professional service, but it is not strictly necessary and in an era of fee competition it is not always practical to achieve. To overcome this problem, the early stages of the architect's work are often carried out on a time charge basis.

It is unfortunately true that many clients are astonished, if they have never built before, that at the end of the initial stages of the architect's work there is often nothing visible except a set of two or three presentation drawings for which they are expected to pay what may appear to be an exorbitant fee. To take this attitude, of course, is to ignore the vast amount of work which has gone before the preparation of drawings. The prudent architect will usually avoid this situation by involving the client as fully as possible in every stage of the work. This approach is in line with best practice, but the architect should assess each client, because some want nothing better than that the architect goes away and returns in a few weeks with his or her proposals. The architect is therefore expected to be something of a psychologist alongside all the other skills required.

The relationship between architect and client is that of agent and principal. The agent exercises contractual powers on behalf of the principal and in doing so the principal is bound by the agent's properly authorized acts. The agency relationship may be created in one of four ways:

- *Expressly*, when the client specifically appoints the architect either in writing or orally. This is the most satisfactory, particularly when done in writing, because there is little scope for misunderstandings or mistakes.
- *By implication*, when it is clear to others that the architect must be acting as agent. Such an instance may occur because the client

behaves as if the architect was acting in an agency capacity or simply because the architect is doing the kind of things normally done by an agent.

- *By necessity*, when the architect acts for the client in an emergency and otherwise there would be no agency. There will be very few instances where an agency comes into being in this way so far as architects are concerned. One might just visualise a situation where the architect must give an instruction on the client's behalf in order to save the destruction of property even though the architect may not be empowered to give that particular instruction.
- *By ratification*, when the architect performs some act which the client subsequently ratifies. Two conditions must be satisfied: (1) the architect must carry out the action on behalf of the principal; (2) the principal must have been capable of carrying out the act at the time it was performed.

The agent's authority is important. It may be actual or apparent (ostensible). An architect's actual authority is defined by the terms of the conditions of engagement. Apparent or ostensible authority is the authority the architect appears to possess so far as parties other than the architect and client are concerned. An architect is liable to the client for acting beyond authority, but provided the architect is behaving in the way in which others expect him or her to act, the client will usually be responsible for such actions to third parties. For example, an architect carrying out functions under a building contract may issue instructions to the contractor. Provided the contract expressly empowers the architect to issue such instructions, the contractor is entitled to carry out the work and be paid. It matters not that the architect may be obliged, under his or her conditions of engagement, to obtain the client's authorization for such instructions. Of course, in that situation, the architect may expect to be required to reimburse the client for any loss sustained.

The duties of an agent are:

- To act. Failure to act if action is called for is actionable.
- To obey instructions. The instructions must be lawful and reasonable.
- To exercise skill and care: the kind of skill and care normally to be expected from a member of that particular profession.
- Not to take any secret bribe or profit. The principal may recover damages including the amount of such bribe.
- To declare any conflict of interest.

- Not to delegate without authority.
- To keep proper accounts.

One of the greatest dangers for an architect is that of exceeding the authority actually given by the client. The possible consequences have already been touched upon. When in doubt, the client's written authority should be obtained. Next best is to confirm instructions to the client. Another danger may arise if the architect fails to disclose that he or she is acting for a client. The architect may become personally liable to the third party in such cases.

Agency may be terminated by the death of the agent or principal, by the performance of the agent's contract, by mutual consent, by breach on the part of either agent or principal and by bankruptcy of the principal, but not necessarily of the agent.

At one time it used to be thought that the architect was in the position of a quasi-arbitrator or acting in a judicial capacity when carrying out some functions under the building contract. Such things as giving extensions of time or certifying monies due were thought to be in this category. Such notions were dispelled with the case of *Sutcliffe* v. *Thackrah* (1974)[1] The architect has a duty to act fairly in these circumstances, but the duty is owed to the client, not to the contractor (*Pacific Associates* v. *Baxter* (1988)).[2] If an architect is negligent in the performance of any duty in this regard, the client may sue direct in respect of any loss suffered, but the contractor must take action against the client, probably in arbitration, under the building contract.

The architect's services fall into two parts:

(1) Services which an architect will undertake as part of the overall design and administration of an entire project from beginning to end.
(2) Services which are available from an architect, but not as part of 'normal' entire project services.

A very detailed description of these services is included in the RIBA Architect's Appointment,[3] commonly referred to as the 'blue book' (see Chapter 7, section 7.2) available from the RIBA. Although at the time of writing a new version of the book is nearing completion, it is thought proper to include a reasonably full treatment of the current version. Commissions based on the current version will continue for some years and architects must be familiar with its terms.

All architects will be prepared to offer the 'normal' services to their clients, but some of the additional services may call for a degree of expertise in fields which not every architect will be prepared to offer.

```
Stages

A       Inception
B       Feasibility
C       Outline proposals
D       Scheme design
E       Detail design
F       Production information
G       Bills of quantities
H       Tender action
J       Project planning
K       Operations on site
L       Completion
M       Feedback
```

Figure 6.1   The RIBA Plan of Work (titles of stages only).

For charging and other purposes, the work is divided into stages. Figure 6.1 shows them in diagrammatic form. This part of the book is divided into the same stages for convenience and what follows is a brief description of each stage, which will receive more detailed treatment in succeeding chapters. It is not always easy to pin-point activities within a particular stage, because the whole process is continuous and some activities can be accommodated in several stages. For example, application for full planning permission and selection of specialist sub-contractors will take place at a time to suit the circumstances.

6.2.1 Normal services[4]

A Inception

During this initial stage, the architect's prime function is to obtain the client's brief. It can be a laborious process if clients are not sure of what they want and sometimes even if they are. It is the architect's task to separate what the client wants from what he or she really needs. The architect will need to ask many questions regarding finance available, time schedule and the function required of the building. It is likely that several meetings will be required before the architect is satisfied. If there is any advice the client requires or the architect thinks it proper to give at this point, it will be given. For example, the architect may say at the first meeting that the project is not feasible because of cost, siting or some other reason.

Generally, assuming the scheme is not aborted, the architect will visit the site to get some idea of what is involved. The client can then be given some preliminary thoughts on the need for consultants and specialist sub-contractors. It is at this stage that the architect will be able to provide a rough idea of the cost, time and fees likely to be involved in proceeding with the scheme. If the work the client has in mind is very small, an extension to a house for example, the whole process may take no more than a day or so. In the case of larger projects, a correspondingly longer time will be required. Where extremely large and complex projects are concerned, this stage may be very protracted.

B Feasibility

On small projects, this stage is combined with the first stage; on anything other than small projects it represents a considerable body of work at the end of which the architect might prepare a report, depending upon the size and complexity of the project, for examination by the client.[5] Instead of a report, the architect's conclusions might be presented orally.

This is the stage during which the architect will check thoroughly that the project is feasible, that it can be built for the money the client wishes to spend, that there are no obstacles in the form of planning objections from the local authority or the site conditions and so on. There will be involvement in discussions with statutory authorities and any consultants appointed, and every matter which might affect the client's intention to proceed must be investigated. For example, if the client is proposing a speculative housing development, it might well be prudent to include, for the client's information, details of local schools, shops and bus services near the site. If the site is in a designated conservation or urban redevelopment area, the architect will explain how that will affect the scheme.

At this stage, alternative ways of tackling the design will be suggested, and the stage will conclude with a request to the client to make certain decisions. The decision may be simply whether to proceed, or it may involve matters thrown up by the investigations.

C Outline proposals

This stage is probably better known as *sketch design*. Taking into account all previous discussions, including the client's decisions at the end of stage B, the architect will prepare drawings to illustrate the proposed solution to the client's problem. The drawings will not be detailed, but they will be sufficient to show what the architect has in mind in a general way. It should be possible to see the general massing and external appearance of the building, its disposition on site and the arrangement of the interior.

To produce these sketches, the architect will have to have analysed and considered all the information gleaned during the previous stages. The client should be asked to approve an approximate estimate of cost at this stage. In giving such an approximate estimate of cost, an architect is wise to ensure that it is a generous estimate because this is the figure that the client will always remember.

D Scheme design

On small jobs, this stage is combined with the previous stage. The architect must take into account any comments the client makes about the outline proposals and work with any consultants who may be appointed to produce a more detailed design for the client's approval. At this stage, the client should have a clear idea of the appearance of the building, the materials proposed and the layout of the interior. A fresh estimate of cost will be prepared and dates proposed for commencement and completion. The architect will require the client's final approval to the scheme, time-scale and cost at this point.

Assuming that the client does approve with little or no amendment, the architect should apply for planning permission. Although an application for outline permission will almost certainly have been made at feasibility stage, and thereafter the planning authorities will have been closely consulted, there is unfortunately no guarantee that planning permission will be granted. In most cases, the procedures adopted by the architect avoid a refusal at this stage, but it is not uncommon for the planning authority to require some changes before they will grant permission. Both architect and client will find it frustrating if this happens; it will also cause the architect much extra work.

At the end of this stage, the architect should advise the client that any subsequent changes of mind will be costly in terms of time and money. The scheme now should be regarded as fixed.

E Detail design

As soon as the architect obtains the client's approval to the scheme design, every part of the scheme must be developed in great detail. This is the first part of what is commonly called *working drawings*. If consultants are appointed, they will be involved in similar detailed design work. The client will be asked to approve many of the details, particularly as regards standards and quality. The cost of building the project must be kept constantly under review as each detail is finalized. In a project of any size at all, this task should be undertaken by a quantity surveyor. The drawings produced during this stage will be highly technical, dimensioned, noted and coded. On the basis of these drawings, all further negotiations and approvals with statutory bodies will be finalized. The architect should advise the client that if any subsequent changes are required which are other than trivial, the building programme will be disrupted and the client will incur considerable extra cost. The client's idea of 'trivial' may well not accord with the architect's views.

Clients often fail to understand why a change of mind which appears to reduce the overall cost of the building should result in additional costs. The architect should therefore clearly explain that if the client changes something, the architect has to begin again the process of consultation with statutory bodies (including, on occasions, re-applying for planning and Building Regulation permission), consultants and any specialist sub-contractors. Drawings have to be re-done, fresh calculations made and new costings carried out. The architect's careful programming of office resources will be upset and there is the very real danger that mistakes will be made. It is the architect's duty to give clear advice in this regard if the client wants any changes. It would be wrong simply to carry out the client's instructions and present a large bill for additional services at the end.

F Production information

During this stage, the architect and any consultants should be busy producing all the information which a contractor will require to proceed subsequently to erect the building. In addition to the drawings prepared during the last stage, details and schedules will be produced together with a specification of all the materials and items of work required.

G Bills of quantities

If the system of procurement warrants it (see Chapter 8, section 8.2), bills of quantities should be prepared by the quantity surveyor from information supplied by the architect and other consultants. The architect must be ready to supply any additional information which the quantity surveyor requires. The architect should know the building in detail at this stage.

H   Tender action

Sometime before this stage, the architect should have advised the client on the most appropriate way of obtaining a price for the work. It may be by means of negotiation or tendering. During this stage, he should arrange everything that needs to be done before prices are obtained and, if tendering is decided upon, he should arrange to have tendering information sent out to all the contractors on a list which the client has previously approved. A prudent architect will have requested references from every contractor on the list and at the same time ascertained by discreet enquiry some idea of their financial stability. The architect will in due course assess all tenders received and advise the client accordingly.

J   Project planning

During this stage, the architect should give advice to the client with regard to contractual matters, insurances and the like and should be ready to answer any questions. Discussions will have taken place concerning the appropriate form of contract (including any necessary amendments) before tender stage, and the contract documents prepared for signature. All the information must be assembled to enable building to commence on the appointed date and it is usual for a number of meetings to be held with consultants, specialist sub-contractors, the contractor and possibly representatives from statutory authorities.

K   Operations on site

During the course of work on site, the architect will carry out his or her duties under the contract and make regular visits to the site to inspect the general progress and quality of workmanship and materials. The client should be kept up to date on the progress of work and supplied with financial reports from time to time depending upon the client's requirements and the size and complexity of the project. The client should be given any additional advice required concerning the project.

L   Completion

When work is completed, the architect must ensure that all loose ends are tied up and generally make sure that the financial aspects are settled accurately with the help of other consultants as appropriate.

The client should be supplied with some general notes on maintenance together with a set of drawings showing the building and the main lines of drainage and the services installations.

6.2.2 Other services

Sites

The architect can advise on site suitability and negotiate on the client's behalf. He or she can prepare survey drawings and undertake site investigations, in collaboration with the appropriate consultant.

Buildings

The architect can produce survey drawings of buildings and prepare schedules of conditions. Depending upon the skills within the office, it may be possible to carry out structural surveys and investigate defects and failures. The preparation of specifications in connection with repairs can be undertaken and work in progress inspected. Advice may also be offered on many other building problems, such as heat loss, fire protection, change of use and economic costs in use.

Development

The architect should be an expert in the production of special plans for many purposes in connection with building development. Elaborate models and perspectives are available from some offices; other specialist services which may be available include montages, detailed plans and specifications for roads and sewers, demolition and environmental studies and conveyancing plans.

Design

The architect should be able to offer a wide variety of services under this general heading. Among them are the design and selection of furnishings and decoration, exhibition design, shop-fitting, and advice on the commissioning or selection of works of art. The architect may be able to offer specialist services in acoustical investigations, development and testing of systems of building including testing of prototypes or models.

Financial

Depending on the disciplines within the architect's office, it may be possible to offer complete cost planning of building projects, advice on cash flow requirements, life cycle cost analyses, valuation of buildings, preparation of schedules of rates or quantities, estimates and negotiations in connection with fire damage and grant negotiations. Otherwise these matters are best left to a quantity surveyor.

Negotiations

It is common for architects to offer services in connection with planning appeals and special negotiations, Building Regulation relaxations, submissions to bodies such as the Royal Fine Art Commission and submissions to landlords.

Legal

The architect should be able to offer a substantial knowledge of the law as it relates to building and provide services in connection with easements, party wall negotiations and rights. With appropriate experience, it should be possible to give expert evidence in proceedings and advise during conferences with solicitors and counsel. Although in theory all architects can act as arbitrators in appropriate cases, in practice only those architects who have had proper training and experience should practise as arbitrators.

Management

Management services include the entire project management of building works, provision of constant site inspection, co-ordination of separate trade contracts, co-ordination and supervision of direct labour contracts and services to either party in connection with design-and-build contracts. 'As built' drawings can be prepared together with detailed maintenance manuals and maintenance programmes.

Consultants

If architects have suitably qualified personnel within their practices, they will be able to offer services normally provided by the appropriate consultant. They will be able to offer these services either on jobs for which they are the project architects or project managers or jobs for which another architect has been engaged (with the agreement of that architect). An architect may also be engaged as an independent consultant on a regular basis if required.

Summary

The services which the architect may offer as part of the normal or additional services cover every facet of building work and the care and maintenance of buildings in use. Although all architects will be willing to offer some of the services outlined above, architects like other professionals tend to develop their own specialisms. If an architect holds himself out as qualified to offer a competent service in something which he is not equipped to do, there will be serious legal implications. In addition, an architect should not offer services for which he or she does not have appropriate professional indemnity cover (see Chapter 17, section 17.4).

References

(1) 1 All ER 319.
(2) 6 Con LR 90.
(3) RIBA (1990) *Architect's Appointment*, RIBA Publications Ltd. A new edition is in course of preparation at the time of writing. The drafts distributed for comment suggest that it will be significantly changed in layout.
(4) Green, R. (1986) *Architect's Guide to Running a Job*, 4th edn, Architectural Press Ltd.
(5) Chappell, D. (1989) *Report Writing for Architects*, 2nd edn, Legal Studies & Services (Publishing) Ltd.

Chapter 7

Stage A: Appointment and Briefing

7.1 *Fee negotiation or tendering*

Architects no longer have a mandatory fee scale. This means that they are free to charge whatever they consider to be the proper rate for the work to be done. It also means that negotiations can take place with a prospective client to arrive at a mutually agreeable figure.[1] There is a point, however, below which the architect cannot give a satisfactory standard of service. To negotiate a fee below that point is commercial suicide, to say nothing of being unprofessional. The fees negotiated will depend upon many factors of which the following are the most significant:

- The amount of work the architect has in progress.
- The size of the office related to turnover and hence the overhead costs.
- Whether the project is 'one off' or simply the first of many similar jobs which the architect can expect to receive from the same client.
- Whether the project is particularly interesting to the architect.

Most architects use the fee scales recommended in the RIBA Architect's Appointment[2] or at least they use them as a basis. A small one-man office may charge less, but offer less resources than a larger firm which may charge more to cover its larger overheads. The smaller firm may argue that it is giving a more personalized service. It is now possible for a client to obtain competitive quotations from a number of architects for the same job. It is necessary to ensure that the terms are absolutely clear and on the same basis for each of the architects involved in giving a quotation.

The basis of fees is usually either:

- a percentage of the total cost of building, or
- a time charge, or
- a lump sum.

7.1.1 Percentage charges

Architects will normally charge a percentage of the actual total construction cost if they are providing the normal full service. The RIBA Architect's Appointment divides buildings into classes and provides graphs showing recommended percentages for each class over a range of construction costs. Class 1 buildings are the simplest; class 5 are the most complex. Stages A and B are not usually included in the percentage charge. The recommendations are detailed, and if the architect does propose using them, he should study the implications carefully. Among points worthy of note are the following:

- Consultants' work is included in the total cost even if carried out under a separate contract.
- Specialist sub-contractors' design fees are excluded.
- If the architect carries out work on parts of the building which are eventually omitted, the total construction cost will be estimated for fee purposes.
- Built-in furniture and equipment is included in the total cost.
- If clients carry out any work direct or supply materials at their own cost, the architect should estimate the value and include it in the total construction cost for fee purposes.
- Where there is a substantial element of repetition, the fees may be reduced.

It is normal for fees to be paid in instalments based upon the estimated final cost. The final fee account will be adjusted to take account of the actual final cost of the building. Payment should be agreed as being made at the end of each stage or, better, monthly.

It is essential that the charge is agreed before the architect undertakes any work. If the work is fairly simple, many architects include the preliminary stages A and B in the total percentage fee, but the precise terms should be stated. Many clients get an unpleasant shock when they learn that all the briefing and feasibility studies are extra to the percentage fee. At best, this leads to a damaged relationship; at worst, the parties can become locked in litigation. This is always undesirable; in the middle of a project it can be catastrophic.

7.1.2 Time charges

Time charges are based on an hourly rate. The RIBA Architect's Appointment sets out no recommendations for principals, but for other technical staff it suggests a formula on the basis of 18 pence per £100 of gross annual income or thereabouts. Principals offering special expertise or experience normally charge a relatively high rate. The rate will also vary with the complexity of the work to be carried out. Work for which an hourly rate would be appropriate could include:

- Stage A and B of the RIBA Plan of Work.
- Constant site inspection.
- Partial services.
- Additional services.
- Any instance where the client has agreed with the architect that a time charge should be made.
- Additional work beyond the architect's control such as:
  - revisions to documents due to changes in the law;
  - changes in client's instructions;
  - delays in building operations from any cause.

The actual amount charged per hour varies from practice to practice and from one part of the country to another. Charges are usually higher in the London area than in the North and larger practices usually charge more than small practices. The large practice will probably argue that the increased cost arises from higher overheads needed to maintain a better standard of service.

It is very difficult to arrive at a figure for an hourly rate, because the rates from practice to practice are not generally known. Thus, an architect fixing an hourly rate for his technical staff may wonder where to start. A commonly used guide is the 1 : 1 : 1 formula where the rate is made up of equal parts of salary, overheads and profit. In practice, the architect works out the amount he pays a staff member per hour, then multiplies by three to find the hourly rate to be charged to his client. It is only a rough guide, but all architects should go through the exercise to see if they are charging anything like this figure. It is our experience that most architects and surveyors, particularly outside London, charge very low hourly rates when compared with other professions.

Many clients are wary of paying on an hourly basis. They tend to liken it to a blank cheque. It is, however, perfectly possible for an architect to state an hourly rate and to give a rough estimate of the length of time needed. Another variant is the hourly rate plus ceiling figure beyond which the architect must not go without further authorization. Rendering monthly accounts in such instances assists both architect and client to keep control of the situation. In certain instances, there is no option but to state an hourly rate. It need not be more expensive than a lump sum (see below) because the architect is certain to make a reasonable profit from an hourly rate, whereas he must add something for contingencies when arriving at a lump sum.

7.1.3 Lump sum charges

There is nothing to prevent the architect from quoting a lump sum fee to cover all the work expected to be carried out. However, this should only be done if:

- The extent of the work required is absolutely clear.
- The time-scale of the service is known.

It would be unusual, for example, if the architect were to quote a lump sum fee for carrying out negotiations with the local authority in regard to development work. However, a small project requiring full services over a comparatively short time-scale is the sort of job architects can cost in their offices and for which they can give a firm quotation.

There is danger for the client if he or she requires a lump sum quotation, and the architect has a duty to explain the implications fully. Clients must know precisely what they want; they must not cause delay nor change their minds. If architects are involved in additional work for which they have not priced, the client can be required to pay additional fees. Where architects are requested to quote on a lump sum basis, they must take care to specify precisely the services which are included, particularly whether or not they are inclusive of VAT, expenses etc.

An architect may not take part in a 'dutch auction' so as effectively to undercut another architect's fee quotation. The RIBA Code of Professional Conduct usefully sets out guidelines for architects asked to engage in fee tendering (see Chapter 2, section 2.6).

The practice of project team fee negotiations is rapidly gaining popularity among some clients.[3] These clients commission buildings which, of their nature, require a considerable input from consultants in several disciplines. Traditionally, such clients may be left to negotiate terms and fees with each consultant individually as recommended by the architect, and there is again the fear of a blank cheque. Moreover, experience has shown that different consultants do not always fit together harmoniously. Indeed, many disputes arise out of conflicts between the approaches of differing disciplines. The idea of project team fee negotiations is that an integrated approach is presented to the client consisting of all the consultants under the co-ordination of a lead consultant (who may not be an architect). Fees and the individual responsibilities are expressly set out including specific professional indemnity responsibilities.

7.1.4 Work to existing buildings

If the work the client requires to be done involves an existing building, a larger fee is chargeable. This is because the architect will be involved in much more work owing to the constraints of the original structure, planning, services, etc. If, in addition, the building is of architectural or historic interest, if it is a listed building or in a conservation area, the client may also be paying for the architect's special skills in dealing with buildings of that type. Even if the building is a new construction to be joined on to an existing building, the client will be charged a higher fee for that portion of the work where new and old connect. RIBA Architect's Appointment gives recommendations. It is very risky, from the architect's point of view, to agree to take on this kind of work for a lump sum.

7.1.5 Termination

Just whether and how much the architect can recover in respect of fees in the event of termination will depend on whether formal conditions of engagement have been entered into and the circumstances of the termination. RIBA Architect's Appointment provides that either architect or client can terminate on reasonable notice. It also provides that the architect is then entitled to fees for all work completed up to the time of termination. The exact method of calculating the fees will depend upon the basis originally agreed. The architect is entitled to charge all expenses arising from the termination. If, for example, an architect is in the middle of producing working drawings, specifications and schedules for the contractor, he or she cannot be expected to move staff on to other work immediately.

If there is no formal agreement between the architect and the client, there will be no provision for termination and no provision for subsequent recovery of fees. In this situation the parties will find themselves locked into litigation unless they suddenly display a streak of reasonableness which, had it been present in the first place, would have resulted in an agreement on clear terms (see section 7.2).

7.1.6 Expenses

There is no automatic right to expenses. A client is entitled to assume that they are included in any fee quoted unless they are specifically stated to be extra. It is also advisable to state precisely what the architect considers to be reimbursable expenses. A distinction must be made between expenses and disbursements. Disbursements are sums which are expended on behalf of a client and they are usually recovered as a net amount. Statutory fees and direct payments to consultants fall into this category. Normal expense items are:

- Postage, telephone, telex and other means of communication or delivery.
- Hotel and travelling expenses (mileage rates should be stated in the agreement).
- Charges for travelling time if the time spent on travelling is exceptional (this should also be agreed in advance).
- Printing, reproduction and purchase of all drawings, documents, photographs and models which the architect must or the client requests him to produce in order to carry out the work.
- Payment for specialist advice which the client has authorized; legal advice, for example.
- Special hire charges for equipment if authorized.

7.2 *Terms of appointment*

The relationship between an architect and his or her client is contractual. There may also, depending upon circumstances, be a tortious liability: that is, liability for breach of a civil duty imposed by the law generally. The most important tort is negligence which depends, among other things, on the existence of a duty of care. Principally, however, the relationship will depend upon the terms of the agreement made between the parties.

There are two types of contract:

- A simple contract (under hand).
- A specialty contract (a deed).

There are important differences. In a simple contract, there must be consideration present or the contract will not be valid. Consideration is something which is given, done or foreborne by one party in return for some action or inaction on the part of the other party. In addition, an action for breach of that contract cannot be brought by one party against the other more than six years after the date of the breach. A specialty contract does not require consideration to make it valid and the limitation period is 12 years from the date of the breach. There are other differences, but the two noted above are the most important so far as architects are concerned. Effectively, the result is that an architect who enters into an agreement as a deed with the client doubles the length of exposure to actions under the contract or for breach of its terms.

A contract is a binding agreement between two or more persons which creates mutual rights and duties and which is enforceable at law. There must be an intention to create legal relations. In the case of agreements between business people, such an intention is implied. In the case of friends or relatives, the intention normally has to be demonstrated. For a valid contract there must be:

- An offer by one party.
- Unqualified acceptance by the other party.
- Consideration (except in the case of a specialty contract).
- Capacity to contract. Certain persons, e.g. drunkards, the insane and minors, have very limited capacity to contract.
- Intention to create a legal relationship.
- Genuine consent, i.e. there must be no duress.
- A legal objective.
- A possible objective.

A simple contract can be entered into in writing or orally. The problem with an oral contract, of course, is uncertainty about its terms. Even if there are witnesses, they may later disagree regarding what they heard. Many architects are engaged purely on the basis of an oral agreement, and indeed some clients may appear offended if asked to put the commission in writing, as though it was some reflection upon their honour. In truth, the purpose of recording the terms in writing is to protect both parties, not only against sharp practice, but more commonly against imperfect memory or plain misunderstanding. At the very least, the architect should confirm in writing the terms of the appointment at the earliest opportunity.

It used to be the case that a specialty contract had to be made under seal. This was usually a round piece of red paper on which a seal was embossed or it could be a rubber stamp or, indeed, anything so long as the parties clearly intended the document to be sealed.[4] However, the Law of Property (Miscellaneous Provisions) Act 1989, in the case of individuals, and the Companies Act 1989, in the case of companies, removed the necessity to use a seal.

In the case of a company all that is required is for the document to state on its face that it is a deed and for it to be signed by two directors or one director and the company secretary. In the case of an individual, the document must state on its face that it is a deed and it should be signed by the person making the deed in the presence of a witness who must attest the signature. Alternatively, but rarely, an individual may authorize another to sign on his behalf in which case there must be two witnesses who must attest the signature. The stamping of such documents is not generally required unless part of a conveyance.

Some bodies insist that the architect contracts on the basis of their own particular terms and conditions. In such cases, the architect should take the greatest possible care including if necessary obtaining expert advice. Wherever possible, the architect is well advised to contract on the basis of standard terms of which the best known is the RIBA Architect's Appointment. Although it is possible to incorporate these terms by stating in a letter to a client that they are so incorporated,[5] such a practice can lead to confusion because the terms are intended to be applied on the basis of a memorandum of agreement which provides for the addition or deletion of terms as appropriate. Simply to incorporate the document as a whole without qualification could lead to ambiguity. Another difficulty which can arise is that the document is drafted with a traditional contractual arrangement in mind. If some other arrangement is intended, such as employment by a contractor or in connection with a management contract, some amendment of the terms will be necessary.

The Architect's Appointment was introduced by the Royal Institute of British Architects in 1982. It is the successor to the *Conditions of Engagement* and follows the report of the Monopolies and Mergers Commission on architects' and surveyors' services and remuneration. There is also a small works edition. The document is in four parts:

(1) Preliminary and basic services provided by the architect.
(2) Other services.
(3) Conditions of appointment normally applying.
(4) Recommended methods of calculating fees.

It is useful to examine the Conditions of Appointment in greater detail.

By *clause 3.1* the architect is to exercise reasonable skill and care in conformity with the normal standards of the architect's profession. This term simply states what is the general law. In *Bolam* v. *Friern*

Hospital Management Committee (1957)[6] where the judge defined the standard required of a professional person:

'But where you get a situation which involves the use of some special skill or competence, then the test whether there has been negligence or not is not the test of the man on top of the Clapham omnibus, because he has not got this special skill. A man need not possess the highest expert skill at the risk of being found negligent. It is well established law that it is sufficient if he exercised the ordinary skill of an ordinary competent man exercising the particular art.'

Clause 3.2 is very important. It sets out the architect's authority to act on behalf of the client. It gives the architect power of agency in respect of the matters set out or implied in the architect's appointment, but it stipulates that the architect must obtain the client's authority before beginning any service or work stage. The architect as agent has been discussed in Chapter 6, section 6.2.

Clauses 3.3 and 3.4 serve to qualify the architect's actual authority in that substantial changes from the approved design must not be made without the client's agreement unless it is a matter of urgency in which case the architect must notify the client without delay. The architect must also inform the client if the overall authorized cost or contract period is likely to be varied. It is good practice to send progress reports to the client at such intervals as seems appropriate to the type and size of project. Unless the client is familiar with the building industry, the reports should be couched in straightforward terms so that the implications can be grasped immediately.

Note that the building contractor is only concerned with whether the architect acts within the powers given by the building contract. If the contract empowers the architect to instruct the contractor to carry out extra work, it matters not that the architect has not obtained the client's permission. The contractor is entitled to do the work and be paid by the employer. In such a situation, however, the employer might well have a valid claim against the architect for exceeding his or her actual authority as set out in these conditions.

Clauses 3.5–3.7 deal with consultants. Either party may nominate a consultant, but the other must agree. This protects each from having to work with a consultant with whom they have had a bad experience in the past. The case of *Moresk* v. *Hicks* (1966)[7] decided that architects have no implied authority to delegate design responsibility, and unless they obtain the client's agreement they will be held liable to the client if a delegated design proves to be defective.

A very important provision states that the client will hold each consultant, and not the architect, responsible for the competence, general inspection and performance of the work entrusted to them. This is the case if the consultant is employed either directly by the employer or through the agency of the architect. That is a very good reason, quite apart from the question of professional indemnity cover (see Chapter 17, section 17.4), why the architect should not undertake to carry out what would normally be consultants' work by direct engagement of consultants. The efficacy of this clause which in effect limits the architect's liability has been accepted by the court in *Investors in Industry Commercial Properties Ltd* v. *South Bedfordshire District Council* (1986)[8] where a similar clause in the previous RIBA Conditions of Engagement was considered. The architect is given authority to co-ordinate and integrate the consultant's work into the overall design. If this term was not expressly included, it would have to be implied to enable the carrying out of the architect's duties.

Clause 3.8 refers to the nomination of a sub-contractor or supplier to design any part of the works in similar terms to consultants. The architect is not to be held responsible for their designs. Once again, it is important that the client gives consent to delegation of design duties.

Clause 3.9 is especially useful to bring home to a client the true situation in respect of the building contract although it only states what is the general law. In practice, a client will always blame the architect if anything goes wrong with a project. This clause makes clear that where the client has entered into a separate building contract, the contractor, not the architect, must be held responsible for the contractor's methods and for the proper execution of the works.

Many problems have been caused by the architect's obligation to inspect the works. Nowhere does it state that the architect must 'supervise' the works although the courts, and architects themselves, regularly refer to the architect's duty to design and supervise. Supervision implies constant inspection and direction. In building contracts, this duty lies with the contractor.

Clauses 3.10–3.12 refer to site inspection. The architect is required to visit the site at intervals appropriate to the stage of construction to inspect the progress and quality of the works and to see that they are being carried out generally in accordance with the contract. It is expressly stated that the architect is not expected to make frequent or constant inspections. If such a degree of inspection by the architect is agreed to be necessary, a part- or full-time resident architect may be appointed or otherwise a clerk of works will be employed.

The clerk of works may be employed by the architect or by the client, but in any event under the direction and control of the architect. In the case of *Kensington & Chelsea and Westminster Area Health Authority* v. *Wettern Composites Ltd* (1984)[9], it was held that the damages awarded against the architect should be reduced by 20% to take account of the negligence of the clerk of works. Being employed by the client, it was held that the client was vicariously liable for the clerk of works' actions. It is clearly in the architect's interest if the clerk of works is employed directly by the client.

Clauses 3.13 and 3.14 are procedural in character and provide that the client will provide necessary information and decisions. Such a provision must be implied or the architect would be unable to function properly. If the client is composed of a number of persons, it must nominate a responsible representative for the giving of instructions. This is a sensible procedure which would probably be adopted in any event.

The copyright position is regulated by the Copyright, Designs and Patent Act 1988. There is also case law which has a bearing on the situation. There is no copyright in ideas or concepts, but only in the way in which they are expressed. Section 1 of the Act states that copyright is a property right in, among other things, original literary, dramatic, musical or artistic works. Section 4 makes it clear that 'artistic work' includes 'a work of architecture being a building or a model for a building' and that 'building' includes any fixed structure and part of a building or fixed structure. 'Artistic work' also means 'a graphic work, photograph, sculpture or collage, irrespective of artistic quality'.

In general, copyright remains with the originator or creator for his or her lifetime and for 50 years thereafter. Work produced by an employee is the copyright of the employer. Section 2 of the Act makes it clear that no one may reproduce a copy of any work without the consent of the originator. Assignment of copyright from the creator of the work to another may only be accomplished in writing. Such assignment can never be implied (s. 90). It is not usual to transfer copyright, but rather to grant a licence to use the copyright material for a particular purpose or for a particular period of time. It is not necessary to register ownership of copyright in any way, but in published works it is usual to indicate a claim to copyright thus: © John Smith (1991).

The Act introduces the concept of 'moral rights' (ss. 77(4) to (5)). An architect has the right to be identified as the originator of the building when 'in the case of a work of architecture in the form of a building or a model for a building, a sculpture or a work of artistic craftsmanship, copies of a graphic work representing it, or of a photograph of it, are issued to the public'. S. 77(5) states that 'The author of a work of architecture in the form of a building also has the right to be identified on the building as constructed or, where more than one building is constructed to the design, on the first to be constructed'. The creator must assert the right to be identified in this way before an infringement can take place.

Architects have copyright in their designs and a client usually has a licence, which may be express or implied, to reproduce the design as a building. In the absence of any agreement, the client must have paid a sufficient fee before a licence will be implied: *Stovin-Bradford* v. *Volpoint Properties Ltd* (1971).[10] In any event, even if sufficient has not been paid for a licence to reproduce in the form of a building to be implied, the client will be entitled to possess the drawings: *Gibbon* v. *Pease* (1905).[11]

Clauses 3.15–3.18 do not attempt to amend the position under the general law. They simply clarify the architect's position. Copyright in all the architect's drawings and documents and in any building produced from such documents is the property of the architect. The client, however, is entitled to reproduce the architect's design once only on the site to which the design relates provided the architect has completed work stage D (scheme design) or has provided information in stages E, F and G and he has been paid any fees due. The client is getting a licence to use the architect's design. The licence is expressly said to extend to works of maintenance, repair and renewal of the buiilding. Otherwise, the client may not use the architect's design without the architect's permission and the payment of an agreed fee. The architect is not entitled to withhold consent unreasonably, but if the architect's involvement is restricted to the making or negotiating of planning permission, consent may be withheld unless an arbitrator decides otherwise.

The architect's normal remedy for infringement of copyright is to take out an injunction to prevent the carrying out of the work. This will not normally be granted if building work has already commenced on site: *Hunter* v. *Fitzroy Robinson and Partners* (1978).[12] The alternative remedy is for the architect to sue for damages. Large amounts of damages will not usually be recovered unless it can be shown that the infringement of copyright was flagrant or a substantial benefit accrued to the infringer. Section 107 of the Copyright, Designs and Patents Act 1988 makes certain instances of infringement a criminal offence with penalties of fines and imprisonment. That particular provision is unlikely to have much application to the architect.

Clause 3.19 prohibits either party from assigning the whole or any part of his duties without the other's written consent. This is simply stating the position under the general law whereby a party may usually assign a right, but not a duty without consent. Applied to architectural practice, it simply means that the architect must perform his or her part of the contract, say to make application for planning permission, and the client must do its part, i.e. to pay the architect's fees. There is nothing to stop the client assigning the benefit of the architect's services to someone else and, similarly, the architect may assign to another the architect's right to receive payment.

It is important to understand the difference between assignment and delegation. If an architect delegates any duties (which as noted above may not be done without permission), he or she still retains responsibility for the proper carrying out of such duties. If, however, some of those duties are allowed to be assigned, the architect is no longer responsible for them. The responsibility passes to the person to whom they have been assigned. To properly carry out an assignment a three-way contract must be drawn up, called 'novation', between the assignor (the person assigning), the assignee (the person to whom the duty is assigned) and the third party (the person to whom the duty is owed).

Clauses 3.20–3.24 deal with the position if the contract is suspended or terminated. Without such a provision, neither party would be entitled to terminate or suspend unless they could establish grounds at common law, e.g. repudiation. It is worth noting that usually there is no right to terminate at common law because the client fails to pay. That is simply a breach of contract for which the remedy is damages. The architect must give immediate notice to the client if any situation arises from *force majeure* which makes it impracticable to carry out any services which have been agreed. An alternative course of action must then be agreed.

This provision begs the question: what is *force majeure*? The most commonly quoted definition is 'with reference to all circumstances independent of the will of man, and which it is not in his power to control': *Lebaupin* v. *Crispin* (1920).(13) Clearly, such things as war and government decree fall under this heading and also fire and flood, but the boundaries are not precisely defined.

The client may order suspension of any or all the services if reasonable written notice is given, but the architect must make a written request if he has not received instructions to resume work within six months. The client has a further 30 days from the date of the request to respond, failing which the architect is entitled to treat the appointed as terminated. Even without a prior suspension, either party may terminate the appointment simply by giving reasonable notice in writing. No reason need be given.

What constitutes reasonable notice will depend upon circumstances. If the project is other than very small, the client cannot expect the architect to be able to switch staff from that job to another immediately. In some instances, it might be reasonable for the client to give a month's notice to enable the architect to reorganize resources. The architect's reasonable notice will depend on the stage of the work. If it has reached a very delicate stage, such as invitation of tenders, the architect will have to give longer notice than if production drawings are being prepared.

The appointment is automatically terminated on the death or incapacity of the architect. This provision clearly refers to the situation where a client has appointed a person. Where the appointment is a firm, it cannot die or become incapacitated (in the accepted sense). If the partner or director in charge of the project dies, the project will simply be carried out by another staff member unless the client has specifically stipulated that he wishes the project to be handled by the partner in question. In very small firms, it becomes a matter of a contract for personal services, in which case death puts the contract at an end.

The conditions stipulate that if the client pays all outstanding fees and expenses, it may make full use of all documents prepared by the architect under the agreement, but only for the purpose for which they were prepared.

Clauses 3.25 and 3.26 provide that the parties shall settle disputes by means of arbitration by a person to be agreed or, failing agreement, a person appointed at the application of either party by the President of the Chartered Institute of Arbitrators. This is an agreement to arbitrate which falls under the Arbitration Acts 1950 and 1979. If the dispute concerns copyright, the arbitrator must be an architect. Prior to the reference to arbitration the parties may, if the dispute is in relation to fees, agree to refer it to the RIBA, RIAS or RSUA for an opinion. There is a proviso that the architect's appointment is based on RIBA Architect's Appointment, it has been agreed in writing, there is a joint statement of undisputed facts and the parties agree to accept the opinion as final and binding. There is an alternative arbitration agreement for use in Scotland. *Clause 3.27* rather unnecessarily states that nothing in the agreement prevents the parties settling any dispute without referring it to arbitration.

Clause 3.28 finally states the law governing the conditions. By use of optional clauses, it may be either the law of England, Scotland or Northern Ireland.

7.3 *Duty of care agreements (collateral warranties)*

Strictly speaking a collateral warranty[14] is a contract which runs alongside another contract and is subsidiary to it. Such documents have proliferated in recent years and it is common for contractors, nominated and domestic sub-contractors and suppliers and all the consultants to be required to execute a collateral warranty in favour of the building owner, the fund providing the money for the project and/ or any number of prospective tenants. It used to be the view that such an agreement was not very important because it merely stated in contractual terms the duties which everyone knew the architect owed to a third party in tort. That view is no longer tenable.

Before looking at some of the provisions commonly encountered in forms of warranty, or duty of care agreements (as they are often called when used in relation to consultants), it should be understood why they are so important to the building owner. There is a fundamental contract principle that only the parties to a contract have any rights or duties under that contract. The principle is called *privity of contract*. For example, in a contract between a client A and an architect B, each has rights and duties to the other. B has a duty to design a building for A, but he has no duty to any third party C to design that building. That would be the case even if the contract stated that he had such a duty.

To put it at its most basic: if A and B include a term in their contract that they will each pay £100 to C, the term will be ineffective in that if they fail to honour it, C will be unable to enforce it, because C is not a party to the contract. In a similar way, if A and B include a term that C will pay each of them £100, they will be unable to enforce it.

Applying this principle to the architect's conditions of engagement, if something goes wrong with the building which is clearly a design fault, only the client can take action against the architect for breach of the conditions of engagement. For example, if an architect designs a house for the client, the house is sold on to a third party and a design defect then becomes apparent, the third party cannot take action against the architect under the conditions of engagement between the architect and client. At one time, the third party would have been able to overcome this kind of problem by suing in the tort of negligence if there was no contractual relationship. A plaintiff suing in negligence must show that:

- the defendant had a duty of care to the plaintiff, and
- the defendant was in breach of that duty, and
- as a result of the breach the plaintiff suffered damage of the kind which is recoverable.

So, in the first place, the plantiff would try to show that the defendant architect owed a duty of care. The courts appeared willing to find such a duty in many instances, the high point being the case of *Junior Books Ltd* v. *The Veitchi Co. Ltd* (1982)[15] where the House of Lords held that a specialist flooring sub-contractor was liable in negligence for defective flooring to the employer with whom the sub-contractor had no contractual relationship. Almost immediately, however, the courts began to retreat from that position by means of a long string of cases which culminated in *Murphy* v. *Brentwood District Council* (1990)[16] which, among other things, overturned the 12-year-old decision in *Anns* v. *London Borough of Merton* (1978).[17]

In broad terms, the decision in *Murphy* means that if an architect negligently designs a building, recovery in the tort of negligence will only be possible if the defective design causes injury or death to a person or if it causes damage to property other than the building which is the subject of the defective design. Even then, the recovery will be limited to compensating for the injury or damage to other persons or property and will not cover rectification of the original design defect. The concept is much the same as product liability and the Lords saw no reason for making any distinction.

The result is that a third party can no longer rely on suing an architect in negligence except in very circumscribed situations. Contracts are concerned with achieving specific results and contain many terms relating to quality. Tort is concerned with remedying wrongs. The courts now emphasize the difference. To take a simple example: if an architect specifies the wrong external cladding which soon deteriorates, that is a breach of contract for which the law lays down remedies as between the architect and the client. If the cladding is so inadequate that it falls off the building and injures a passer-by, that may be negligence for which the passer-by has a remedy against the architect in tort.

The purpose of a duty of care agreement is to create a contractual relationship between the architect and third parties who would otherwise be unlikely to have any remedy if design defects became apparent after completion. At the time of writing, there is a standard form of warranty, for use by funders, which has been agreed by the RIBA, RICS, ACE and the BPF. There are also a great many other forms of warranty in circulation, some of which have been especially drafted by solicitors with a greater or lesser experience of the architectural profession and the building industry generally. The following are points which architects should bear in mind when called upon to sign a duty of care agreement.

7.3.1 General

The basic problem is that, by virtue of the agreement, the architect acquires liabilities towards a party who has paid no fee for the privilege. If the architect does not take care, greater duties may be undertaken towards the third party than those which the architect already owes to the client under the conditions of appointment. If it can possibly be avoided an architect should not enter into a duty of care agreement. Some architects take the view that they should not resist requests to execute duty of care agreements because, as professionals, they should be prepared to take responsibility for their actions. This is a most laudable sentiment, but architects should consider whether they wish to accept a greater burden of liability than the general law would impose. That is the situation where a duty of care agreement is executed as in any other freely negotiated contractual situation. If architects do execute such agreements, there seems to be no good reason why they should not charge an appropriate, rather than a nominal, fee for the warranty.

7.3.2 Execution

The essential differences between a deed and a simple contract have been explained in section 7.2. Architects will usually be asked to enter into a duty of care agreement in the form of a deed, because it extends the potential liability period to 12 years and no consideration is necessary. If the original conditions of engagement are under hand, an architect could be in the position of having a longer period of liability to the third party than to the original client. In duty of care agreements executed as simple contracts there will always be a term stipulating that the architect receives a small sum, usually about £10, in order to make a valid contract. This is because the agreement is always very one-sided and, without the nominal sum, no other consideration on the part of the third party would be present.

7.3.3 Skill and care

There is usually a term by which the architect warrants reasonable skill and care in the performance of his or her duties. This is the normal professional standard of care and as such it is not inherently objectionable. There should also be a proviso that the architect will under no circumstances have a greater liability to the third party than the architect already owes to the client. An architect should never warrant fitness for purpose. That is clearly a very much higher standard of care.

7.3.4 Materials

Architects are often asked to warrant that they will ensure that certain materials will not be used in the construction of the building. An architect cannot warrant any such thing. The best that can be done is to warrant that the architect will not specify certain precisely defined materials. References such as 'any materials known to be deleterious' are to be avoided.

7.3.5 Copyright

There is no sensible reason why a professional should surrender his copyright. It is enough to grant a licence for certain specific uses such as repair and maintenance. If an architect does agree to assign copyright in the designs, there could be problems if the architect later wishes to use some distinctive detail on another building.

7.3.6 Assignment

This is a provision which allows the party to whom the architect gives the warranty to assign the benefits of the warranty to other parties. It is this clause which gives the agreement much of its value. The worst clauses allow assignment, without consent to unlimited numbers of people for an indefinite period of time. If the architect agrees to an assignment clause, it should allow assignment once only within a limited period of time, say two or three years subject to the architect's consent.

7.3.7 Professional Indemnity

The party taking the benefit of the warranty will principally be interested in the architect's professional indemnity insurance. Many architects enter into duty of care agreements with terms so onerous that the insurance would be repudiated by the insurers if ever a claim was made. Every agreement must be put to the insurers before it is signed, or the indemnity insurance will be at risk. A term by which the architect agrees to maintain indemnity insurance cover at a particular level for a specific number of years is virtually useless for practical purposes. The most an architect can do is to agree to use best endeavours to keep such a policy in force provided cover remains available at commercially viable rates.

7.3.8 Funders

Where the third party is providing financial backing for the development, they will require some kind of control over the situation if things go wrong between architect and client. It is usual for a term to be inserted which provides that if the architect wishes to terminate the appointment, the architect must give a specified number of days notice to the funder. If the funder then gives notice to the architect, the architect loses the right to terminate or accept repudiation, and must thereafter accept the funder's instructions in respect of the development. This type of clause poses two basic difficulties: (1) the original client may object if it is not a party to the warranty; (2) the architect loses the right to terminate. If architects agree to the inclusion of this type of term, they should ensure that the funder can only take over the appointment by novation subject to payment of all outstanding fees.

7.4 *Consultants*

A consultant is someone who gives expert advice or assistance. Common types of consultants in connection with building work are:

- Quantity surveyor.
- Structural engineer.
- Electrical engineer.
- Mechanical services engineer.
- Planner.
- Interior designer.
- Landscape architect.

A consultant, of course, can be anyone the architect considers necessary to assist in the development of the project. The architect may be a consultant on the same basis as the others in those instances when another construction professional has been chosen to be the lead consultant. In most cases, however, the architect is the lead consultant because of the particular breadth and scope of training he or she has undergone, and we will assume that this is the case in this instance.

If the project is small, the architect may feel capable of carrying out the whole of the design work. The professional indemnity insurance, however, must always include all the kinds of work the architect undertakes to carry out. On larger projects, the architect must nominate consultants as required to deal with those areas of work which are outside the architect's competence. Consultants are employed either directly by the client or by the architect. It is better for the architect if the consultant is employed directly by the client, because there is a direct contractual link established between consultant and client which is clearly useful in the case of problems with liability and fees (see section 7.2). Where the architect appoints the consultant, any action in respect of the consultant's negligence will be taken by the client against the architect. In order to recover the whole or a contribution to any damages, the architect will join the consultant as third party. Therefore, care must be taken that the consultant has appropriate professional indemnity insurance and provides the architect with an indemnity in respect of the work carried out.

It is good practice, indeed almost essential, to employ consultants as soon as the need is identified. In practice, this will be shortly after the architect has clarified the brief with the client. It is sometimes difficult to convince a client that consultants are necessary. The client is conscious of the additional fees. It is part of the architect's duty to advise the client when consultants are required. To delay the appointment of consultants may result in the redesign of large parts of the project at a late stage.

However consultants are appointed, they must be made aware of the extent of the services required from them. Ideally, this information should be imparted during the first design team meeting (when all consultants and the client are present), carefully recorded and made the basis of the contract of engagement. All consultants must report to the architect unless another construction professional has the co-ordinating role.

The standard forms of contract do not generally make any reference to consultants other than the quantity surveyor. The exception is the JCT Management Contract 1987, but there the reference is confined to the Articles and they are not mentioned in the conditions. All consultants should report to the architect. Obviously, it is essential that they inspect their own work on site, but no contract gives them power to give instructions. A consultant who wishes to issue an instruction should first submit it to the architect who may incorporate it into an architect's instruction. Indeed strictly they can only enter the site if the architect makes them authorized representatives for the sole purpose of inspecting their own portions of the works.

The architect should obtain an appropriate certificate from each consultant in respect of the practical completion of each specialist section of work.

7.5 *Sequential framework and plan of work*

For every activity there is a need for a sequential framework so that the correct operations can be carried out at the right time and, probably most important, in the right order. The things which an architect has to do throughout the process of design and construction of a building are so numerous, complex and interactive that, without such a framework, chaos would soon result. Architects have long produced such frameworks for themselves. Sometimes they were not much more than lists. In 1964, the RIBA Plan of Work was first published in the RIBA *Handbook of Architectural Practice and Management*.[18] The intention was to provide a model procedure for the design team. It was never the intention that the Plan of Work would be slavishly followed under all circumstances. Indeed, certain assumptions were made:

- A building cost of about £300 000 and a full team of designers. It is now considered relevant to most building projects.
- The architect is responsible for leading the building team.
- The earliest possible appointment. What the architect does may vary according to the time of his appointment.
- The degree of complexity was such as to involve the stages set out in Figure 6.1, the objective of each stage being to commence the next.
- In each stage the cycle of work is:
  - stating objective and assimilation of relevant facts;
  - assessment of required resources and setting up of appropriate organization;
  - planning the work and setting timetables;
  - carrying out work;
  - making proposals and recommendations;
  - obtaining client decisions;
  - setting out objectives for the next stage.

The Plan of Work is an ideal tool provided it is remembered that it is only the basic outline. There are many instances when two or more stages may be combined. The stages may often interweave and it is rare, certainly up to stage H, that there is any definite point at which it can be said that the project is moving from one stage to another. The Plan, in its complete form, indicates the principle tasks for the major participants at the stage when the tasks are usually carried out and shows the architect's tasks in two sections: Design Function and Management Function. The architect should not slavishly follow this time schedule, but must carefully assess each project in the light of the Plan and adjust the Plan to suit. A very full fleshing out of the Plan of Work is represented by the RIBA *Architect's Job Book*.[19] The use of the Plan of Work will not eliminate mistakes, but it will very much reduce their incidence by ensuring that crucial steps are taken in logical order and by paving the way for the architect to co-ordinate the members of the design team.

7.6 Site and building acquisition

In most instances clients already have a site when they approach an architect for the first time. Giving advice on site or building acquisition is one of the additional services which the architect can offer. Clearly, the choice of site should follow the architect's assessment of the client's brief (see section 7.8). If a new building is being considered, the shape of the site, the contours and the location can have a marked influence on the finished building. There are some buildings, such as factories, which require virtually flat sites; others need sites in sunny locations, by a railway or central road network, in an urban centre and so on. A key factor is the size of the site and whether it is acceptable to erect a high-rise building. There are several factors which can influence this kind of decision. Among them are the attitude of the planning authority, market value of floor area at different storey heights above ground level and, particularly in the case of dwellings, social considerations.

It is even less likely that an architect will be asked to advise on the acquisition of a suitable building although it does sometimes happen if the client is seeking a suitable building to convert to a specific purpose. In such a case, the architect has to start from the brief and assess the ease with which any particular building can be converted to its new purpose and the degree to which it is capable of fulfilling the client's brief when so converted. It can be a difficult and complicated task. The key factors to be considered are as follows.

- *Structure*   In most instances a structural survey will be required.[20]

In addition it will be necessary to consider the constructional implications of:

Columns.
Internal heights.
Changes in floor level.
Unusual roof shapes.
Towers, spires, etc
Basements.
Windows and doors.
Special architectural features, e.g. finials, drip moulds.
Decay.

- *Heating and insultation*
  Need to change.
  Compatibility of electricity, gas, solid fuel, solar heating, organic heating etc.
  Compatibility of systems such as radiators, warm air, pressured air, underfloor heating, ceiling panel.
  Insulating qualities (heat and sound) of existing fabric.
  Ease of upgrading the insulation.
  Any obvious restrictions on materials.

- *Materials*
  Durability.
  Appearance.
  Appropriateness.
  Consider floor, walls and ceiling and roof.
  Heat-retaining qualities.
  Susceptibility to condensation.

- *Ventilation*
  Natural.
  Artificial.

- *Lighting*
  Natural.
  Artificial.

- *Acoustics*
  Materials.
  Room shape and volume.

- *Design considerations*
  Possibility of division vertically and/or horizontally.
  Possibility of creating large unobstructed spaces.

Means of escape in the event of fire.
Pedestrian and vehicular access.
Disabled access.
General shape as existing compared to the required or ideal shape.

- *Environmental requirements*
  Internally: problems in heating, lighting, humidity, ventilation, damp penetration.
  Externally: effect of alterations on external appearance and the relationship to other buildings and spaces.

- *Possible adaptation techniques*
  Complete gutting.
  Partial gutting.
  Virtually complete retention of existing structure.

- *Likely costs.*

In practice, the architect will not separate the above into separate categories. Indeed, it can be seen that some factors fall into or have relevance in several categories. Part of the architect's skill in assessing whether an existing building is appropriate for a particular use is to keep all these factors in mind and weigh one against another in arriving at a considered view.

There are certain other legal considerations which are considered in Chapter 8.

7.7 *Surveys*

Whether the architect advises on the acquisition of land or buildings or whether the client presents a *fait accompli*, a survey will be required before the architect can proceed with design work. 'Survey' is an imprecise term referring to an activity which may range from taking a detailed set of measurements, including levels and translating them into careful drawings, to an inspection of varying degrees of thoroughness resulting in a written report. It is, therefore, very important for the architect to establish from the outset the kind of survey which will be required.

For example, if the client is simply considering purchase and development of existing property, an inspection and written report is indicated together with a rough sketch containing a few key dimensions. If the architect is presented with a site and instructed to produce a feasibility study, a very general idea of the dimensions, levels and other features is required sufficient to determine whether the project can be fitted on to the site. A wholly different set of information must be considered (see section 8.1). In practice, however, the most common kind of survey in which the architect will be interested is the measured survey.

The next thing the architect must decide is whether to advise the client to engage a surveyor (land surveyor or building surveyor as appropriate) to carry out the work. If the site is relatively small and uncomplicated, or the existing building and its proposed alterations are simple in character, the architect can probably do the survey work without difficulty.[21] For anything other than the simplest sites or buildings, a survey is indicated. The main reason is that surveying is becoming very sophisticated and the equipment tends to be highly expensive. It makes no economic sense for the architect to have that kind of equipment unless he can use it on a regular basis. Moreover, in the case of complex surveys, the architect cannot hope to compete with the surveyor who is doing the job full-time.

7.7.1 Preliminary enquiries

Before tackling the survey or instructing the surveyor to do the work, the architect should make certain enquiries. Some of these enquiries will produce information which is vital to the survey or which assists the architect at feasibility stage. It is suggested that the following should always be consulted.

- *Local planning authority:* They have a wealth of information and they will advise on such things as the structure plan for the area, local plans, urban redevelopment areas, enterprise zones, conservation areas, listed buildings and trees with preservation orders. In addition, of course, they will have a view on the acceptability of the proposed development.

- *The building control office:* Old deposited drawings may be very revealing, but often the building control officer may be the best source of information.

- *Local history department of the public library:* The curator will normally have a great deal of information in the form of old maps and plans of the area or of the building. Such things as ancient quarries, rivercourses and even tunnels may be discovered in this way.

- *Local inhabitants:* They can give helpful information, but it should always be supported in some other way if possible. Pointers to the possibilities of easements may be obtained (see Chapter 9, section 9.6.6), but watch out for petty rivalries which may fog the memory. It has been known for an elderly person positively to remember that the site in question used to harbour an old mineshaft only for it to be discovered much further down the road.

- *The mineral valuer:* Useful in respect of the nature of the subsoil and the possibility of faults, filled ground, etc.

- *British Coal:* For a fee they will provide a short report about the past and projected mine workings which may affect the site. For a larger fee, they will supply more detailed information which may require an expert to interpret.

- *Deeds Registry or County Office:* Tend to be the repository of legal information and deed plans, but it is amazing what can be discovered in the conveyancing history of a piece of land.

- *The client's solicitor:* With the client's permission, of course, for advice on any matters affecting the land such as covenants or easements.

7.7.2 Site investigation

This term has come to mean the investigation of the ground under the site. Some of the information discovered when conducting the preliminary enquiries will give valuable hints regarding the kind of site investigation which should be carried out. If the building is other than relatively small and light, a specialist consultant engineer should be engaged by the client to advise on and oversee the investigation. Such a consultant will usually be nominated by the architect. There are firms which specialize in ground investigations, but it is essential that they are given a proper brief so that they can form conclusions regarding the scope of the investigation. Even where the proposed building is very light and the ground has no known problems, the architect will have some trial pits dug in order to confirm that all is well. It is usual to set out the positions of the pits with regard to the actual siting of the building.

If a specialist firm is employed, the type of investigation proposed will depend on the proposed building and the kind of ground conditions expected. The usual method is to sink boreholes and measure the samples, taking various tests for acidity, sulphate content, strengths under varying conditions and so on. If the height of the building suggests that piles will be required, the boreholes may well be sunk to great depths. The firm will prepare a report which will repay careful study. If in doubt, the architect should never hesitate to request the firm or specialist to produce a further report to explain the first.

7.7.3 General considerations

Other considerations which should be carefully studied are the aspect, orientation, shelter, overshadowing from adjacent buildings, existence of services such as sewers, water, electricity and gas, means of access to the public highway and communications. In rural districts the suitability of the site for sewage disposal plant or the sinking of a well may also have to be considered. Topographical and other features of the site must be recorded: such things as levels, dimensions, benchmarks, positions and types of trees, existing buildings on and near the site and their character, overhead cables and poles, rivers, lakes, springs, rocky outcrops, fissures and the type of vegetation.

The architect must never make the mistake of thinking that a first-class survey is a substitute for visiting the site. Not even a superb set of photographs taken from every angle or a video of the site will suffice. It should not be discounted how often an architect will get a feeling for the kind of building required during the first site visit. It may be because of a particular view or a grouping of existing buildings or something as intangible as the atmosphere. Certain it is that site visits are essential.

Even if a surveyor has been engaged to carry out the survey, the architect should make a point of walking all over the site or, in the case of a building, throughout the building and actually entering every room. Only by doing this will the architect throughly know the site or building and be able to carry out the duty of care owed to the client.

7.7.4 Surveys of existing buildings

Unless it is absolutely out of the question, the architect should always carry out an existing-building survey.[22] Not only will the architect know precisely what is required in the form of illustrative drawing so far as difficult details are concerned, he or she will also learn about the way the building is constructed by the very process of carrying out the survey and plotting the results.

If a simple extension is to be made to an existing building as opposed to the alteration of the building itself, it will be sufficient to survey only the part of the building immediately adjoining the proposed extension.

Some suitable point on the existing building will probably be chosen as a temporary bench-mark which may or may not be related to ordnance levels. The exact positions of all plinths, string courses, openings and other features on the elevations have to be taken into consideration. Not least is the establishment of the precise level of every floor, carefully checking that the floors are themselves level and, if not, the taking of several levels along the edge of each floor at the point of extension. The thickness and construction of any walls to be cut through should also be determined. In old buildings, it is not unusual to find dummy columns and pilasters, even the wall thickness itself may consist of battened-out voids covered in thick plaster or stucco. The levels of the external ground must be established.

The first thing the architect will do after arriving at the building is take a general walk around and observe the surroundings, the condition of boundary walls and fences and any outbuildings. After looking at the outer elevations and looking into each room internally, the architect will be able to form an opinion regarding the overall condition and place it in one of the following categories:

- In good repair.
- Neglected, but basically sound structurally.
- In poor condition structurally, perhaps in a dangerous state.

In some instances, the architect will find a very serious problem during the initial walk about. In such circumstances, there is no alternative but to telephone the client immediately for further instructions. Clearly, there is little point in continuing to survey a building which is only fit for demolition. Whatever the client's instructions may be, the architect should always confirm them in writing.

During the survey, it may be necessary to obtain the client's authority to employ a contractor to assist the investigations by taking up floor boards or exposing part of the foundations. This kind of investigation cannot be carried out if the client does not own the property unless the actual owner has given express permission. The architect is always wise to get such permission in writing through his client.

Investigations should encompass the various services: whether they exist and, if they do, what their condition is. Gas, water, electricity, drainage, hot water, cable TV, etc. may all require substantial overhaul or renewal. The condition of the roof, eaves, flashings, rainwater pipes and gutters, damp-proof course and any other features which prevent moisture from penetrating into the building deserve particular attention, as all the money spent on improving or redecorating the property may be wasted if some fault in these areas is overlooked. It would not be overstating the point to say that damp is at the root of most building defects.

Although it may be that the eventual scheme for the building will only affect certain parts, it is usually best to make an accurate measured survey of the whole, including all internal heights, so that sections can be drawn through any part without much difficulty. The only exception to this general rule is if the architect knows clearly in advance just which parts of the building are to be affected. Some architects advocate the making of a rough survey in the first instance, to be followed by a thorough survey only when the new design has been approved by the client. Down that road lies disaster. The architect will often find that he or she is faced with trying to make a scheme work which the later detailed survey shows cannot work, possibly because of an impossible change in levels or of headroom.

The golden rule is never to make assumptions. Inevitably, the architect will discover, when plotting, that certain dimensions have been forgotten. There is no alternative but to return to the building and check them. This can be difficult if the building is some distance from the office. In those circumstances, the prudent architect will take a small drawing board along to enable the building to be roughly plotted out as a check.

Each room or space on the survey drawing must be given a number so that they can be identified easily by giving them the same number on the alteration drawings. It is good practice to provide the contractor with a set of drawings of the building as existing so that comparison of existing and proposed can be readily made. The following is a brief checklist covering the major areas to be considered when carrying out a survey.

Building site

- *Development*
  Permitted development and restrictions under the local development plan or action area plan.
  Zoning, density, floorspace index, etc. as applicable.
  Improvement lines.
  Proposed adjacent development.

- *History of the site*
  Rights of public and adjoining owners.
  Boundaries or party walls or fences.

- *Nature of ground and subsoil*
  Trial holes or other evidence of nature of subsoil.
  Precautions against subsidence, seasonal variations in subsoil and
    water table.
  Safe bearing capacity of subsoil.
  Report from mineral valuer and geologist.
  Liability to flooding.

- *Condition of site*
  Levels and gradients.
  Bench-marks.
  Shelter or exposure from surrounding ground.
  Direction of prevailing wind.
  Aspect and orientation.
  Dimensions and area of site.
  Existing trees and features.
  Existing buildings on the site and on adjoining land.
  Overhead cables and poles.

- *Services*
  Position, size and depth of public sewers.
  If no sewer, suitability and possible siting of septic tank and
    overflow outlet.
  Utility services available, such as gas, water, electricity, with names
    and addresses of supply undertakings.
  Position and pressure of water main.
  Electricity supply, voltage, capacity of any existing cables.
  Position and size of gas main.
  Telephone service.
  Possibility of sinking well.

- *Communications*
  Means of access
  Nature and proximity of public highway.
  Rights of way across site.

Existing buildings (in addition to the foregoing, so far as applicable)

- *Drawings*
  Plans, elevations, sections, details as necessary, drawn to scale.

- *Construction*
  Type and method of construction of foundations, walls, floors and
    roof.
  Wall and floor thicknesses.

Hidden construction features.
Special finishes.

- *Condition of structure*
Signs of rot, beetle or other infestation in timber.
Looseness of plaster surfaces.
Damp penetration through roofs, flashings and gutters.
Condensation.
Damp-proof course to walls.
Settlement cracks.
Windows and doors, etc.

- *Condition of services*
Gas, water, electricity, drains, central heating, hot water, TV cable
   or aerial, vacuum, computer, specialized gases or other links.
Possibility of extending the services.

- *History of the building*
Age.
Purposes of previous occupation.
Quality of previous maintenance work.

7.8 The brief

One of the architect's most important functions is the taking of an
accurate brief from the client. Yet many architects are very careless in
this respect. The brief is the client's instructions to the architect. It may
be intensely detailed and complex and, since the architect's task is to
satisfy the brief, it is essential that it is as clear as possible. Of course,
it may not be possible to produce a very clear brief. Indeed the very
essence of some briefs is the vagueness and the freedom of the
architect to produce a solution within very broad parameters. This is
probably because, in those instances, the client does not know what he
or she wants.

This raises another important point. The architect's function is to
produce not what the client wants, but what the client needs. That is
the function of every professional person. The process of setting down
what the client needs may take a long time. Once this is accomplished,
the design process may be swift. In some cases, such as the brief for a
new hospital, the pace of development may be so quick that there is
never any hope of the architect's producing anything more than a
loose brief designed, hopefully, to accommodate as many changes as

possible so that the design will never be finally fixed until the contractor has left site.

The traditional method of taking a brief would result in a schedule of accommodation required. That system should long since be defunct in favour of a user requirement study or some development of that principle. The idea is that the architect analyses the client's needs in terms of activities, and identifies in respect of each activity a number of key criteria including areas, volumes, requirements for finishes, orientation and aspect, interaction with other activities and to what extent, numbers of persons involved, special requirements ancilliary to the activity, social and psychological needs.

A great deal of work may be necessary to produce a brief of this nature, in terms of research or operational study or both. In many cases, it will not be justified if the proposed building is a common building type. Even if that is the case, the architect should always be wary that the brief which the client has come to know and love over the years may be flawed or may have become flawed with the passing of time and the introduction of new processes, etc.[23]

The result of any briefing exercise will be something in writing or, in some instances, in graphical form. Wherever possible, the architect should try to schedule information in logical form and to confine other written material to note form. There will be much information in the form of hard facts, but there will also be much in less tangible form. It is often useful to separate the two. The brief should always be confirmed to the client before the next stage is commenced.

References

(1) Moxley, R. (1984) *Architect's Guide to Fee Negotiations*, Architectural Press Ltd.
(2) RIBA (1990) *Architect's Appointment*, RIBA Publications Ltd. A new edition is in course of preparation at the time of writing. The drafts distributed for comment suggest that it will be significantly changed in layout.
(3) Anon (1986) Project team fee negotiations. *Architects' Journal*, 5 November, p. 71.
(4) *Whittal Builders Co Ltd* v. *Chester le Street DC* (1987) 11 Con LR 40.
(5) *Kilby & Gayford Ltd* v. *Selincourt Ltd* (1973) 3 BLR 104.
(6) 2 All ER 118.
(7) *Moresk Cleaners Ltd* v. *Thomas Henwood Hicks* (1966) 4 BLR 50.
(8) 5 Con LR 1.
(9) 1 Con LR 114.
(10) 3 All ER 570.
(11) 1 KB 810.

(12) 10 BLR 84.
(13) 2 KB 714.
(14) Winward Fearon, (1990) *Collateral Warranties*, BSP Professional Books, Oxford.
(15) 21 BLR 66.
(16) 50 BLR 1.
(17) 5 BLR 1.
(18) Cox, S. & Hamilton, A. (1991) *RIBA Handbook of Architectural Practice and Management*, 5th edn, RIBA Publications Ltd, London.
(19) Beaven, L., Cox, S., Dry, D. & Males, R. (1988) *Architect's Job Book*, 5th edn, RIBA Publications Ltd, London.
(20) Milka, S.L.J. *Structural Surveying*, 2nd edn, Macmillan.
(21) Clancy, J. (1991) *Site Surveying & Levelling*, 2nd edn, Edward Arnold.
(22) Hollis, M. & Gibson, C. (1991) *Surveying Buildings*, 3rd edn, RICS Books, London.
(23) Shoshkoo, E. (1989) *The Design Process*, ADT Press.

Chapter 8

Stage B

8.1 Feasibility studies

Once the architect has found out what the client wishes to build, where and when, the next stage is to decide whether it is feasible to build. If not, the project will abort at that stage. Feasibility, however, may depend upon any one of a number of factors or a combination of several factors. The decision to proceed or to stop lies with the client of course, but it is the architect's function to present the appropriate information to the client in a structured way so that it is made as easy as possible for the client to come to a decision. Clearly, the client's decision may be influenced by matters which are not known to the architect, therefore it is always wise for the architect to investigate more rather than less widely. Because it is difficult at this stage to decide just what data might be relevant, the architect should always include rather than exclude information.

There are some very small projects for which a formal feasibility study may be inappropriate. Remember, however, that it is not the size of the project which determines whether a feasibility study should be done, but the associated factors such as complexity, situation, and type of development. It is sensible for the architect always to approach a feasibility study as though the client requires a formal report to be prepared. In some cases, particularly in the case of a large company or any organization whose officers have to satisfy others beside themselvs, a feasibility report will be mandatory.

Whether the architect is to produce a report or simply to investigate and report orally to the client, it is vital to have a checklist in order to prevent the inadvertent omission of an important item. The following checklist and brief notes are not intended to be exhaustive, and some of the items will apply only to certain developments, but they provide a suitable basis which architects can mould to suit individual requirements.

Terms of reference

It is always sensible to bear in mind the terms of reference or, to put it another way, what it is that the architect is trying to do. It is prudent to make a list of the assumptions being made so that the client knows what is certain, what is estimated and what is merely assumed for the moment. A proper measured survey may not have been carried out, in the case of an existing building a structural analysis may not have been done, and the structural stability of the building may be assumed. If there is any reason to doubt the structural stability, short of a detailed structural survey and calculation, no assumption should be made and the architect should obtain authority to have the structure properly investigated. Other assumptions which may have to be made concern boundaries and the ground condition.

Consultants

Consultants who might be involved in the study include:

- Quantity surveyor.
- Structural engineer.
- Geotechnical engineer.
- Electrical engineer.
- Heating and ventilation engineer.
- Mechanical engineer.
- Acoustics engineer.
- Landscape architect.

Authorities

Statutory and other authorities who may be involved are:

- Planning.
- Highways.
- Drainage.
- Housing.
- Education.
- Fire brigade.
- Transport.
- British Coal.
- Electricity.
- National Power.
- Water.

- Gas.
- British Telecom.
- Police.
- Forestry Commission.
- Royal Fine Arts Commission.
- National Trust.

Site location

This should be considered in relation to the distance from the nearest centre of population and the general topography. Neighbouring watercourses, use of adjoining land and any possible nuisance should be examined.

Access

Means of getting to the site is always important; in some cases it can be crucial to the success or otherwise of the project. Bus, train and air services can be vital to a building which hopes to prosper as a conference centre. Road routes are also important.

Shops

The type of project will determine the importance of nearby shops on its viability. Housing must be reasonably near to shops and elderly people's accommodation is more attractive if it has a few small shops nearby such as newsagents, chemists and general stores. Mobile shops should not be forgotten and the distance of the project from, and ease of access to, the nearest large shopping centre should be recorded.

Health

The following are important:

- Doctors' surgeries.
- Dental surgeries.
- Opticians.
- Chiropodists.
- Clinic.
- Health centre.
- General hospital facilities.
- Proposed future provision.

Social and recreational

It is worth while making a complete list of this type of provision in the area for certain kinds of proposed development. The only accurate way to compile such a list is for the architect to walk over every part of the surrounding area.

Education

A wide range of educational provision is possible and in the case of residential development it is essential that appropriate provision is available. Any projected educational developments in the area must also be noted.

Employment

The names and locations of principal employers in an area may be a crucial factor in the viability of dwelling-houses.

Rights

The following rights should be recorded if existing or if thought to exist:

- Light.
- Way.
- Support.
- Party walls.
- Easements.
- Covenants (restrictive or otherwise).

Planning points

- Whether there is any agreement in principle.
- Whether there is any earlier permission concerning the same site.
- What are the usual standard conditions inserted in planning permissions in that area?
- Specific requirements in regard to storey heights and number, densities, access provision, permitted materials, parking provision.
- Any other planning permissions for nearby sites.
- Building lines.
- Improvement lines.
- Road proposals.

Licensing

If required.

Drainage

General provision and problems.

Architectural/historical

Whether the building (if an existing building is being examined) or the site is in a conservation area. Even if there is no statutory protection for the building, the architect will want to record any interesting and attractive features. The reaction of local amenity societies should also be considered. Although not decisive, opposition from such a quarter can cause serious delays to the process of obtaining appropriate statutory approvals.

Geological factors

Fault lines, unusual ground conditions, mining subsidence are all problem areas.

Statutory undertakings and services

What services, if any, are readily available to the site or can be connected without undue problems. Any easements or diversions required. Other points regarding street lighting, high voltage cables overhead or underground, substations.

Policy

Whether there is any local or central government policy which affects the scheme.

Grants

If any are available.

Structural analysis

Comments on existing structures, if any, in relation to the proposals.

Access

Number of entries to site and width, if metalled surface or special difficulties.

Design possibilities

Options available in broad terms with regard to disposition of various elements set against the site factors, structural options, aesthetics, historical and urban factors.

Estimate of cost

In broad terms, stating the basis of the estimate (i.e. 'current prices'), whether VAT included and so on. Some clients insist upon a fairly sophisticated life cycle analysis which the architect would usually request the quantity surveyor to carry out. In fact, there is little to be gained from such an exercise at this stage, when very little is known about the building.

Programme

Possible design team programme and future building programme in the form of key start and finish dates.

Conclusions

Advice to the client, with short reasons.

Approvals/decisions

A list of the approvals and decisions required from the client and a time schedule for receipt if the programme indicated earlier is to be implemented. This is a valuable method of getting the client to respond.

Additional material

Whatever is useful to assist the client in understanding the issues and reaching a decision such as charts, graphs, maps, drawings and photographs.

8.2 *Procurement paths and implications for the professional*

The procurement system should be the most appropriate in the light of the criteria signalled to the architect by the client during and after the briefing stage. In choosing a procurement path, the key criteria are the client's priorities in respect of:

- Time: economy and certainty.
- Cost: economy and certainty.
- Control: apportionment of risk.
- Quality: in design and construction.
- Size/value: small/medium/large.
- Complexity: complex/simple.

There are as many different procurement systems as there are pebbles on the beach, but some of them are different only in detail. The principle systems may be expressed as follows:

- Traditional.
- Project management.
- Design and manage.
- Design and build.
- Management contracting.
- Construction management.

8.2.1 Traditional

Very broadly, this is where the client commissions an architect to take a brief, produce designs and construction information, invite tenders and administer the project during the construction period and settle the final account. If the building is other than small, the architect will advise the client to appoint other consultants to deal with particular items, such as quantities and costs generally, structural calculations and heating design. The contractor, who has no design responsibility, will normally be selected by competitive tender or there may be good grounds for negotiating a tender.

The essentials are that the architect is the independent adviser to the client carrying out the design. The contractor is only responsible for executing the work in accordance with the drawings and specifications produced by the architect and other professionals. Figure 8.1 shows the relationships of the parties in diagrammatic terms.

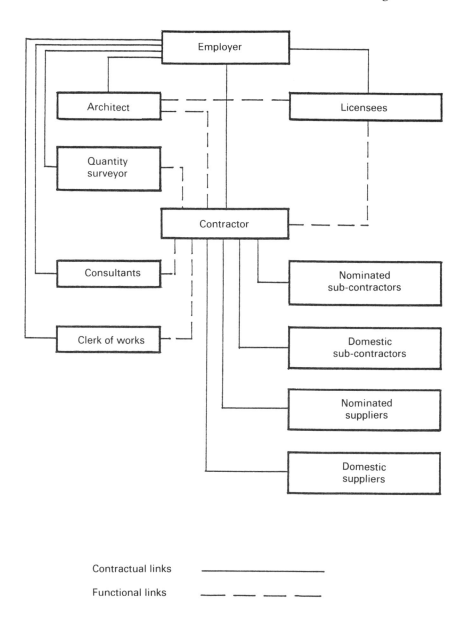

Contractual links   —————————————

Functional links   —— —— —— ——

Figure 8.1   Traditional contract.

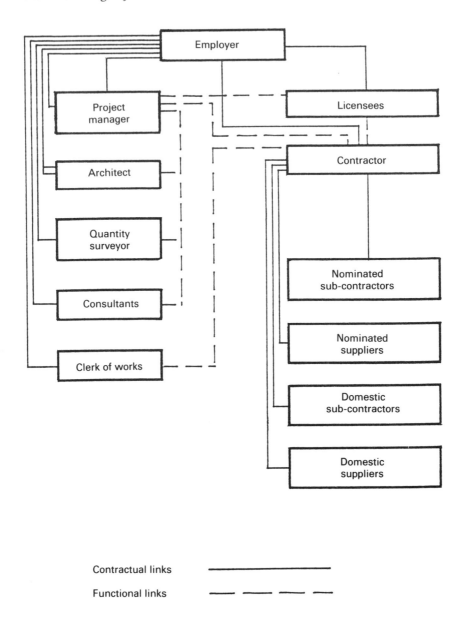

Figure 8.2 Project management.

8.2.2 Project management

Although this is a somewhat imprecise term, it has much in common with the traditional system. However, the architect is not the leader of the team; the project manager is the leader. The project manager, of course, can be an architect and most architects would say that an architect is the obvious choice for the post in view of his or her particular training. Essentially, the project management system places most emphasis on management. Therefore a person, whether architect, engineer or surveyor, with the relevant project management skills is required. The project manager manages the project, including organizing and co-ordinating all consultants. The project manager acts as a link between the client and the design team. Depending upon the particular kind of project management chosen, the contract administrator may be the project manager or the architect. Figure 8.2 shows the relationship of the parties in diagrammatic terms.

8.2.3 Design and manage

This is not as yet very common in this country. Single point responsibility rests with a professional who may be architect, engineer or surveyor. Besides being responsible for the design of the project the professional also manages the project in the sense of managing the other professionals and also the construction process in the form of, probably, a number of sub-contractors and suppliers. Figure 8.3 shows the relationship of the parties in diagrammatic terms.

8.2.4 Design and builid

This is a system which is growing in popularity. It places responsibility for both design and erection in the hands of the contractor. There are variations in the name and there are subtle differences in meaning. *Design and build*, for example, refers to the basic system where a builder carries out the two functions. *Design and construct* includes design and build and other types of construction such as purely engineering works. *Package deal* can be used to refer to either of these. In theory, the term suggests that the contractor is responsible for providing everything in one package and it is particularly apt when referring to an industrialised building. *Turnkey* contracting is a system in which the contractor really is responsible for everything, including furniture and

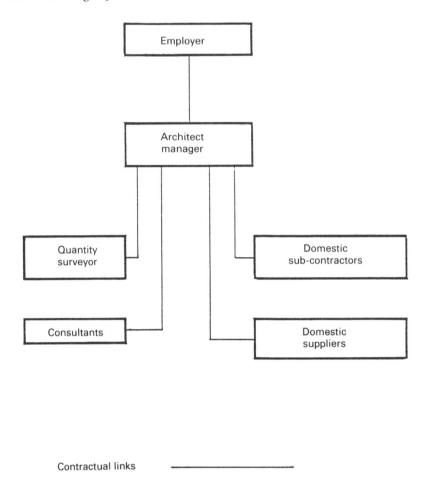

Figure 8.3   Design and manage.

pictures on the walls if required. The idea is that the employer simply turns the key and begins using the building: hence the name.

Many architects are unduly concerned about design and build as though every such contract is one less for an architect to design. Nothing could be further from the truth. Unless the building is very simple, the contractor will seek an architect to carry out the design including all the preliminary briefing and feasibility work where necessary and also the preparation of constructional drawings. From the client's point of view, an independent adviser is required to look after the client's interests before, during and after construction. There is no doubt that the architect's role is different from the traditional image, but that should not be a problem. Because an architect has a contractor for a client, it does not mean that he or she will be unable to produce good architecture. It is very much in the contractor's interest that the client is happy with the finished building.

The employer may approach a design and build contractor as soon as the intention to build starts to form. The contractor then takes charge of the project until completion. The architectural function will either be carried out in the contractor's own architects' department or, more commonly, by subletting the work to a firm of architects in private practice. An architect in such an instance will owe a duty to the contractor which will depend on the conditions of engagement agreed for the work. Generally, the duty will probably be to carry out the architectural functions in obtaining and satisfying the brief and perhaps to carry out quality control duties on behalf of the contractor during the construction period. An architect in those circumstances will have no duty to the employer other than the common law duty to ensure that the design will not result in injury or death to the employer or those who will use the building and damage to property other than the building itself.[1]

Alternatively, the employer may engage a full design team to complete the design of the building and a great many production drawings in some detail before seeking tenders from contractors to complete the design and construct the building. Most commonly, the employer will engage an architect to prepare an outline scheme together with a performance specification on which contractors will be invited to tender. The contractor will engage an architect to do the detail design development work and to produce the production information to satisfy the performance specification.

A system which is increasing in popularity involves what is known as a *consultant switch*. In this system, an architect or even a full design team is engaged by the employer to prepare all the initial material and tenders are invited on the basis that the successful contractor will take the design team on board as the contractor's consultants to complete the work. The architect must remember who the client is at any particular moment, because the contractor will require somewhat different service than that which was given to the employer. After the switch, the employer must either do without independent advice, or engage another architect for that purpose. The very worst thing that an architect could do would be to try and act for both employer and contractor. There is a clear conflict of interest.

A particular point which architects should watch if they are asked to carry out work for contractors in a design and build scenario is the extent of the design obligation. An architect's normal obligation, like that of any other professional, is to use reasonable skill and care. In contrast, the normal design and build liability, unless expressly amended, is to produce an end result which is fit for its purpose if that purpose is made known. The contractor may well attempt to engage an architect on 'fit for purpose' terms. Quite apart from the fact that such liability is very onerous and admits of no 'state of the art' defence, the architect's insurers are almost certain to refuse cover (see Chapter 17, section 17.4).

Figure 8.4 shows the relationship of the parties in diagrammatic terms.

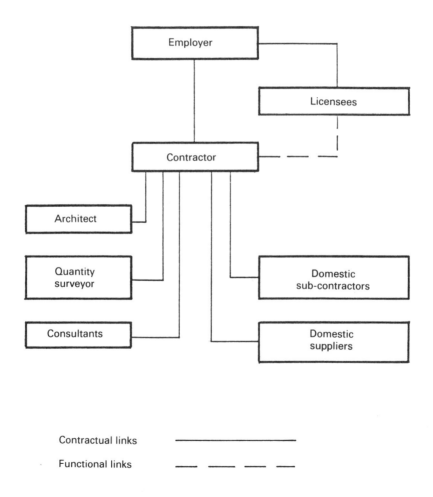

Figure 8.4　Design and build.

8.2.5 Management contracting

This system seems to be waning in popularity as design and build increases its stake in the construction market – or perhaps design and build is gaining in popularity as management contracting is decreasing.

The contractor is selected at an early stage. Although not normally responsible for carrying out any of the construction work, the contractor simply has a management function for which a fee is paid. The construction work is divided into a number of packages with the contractor's advice and tenders for these individual packages are invited as appropriate to suit the programme. The works contractors are in contract with the management contractor.

This type of contract has much in common with a traditional contract in which all the work is sub-let to nominated sub-contractors. The system is commonly said to allow the employer considerable freedom for change of mind while preserving price and end date. Such a contention is clearly contradictory and management contracts in practice appear notable for escalating costs and shifting end dates. The employer takes more risk under a management contract than would be the case under a traditional procurement system, but this is the price paid for greater control over the work.

This is the system most often referred to as *fast track*, the idea being that work begins on site as soon as sufficient information has been produced to enable the first works contractors to start. The architect is then involved in a constant race against time to produce the remainder of the drawings in time for the succeeding works packages. The architect must also be sufficiently organized to ensure that subsequent drawings do not necessitate the reconstruction of work already executed.

A few years ago, architects who worked in this way were heavily criticized by quantity surveyors, contractors and clients alike. From that point of view management contracting could be said to have made a virtue out of necessity. Architects should not be misled, however, by the apparent glamour of fast track. The architect's liability is exactly the same. The system imposes a tough discipline on all sides. The employer must be precise in requirements and prepared to hold fast to decisions. The preparation of information must be scheduled and on target, and the management of the contract must be tight. Any disputes which may arise can usually be traced to a failure to adhere to these principles.

It is, of course, quite difficult to perform under conditions of stress such as occur during fast building. It can be compared to driving a car: the faster the car is driven, the better the road and the mechanics have

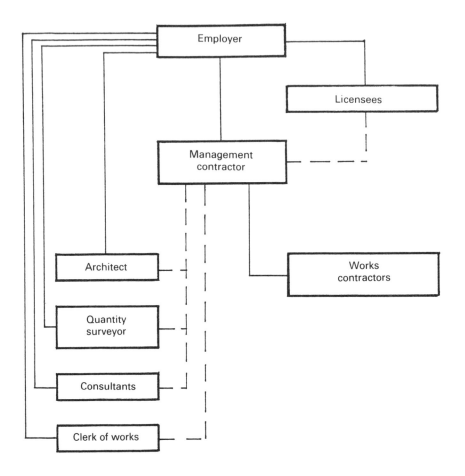

Contractual links ——————————

Functional links — — — — —

Figure 8.5   Management contracting.

to be, and the further the driver has to see ahead. The driver is called upon to exercise more, not less, skill. The fast driver who has an accident is told that he or she should not have been driving so fast. The architect who makes a mistake purely as a result of fast building techniques must be told to get out of the fast lane.

Figure 8.5 shows the relationship of the parties in diagrammatic form.

8.2.6 Construction management

Once again, this system calls upon the contractor to act simply in a management capacity for which a fee is paid. The design team is often appointed directly by the employer, but in some instances the contractor may appoint. In such cases, the system has some of the flavour of project management. The key difference between this system and management contracting is that the individual works contractors (they are usually termed *trade contractors* under this system) are in contract with the employer.

This overcomes a number of problems encountered under the management contracting system: the contractor, as construction manager, can become one of the team alongside the architects, engineers and quantity surveyors, and the trade contractors are liable for their breaches directly to the employer without the problems of an intervening contractor in the contractual chain. Some very large projects have been carried out using this system which calls upon the same kind of skills from the design team as required under the management contract. Figure 8.6 shows the relationship of the parties in diagrammatic form.

There are other ways of separating systems such as by method of price determination, i.e. measurement or cost reimbursement contracts which must in any event be taken into account, and by reference to the method of contractor selection, i.e. competitive tender or negotiation.

8.3 *Reporting*

Architects are expected to report to their clients at various stages throughout the design and construction period. Stage B is probably the earliest stage at which a client can expect a report and, of course, such a report will not always be in writing. Indeed, for a very small

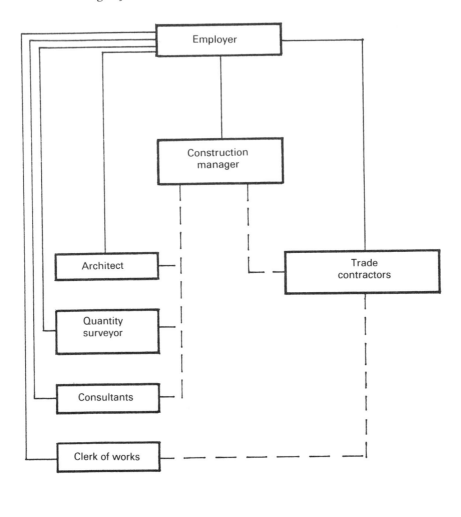

Figure 8.6   Construction management.

project and an unsophisticated client, a written report is probably quite inappropriate.

It is often difficult to decide when to report and when a report is unnecessary, but it is usual to make a report of some kind whenever an architect wants some kind of decision from the client. The purpose of the report in such an instance is to acquaint the client with the appropriate information on which to base a decision. There will be other instances when the architect requires no decision, but it is simply good client relations to report on progress. A client, like anyone else, always likes to know that he or she is not forgotten.

The following list indicates typical reports the architect may produce while running a project, not all of which will be applicable on every project:

- Feasibility.
- Outline proposals.
- Scheme design.
- Progress reports.
- Extension of time.
- Loss and/or expense.
- Special reports, e.g. before determination, after insurance risk damage, etc.

The architect will also be responsible for passing on and, if appropriate, commenting upon reports received from other consultants: for instance, cost reports from the quantity surveyor, reports on structural condition from the structural engineer. Sometimes such reports are submitted direct by the consultant concerned, but it is better that they pass through the hands of the architect so that the employer deals with one person and a possible clash of professional interests is avoided. Some brief comments on report writing are covered in Chapter 15, section 15.4.

Reference

(1) *Murphy* v. *Brentwood District Council* (1990) 50 BLR 1.

Chapter 9

Stages C and D

9.1 Design data

The RIBA Plan of work describes Stage C as:

'To determine general approach to layout, design and construction in order to obtain the authoritative approval of the client on the outline proposals and the accompanying report.'

During this stage the architect will be involved in developing the brief, carrying out user requirement studies, gathering appropriate information, trying out solutions in consultation with other members of the team and preparing an outline proposal. It has already been seen (Chapter 7, section 7.8) that the architect must prepare a brief on the basis of client needs rather than client wants if there is a conflict. If the brief is considered as a problem, the architect can only start to find the answer when all the necessary data have been assembled.

Much of the data will be collected as part of the feasibility study (see Chapter 8, section 8.1). Other factual material will concern relevant Acts of Parliament, Statutory Instruments and Regulations and the recommendations of appropriate bodies (e.g. the Sports Council). In addition to this material, the architect will be concerned with user requirement studies. Some of this work may have been carried out while preparing the brief, but it is usual for more detailed studies to take place after the feasibility stage has been completed.

User requirement studies, put simply, attempt to encapsulate in easy reference form all the criteria which the user requires of the building. All buildings have more than one user, and there is the problem. Each user may have slightly, or even widely, differing requirements. Sometimes different classes of person use the same building but have almost opposing requirements. An example of a building where this is the case is a court-house, where not only are the requirements of judges, prisoners and public quite different, the circulation routes must not cross. When one takes into account the needs of police, court officials, solicitors and others involved in the cases for trial, not to mention the complex administration requirements, a court-house of any size becomes a very complex building. There are other buildings with equally complex user requirements.

Some part of the user requirement study will be factual; other parts will be more subjective and will need to take into consideration such things as suitable environmental, social and psychological factors. During this stage, the architect will try to visit some good examples of the building type under consideration. Much other design data will be standard for most projects (see Chapter 5, section 5.3).

The point to appreciate is that all relevant design data must be available before the architect can seriously attempt to formulate even outline proposals. It is essential to emphasize this point because it can be hard to resist the temptation to launch into the design stage of an interesting project before all information is to hand.

9.2 *Outline proposals and development*

This is not the place to discuss architectural design. It is beyond the scope of this book. Most clients are not at all interested in design theory; they are only interested in results. If the results are bad, the theory is irrelevant.

As a basic principle, the architect should always keep the client informed of the progress of the design work. This is especially the case if the architect wants to attempt something rather different from the norm. In such a case, the client's agreement should be obtained first. In most cases, a client is interested only in such fundamentals as whether the building will successfully keep out the rain, the cold, how well it works and how much it will cost to build and to run. An architect who can keep a client happy on those points will have little to worry about.

As a general rule, the architect should only present one proposal to the client. There are exceptions to this as to every other rule, but they will be rare. The client looks to the architect and other members of the design team to produce a solution to the problems contained in the brief. Above all, a client expects advice. The team may well come to the conclusion that any one of a dozen different schemes could be developed into an acceptable project, but it is their function to recommend the one they consider to be the best. Unless the client has expressly asked for alternative proposals, a single proposal shows that the architect is carrying out the job of eliminating options. Most options should be eliminated by a consideration of the brief, and the rest at feasibility stage. To present proposals which show major differences at this stage suggests that the architect has not carried out earlier tasks adequately.

During this stage the architect will perform certain management functions. Co-ordination of the design team is an ongoing process throughout the design and construction stages of any medium to large project. As part of this process, during this stage the architect will be concerned with putting in place the procedures which will ensure that the team works as a team and not as a group of individuals, although it must be admitted that the ideal is easier to envisage than to achieve. A key factor will be the lines of and frequency of communication. As a general rule, all communications should be to the architect whose job it is to see that the appropriate information is properly distributed. Although it is vital that the structural engineer has all the information needed to enable a proper contribution to be made to the project, the architect must take care that individual team members are not swamped with information 'just in case' it might prove useful. This is where the managerial qualities of the architect should come to the fore.

It is useful to have a meeting for the team at the beginning of this stage to establish the following (adapted from the RIBA Plan of Work):

- The objectives (often overlooked; see Chapter 14, section 14.1).
- Available information regarding the brief, basic design data (see section 9.1), cost limits, timetable set by client or other restraints.
- Matters to be dealt with as priorities.
- Design team procedures, including roles and communications.
- The very important topics of procurement systems and contractual arrangements, tendering, type of bills, specification, schedules, and work methods.
- Any special drawing techniques or systems (such as computer-aided design). It may indeed be a little late in the day to decide this point and it is something which the architect should consider at briefing stage. The reason is that some consultants may not be willing to work within any given system of drawing. They may in fact have a fully operational computer drawing system which is incompatible with the architect's own system.
- System of carrying out cost checks during design.
- List of actions to be taken.
- Programming and progress techniques for the design team and for the project in construction.

Either at the end of Stage C or in the early part of Stage D the architect will apply for outline planning approval. At the end of Stage

D or during the early part of Stage E, full planning permission should be sought (section 9.4).

The RIBA Plan of Work describes Stage D as:

'To complete the brief and decide on particular proposals, including planning arrangement, appearance, constructional method, outline specification, and cost and to obtain all approvals.'

The team should have a very clear idea of the brief during this part of the work. Indeed, there should be no question of changing the brief once this stage is complete and the client should be so informed, otherwise much wasted time and money will be involved. What was thought of in terms of concepts during the last stage now has to be developed into a design which is quite detailed: i.e. the staircase must be capable of being made to work without altering its dimensions; space allocations for columns, beams and service ducts must be adequate; and the advice of appropriate consultants must have been taken. It is during this stage of work that every member of the team has to make a determined effort to work together. It really is no use the architect's saying that all the other members must fit their designs into his or her master design; nor should any other consultants stick out for their own particular choice. Unless the final design is a true combination of all the team working single-mindedly to solve the client's problems, the end result will be lacking in validity. A modern building is so complex that single-handed design is not feasible.

At the end of this stage, the architect should be able to present the client with design drawings which show how the building will work and look and, if up-to-date computer techniques are employed, how the users will experience living and working in and around the building as part of the overall environment.

The management function is much the same as in Stage C, except that the procedures set up then should be fully operational and the architect is simply in the position of setting fresh objectives and time-scales, and ensuring that every member co-operates properly and at the right time. In addition, the architect will be ironing out any problems with relevant authorities, the most important of which will be:

- Water.
- Electricity.
- Gas.
- Highway.
- Fire.

- Telephone.
- Environmental health.
- Cleansing.

Many of these authorities require layout plans before they can comment sensibly and it is essential that the architect has agreements before this stage is completed or the whole scheme can be put at risk. Even something like refuse collection may pose severe problems if not tackled early with the support rather than the opposition of the local cleansing department.

It is useful for the architect to submit a written report with the presentation drawings in which the major strengths can be emphasized and any weaknesses made clear. The architect should ask the client for agreement to proceed to tender stage through the more detailed design, production information and bills of quantity stages.

9.3 Cost estimates and planning

The quantity surveyor is the expert on costs. There is a world of difference between producing an estimate of the probable cost of a building from a set of drawings and producing a similar estimate from a brief and, as the design develops, putting together a cost plan which enables the architect to work within known cost limits in respect of each element. An experienced architect may make a reasonable attempt at the former, but only a skilled and experienced quantity surveyor will be able to carry out the latter with sufficient accuracy to be useful.

The client will have stated what can be afforded, but the architect may have to use some strategy in getting the true figure. On the basis that all building work costs more than expected or planned, the client will often present the design team with a reduced figure. When this happens, the team set their sights accordingly and when construction is nearing its end the client sometimes indulges in an orgy of expenditure and uses up his hidden balance in pointless extras when it would have been put to better use in perhaps increasing the overall floor area, or heights, or other fundamental provision. Be that as it may, the team can do no other than to work to the figure given by the client. To do other would amount to negligence and, at the very least, the professionals would lose their fees.[1]

Although the client may say that the maximum expenditure is, say, £5 000 000, that information is of little help to the architect except in very general terms. It can be translated into rough areas or volumes on the basis of different constructional systems and finishes (expensive or cheap). What the quantity surveyor can do is to produce a cost plan for the designers which allocates a sum of money to each element. For example the cost of walls may be expressed as £x per square metre, and similarly for floors, roofs and so on. Allocations for furniture can be made on a room-by-room basis. More importantly, the quantity surveyor can give the architect an idea of what those sums of money represent in terms of construction and finishes by giving a range of examples in each case. In order to be able to do this, the quantity surveyor has to be able to call upon a file of cost information and trends built up over a considerable period.

The cost plan can be divided in different ways, so that if a housing estate is being considered, a price per dwelling may be expressed together with a figure for district heating, another for roads and footpaths, landscaping and so on. The plan can be as coarse or sophisticated as required although the finer the tuning, the less accurate it will be because it is simply an estimate and it depends very much on the level of tendering and many other factors on the day. Over the years, several professional journals have featured buildings whose costs have been split in this way.[2]

9.4 Town planning applications and approvals

9.4.1 Introduction

Town planning legislation is now consolidated in four Acts:

- The Town and Country Planning Act 1990.
- The Planning (Listed Buildings and Conservation Areas) Act 1990.
- The Planning (Hazardous Substances) Act 1990.
- The Planning (Consequential Provisions) Act 1990.

Recently, the procedures for enforcement, established use and planning agreements have been modified by the Planning and Compensation Act 1991. The control of planning matters is delegated to local planning authorities (county councils and district councils or the London boroughs or metropolitan districts) by the Secretary of State for the Environment, but certain matters must be referred for his decision.

9.4.2 Development plans

Part II of the Town and Country Planning Act 1990 sets out the types of development plan. For the London boroughs and metropolitan districts the unitary development plan is replacing the structure plans and local plans. Elsewhere, there is a two-tier local government structure in which the county council will prepare the structure plan and the local plans will be prepared by the district councils. Together, they form the development plan for that area. They are legally binding, but they do not confer a right to develop.

The county councils and certain other bodies have the duty to carry out surveys of their areas, consult with the public and produce *structure plans*. These are written statements of policy for the area together with a set of small-scale plans to form a long-term strategy for the region and a basis for local plans. There is an elaborate procedure to ensure full public participation although it must be said that the percentage of members of the public who are interested enough to make comment is very small.

The authorities also take soundings from local societies as being representative of a wider spectrum of opinion. The plan must have proper regard to national and regional planning and the strategies of neighbouring authorities. The finished plans must be approved by the Secretary of State before they are published.

Structure plans must be updated on a regular basis, normally every ten years, but some authorities fall well behind that target. Evaluation and monitoring of the plan is continuous to meet changing circumstances.

Local plans fall into three types:

- *District plans*   These show the development of large areas such as towns. They are normally produced to a small scale showing broad policies.
- *Action area plans*   These show the comprehensive treatment of areas urgently needing improvement or re-development within a ten-year period. They are very detailed.
- *Subject plans*   These are detailed investigations of specific topics, often problem areas; for example, the treatment of quarries, recreation areas, disused railway lines and waste disposal sites.

For unitary development plans, after the Secretary of State has given the commencement order and issued regional strategic guidance, the local planning authority must prepare the plan in two parts, (1) a broad development framework and land-use strategy, and (2) a written statement and plan on Ordnance Survey base, together with a reasoned justification of policies.

In practice, it is assumed that many of the policies in existing local plans will be widely adopted into the unitary development plans. An early opportunity is given for public comment by publishing a draft plan. After considering representations and preparing the plan, it is placed on deposit during which formal objections or supporting representations can be made.

Where objections are received and are not withdrawn, the planning authority must hold a local public inquiry to be conducted by an inspector appointed by the Secretary of State. The inspector must report to the local authority about all representations received and the authority must decide what action to take on each recommendation. The local planning authority then finally adopts the plan. The Secretary of State retains the power to call in the plan, but it is likely that this power would be exercised only in exceptional circumstances where the policies are not in conformity with the strategic guidance or part 1 of the plan.

Until 1991, there has been a presumption in favour of granting planning permission. The Planning and Compensation Act 1991 changes that by stating that planning decisions must accord with the development plan unless material conditions indicate otherwise (s. 26).

9.4.3 Development control

With few exceptions the development of land in the UK may only be undertaken with permission of the local planning authority. *Development* is defined by s. 55 of the Town and Country Planning Act 1990 as the carrying out of building, engineering, mining and other operations in, on, over or under land or the making of any material change in the use of any buildings or other land.

Certain operations which fall under this definition are allowed by the Town and Country Planning General Development Orders. They are referred to as *permitted development*. Examples are:

- Certain enlargements carried out to dwelling houses, e.g. garages.
- The erection of fences, walls and gates.
- Building operations carried out on agricultural land for agricultural purposes.
- The erection of most kinds of temporary building, e.g. contractors' site offices.

- Some local authority operations.
- Some developments carried out by statutory undertakers.

Generally, a material change of use will be a change between 'use classes' as defined by the Use Classes Order 1987: for example, A1 retail to B2 industry. Some changes are permitted by the General Development Order. Permitted development rights can be removed by conditions put on a planning permission by the authority or by a direction under Article 4 of the Town and Country Planning General Development Order 1988. Permitted development falls under schedule 2. There are a total of 75 classes divided into 28 parts.

The architect should always consult the planning authority at an early stage (see Chapter 8, section 8.1). It is usually prudent to get *outline planning consent* as soon as possible. This is defined as any consent within which any of the specified five matters are reserved: i.e., means of access, siting, design, landscaping and external appearance. It relates only to proposals where building works are involved and not to change of use. It is more commonly used to refer to permission which is given in principle to allow the development of the project to proceed. It does not confer the right to carry out any building operations until the detailed reserved matters have been approved.

Generally, it is only necessary to supply the authority with basic information such as the address of the site, the nature of the development and a small-scale plan showing the site in red and other land in the applicant's ownership in blue together with the appropriate fee and ownership certificate. There are appropriate forms for the purpose. Occasionally, the authority may require the submission of more details. This is particularly the case if the site is particularly sensitive: for example, if it is in a conservation area. Ideally, outline permission should be obtained at feasibility stage, but the time-scale may preclude this. An outline permission is valid for the period stated on the permission, normally three years.

Application for full planning permission must be made on the appropriate forms. The appropriate fee must be enclosed together with drawings explaining the proposals and a certificate of ownership. The basic information required by the authority includes:

- Site address.
- Name and address of owner of the site.
- Type of development proposed.
- Current usage of the site.
- Access from the highway (existing and proposed).
- Means of foul and surface water drainage.

- Area of the proposed development.
- Method of storage of any materials classified as hazardous.
- Employment position (existing and proposed).
- Parking provision.
- Description of materials proposed.
- Relationship of proposal to surrounding development.
- Full details of the proposal.

In addition, the applicant must submit a certificate setting out the ownership position. Briefly, there are four certificates as follows:

A: used where the applicant is the owner of all the land which is the subject of the application.
B: used if the applicant has given an appropriate notice to everyone who was an owner of any part of the land during the period 20 days before the application date.
C: used if neither certificate A nor B can be issued and the applicant has given notice of the application to known owners and stating steps taken to identify unknown owners.
D: used if no owners are known.

Notice must be served on any agricultural tenant who was a tenant during the 20-day period. Where owners are unknown, an advertisement must be put in the local newspaper and copies sent to the authority with the application.

The authority must come to a decision within eight weeks of the application date unless the applicant and the authority agree to an extension of this period. The authority may grant permission, or grant it subject to conditions, or refuse it giving reasons.[3] If the authority simply fail to respond within the eight weeks or any extended period, the application is deemed refused. In such a case, it is possible to appeal against the 'non-determination', but if discussions are continuing, it is possible for further time to be allowed in which a decision can be made whether or not a request for extension of time has been made by the local authority. It is for the applicant and his or her agent to decide if it will be more productive or quicker to go to appeal. Permission is usually given for the land; it is rarely personal to the applicant. Therefore, when the land is sold, the permission is transferred also. It is very common for a planning authority to impose standard conditions on every permission together with special conditions to suit particular sites.

In the case of certain 'bad neighbour' proposals such as scrap yards, boarding kennels, bingo halls, etc. known as the *designated classes*, the applicant must submit a s. 65 notice with an application, and carry out advertising procedures.

An applicant can find out if planning permission is necessary by formally seeking a determination of the matter from the planning authority and submitting a written description of the proposal together with a location plan under s. 64 of the 1990 Act.

When permission is granted, the applicant must commence work on site within five years.

9.4.4 Remedies

Completion notice

The authority may serve this notice on the building owner where progress on building works is very slow, to the extent that it is clear the work will never be completed. The notice comes into force after not less than one year from the date of the notice to give adequate time for the building to be completed. The effect is that all work shown on the approved drawings which is not completed loses its planning permission. This kind of notice is rarely given.

Enforcement notice

The authority has the power to serve this notice where there has been a breach of planning control, such as development undertaken without permission or in contravention of the condition imposed by the authority.[4] The notice must require the building owner or occupier to do whatever is necessary to remedy the breach. A reasonable time limit must be imposed. An appeal on specified grounds may be lodged with the Secretary of State within 28 days. While the Secretary of State is deciding the appeal, the notice is of no effect. It is not unknown for a building owner to appeal for that very reason. The authority has other powers, however.

Stop notice

The authority may serve this notice[5] to ensure that construction ceases or to prevent a material change of use. It can only be served after an enforcement notice if it seems that the building owner is intent to press ahead with work during the appeal procedure. There is no appeal against a stop notice. If the appeal against the enforcement notice is successful, the stop notice is automatically void. Failure to observe a stop notice results in very heavy penalties and further daily penalties for continuing failure. In some instances, a building owner may be able to obtain compensation after a successful appeal against an enforcement notice which was followed by a stop notice. For this reason alone, planning authorities are reluctant to serve stop notices.

Planning contravention notice

This is a procedure introduced under the Planning and Compensation Act 1991 whereby a local planning authority can obtain information about activities being carried out on a site where a breach of planning control is suspected. The owner, occupier or any other recipient is required to reply within 21 days.

Breach of conditions notice

From 27 July 1992, the local planning authority has power to serve a notice requiring compliance with a condition in a planning permission. There is no appeal against such a notice and failure to comply within 28 days is a summary offence.

Appeal

An applicant may appeal against refusal of planning permission, conditions attached to the permission and various other matters. Notice must be given to the Secretary of State in the appropriate form within a stipulated period from the date on which the refusal was received or, in the case of non-determination, within the period from the date on which the determination should have been made. The actual period allowed for lodging the appeal varies depending on the subject matter of the appeal. The range is from 28 days to six months. An appeal may be dealt with in one of three ways:

- Written representation: if the parties waive their right to an inquiry and the Secretary of State agrees.[6] This is the most common type of appeal and is used in about 85% of planning appeals. It has the benefit of speed and relative cheapness.
- Public local inquiry: The Secretary of State must hold an inquiry if either the appellant or the local authority so desire. These inquiries will deal with the most complex applications and they usually involve legal representation and the cross-examination of witnesses.[7]
- Informal hearing: a simple procedure with some characteristics of

written representations and public local inquiry. It may occur where the Secretary of State considers the case to be appropriate and where one or both parties has indicated their wish to be heard by an inspector. The purpose is to save time and money for the parties and to allow the inspector to lead a discussion about the matters at issue. It is a more relaxed and less formal atmosphere than a public inquiry.

The local planning authority will provide details of the appeals procedure.[8]

9.4.5 Other permissions

Renewal of permission

Renewal of an existing permission is not automatic because there may be a change in circumstances following the original permission. A full permission is normally valid for five years and renewal must be sought before the expiry of this period.

Listed building consent

The Secretary of State has power to compile lists or approve lists compiled by other bodies of buildings of special architectural or historic interest.[9] A building may be listed for its exterior, interior or any feature. The local planning authority must notify owners and occupiers of listed buildings. It is worth noting that ecclesiastical buildings belonging to the Anglican Church are subject to the same listing system as other buildings, but they benefit from 'ecclesiastical exemption' and they do not generally need listed building consent.[10]

It is an offence to demolish, alter or extend a listed building unless the planning authority or the Secretary of State has granted a written listed building consent. If work is carried out without such consent, it may be possible to make out a defence on the grounds that the works were urgently necessary for safety, health or to preserve the building, but the local planning authority must be notified in writing as soon as possible. Temporary protection can be given to an unlisted building which is in danger of demolition or alteration, by the service of a building preservation notice by the authority. Its effect is immediate and it lasts for six months during which time the Secretary of State can decide whether or not to list it.

Conservation area consent

The planning authority has power to declare certain areas to be of special architectural or historic interest as conservation areas where it is required to preserve and enhance their character.[11] The controls in a conservation area include the need for consent for demolition of buildings and for the felling of trees. Planning applications must be advertised and consideration has to be given to preserving and enhancing the character and appearance of the conservation area. The controls on development are not as extensive as for listed buildings, but more restrictive tolerances may be applied in certain instances.[12]

Trees

Each local planning authority has the duty to ensure that adequate provision is made for the preservation and planting of trees when planning permission is granted.[13] It may also make tree preservation orders for trees, groups of trees and woodlands which contribute to the amenity of the area. Notice must be given to the owners and occupiers of the land, who are entitled to object.

It is an offence to cut down, lop, top or wilfully damage such trees without the consent of the local planning authority unless they are deemed to be dangerous, dying, dead or the work is executed in compliance with another Act of Parliament. Even in such cases, the prior consent of the authority should be sought. The authority are entitled to insist on the replacement of a tree by another of appropriate size and species. A provisional tree preservation order can be made which is valid for six months.

Certificate of established use

Such a certificate may be sought in certain areas where there is no extant planning permission referable to the site. In order to claim established use it is necessary to be able to show and to prove that a use was begun before the end of 1964 and has continued since then without a break and that it is still continuing.[14] The certificate states that enforcement procedures will not be used despite the lack of planning permission; with the passage of time, however, such continuous use is becoming increasingly difficult to prove.

The established use certificate is to be replaced by a new *lawful development* certificate which comes into operation on 27 July 1992 under the Planning and Compensation Act 1991. This will enable the planning authority to determine whether development has become 'immune' from enforcement action or whether planning permission is required for an existing or proposed use or operation. There is a ten-year limit for enforcement action on most changes of use of land or breaches of planning conditions.

Advertisements

The planning authority has the power to control the display of advertisements in the interests of amenity and safety.[15] External advertisements of any kind, including those which are located inside, but visible from outside, require permission. Applications must be made using special forms and accompanied by a fee. Some classes of advertisement do not require express consent; they are considered to have deemed consent. The control of advertisements is exercised in the interests of public safety (often road safety) and amenity.

Planning agreements

An applicant may agree with the local planning authority to carry out certain works or to restrict the use of his or her land in ways which would not be legally enforceable through planning conditions.[16] By doing so, the local authority may be willing to grant planning permission. Common examples are the carrying out of off-site highway or drainage works to allow land to be developed or in relation to agricultural workers' dwellings which tie existing land and property to the agricultural holding.

The planning agreement is to be replaced by a *planning obligation* which does not require the agreement of the local authority, but can be made unilaterally by the applicant. This will allow more flexibility for the applicant especially with regard to any applications which are the subject of an appeal.

9.5 *Other approvals*

A development may be subject to a great many approvals other than planning and building control (see Chapter 10, section 10.2). The following are building types which require special approvals of various kinds:

- Licensed premises and restaurants.
- Music and dance halls.
- Cinemas and theatres.

- Petrol stations.
- Nursing homes.
- Abattoirs.

In addition, approval may be required from landlords or funders of development.

9.6 *Property*

9.6.1 Boundaries

Boundaries are the demarcation lines between separate properties. They can be the source of many problems when the properties either side of the line are in different ownerships as is usually the case.

When investigating the feasibility of building, the architect should make it an early task to establish or verify the apparent boundaries of a site. The only safe way to do this is for the architect to request verification from the client's solicitor. Since deed plans and the deeds themselves are often unclear on the matter, the solicitor will often be loath to put forward a definitive view. On occasion, boundaries are so vague that all the adjoining owners have to agree the boundaries afresh. Certain presumptions may be made from inspection of such things as fences, ditches and hedges.

Very great care must be taken when dealing with old properties which adjoin. Ownership of a cellar may extend under the ground floor of the other property and the buildings themselves may actually interlock: e.g. the first floor may project over the neighbouring ground floor and under the second floor. Such cases, however, would more usually fall under a consideration of party walls (see section 9.6.2 below).

If a building is constructed so as to infringe a neighbouring boundary, the building owner will have committed trespass against the neighbour. The matter can only be rectified by the removal of the building or the purchase of the portion of neighbouring land on which it stands, probably at an inflated price. Common infringements occur in the projection of footings or eaves across the boundary. Where a neighbour permits an eaves to project onto his or her land, the building owner is said to have a 'right of eavesdrop'.

9.6.2 Party walls

There are three types of party wall. The most common situation is where the wall is divided vertically and reciprocal easements are in force over the whole wall. In the second type, the wall is divided vertically into two strips, one strip belonging to each owner. In the third type, the wall belongs completely to one owner and the adjoining owner has the right to have it maintained as a dividing wall.

There are special procedures for party walls in inner London.[17] If anything is to be done to a party wall as defined by the Act, notice is to be given in certain forms. If the two adjoining owners do not agree (and it is often unwise to agree in advance), each party must appoint a surveyor to whom certain powers are given by the Act to determine the difference and to decide, subject to the provisions of the Act, what contribution each party is to make to the cost of the works. Both building and adjoining owners have statutory rights which they can exercise under the Act and those rights can never be overlooked or set aside. Printed forms for the various notices are available and care must be taken to adhere to the periods of notice laid down.

When acting for the building owner and in view of the time required for notice, counter-notice and negotiation, the architect must take early steps to set the machinery in motion. Under s. 47(2) of the Act, two months' notice must be given of proposed work to a party wall structure. In case of difference, s. 55 specifies the periods of notice required if a party refuses to appoint a surveyor, if two surveyors appointed fail to appoint a third or if a surveyor refuses to act.

A notice setting out details of the proposed work will normally be accompanied by a drawing giving plans and sections of the party wall in question and as much of the proposed new building as may affect negotiation. The notice would be served on the adjoining owner, who would either pass it directly to a surveyor or to a solicitor to instruct a surveyor. Section 55(a)(i) of the Act provides for the possibility of both parties agreeing on a single surveyor, but it is more usual for each party to appoint one. In the absence of consent to a notice within 14 days a difference is deemed to have arisen (s. 49). Where there are two surveyors appointed, the one acting for the adjoining owner will, on receipt of instructions, communicate with the building owner's surveyor.

Before discussing the notice, the first duty of the two surveyors is to appoint a third surveyor in writing. This third surveyor will not be referred to unless a difference arises between the other two surveyors. Having made the appointment, the two surveyors will then arrange to meet on the site to discuss the proposal, setting out their decisions in the form of an award, on signature of which the works can proceed. It is advisable, although not compulsory, to register the award by depositing a copy with the Land Registry.

The adjoining owner's surveyor will watch his or her client's interests during the progress of the works, and further awards on matters arising and not settled by the first award can be made if necessary, with reference if needs be to the third surveyor. The amount of the adjoining owner's fee is usually determined in the award, which will state that it is to be paid by the building owner. Outside London, there is no statutory control, but the normal common law rights of property must be respected.

9.6.3 Trespass

This is a category of the law of tort. Trespass to land is of most concern to the architect. The general rule is that if a person enters upon, remains upon or allows anything to come into contact with another's land, that person is committing trespass. Trespass can occur under land, on the surface or to a reasonable height over the land. Contrary to popular misconception, there is no necessity to prove damage in order to sue for trespass. There is a requirement for damage before action in the case of nuisance, however, with which trespass is often confused. If a person demolishes a wall by pushing it onto adjoining property, that is trespass; if the wall simply collapses with old age and falls onto adjoining property, that is nuisance. Building a foundation across a boundary is trespass; allowing tree roots to grow across is nuisance. Trespass is a direct invasion of another's land.

The usual legal remedies for trespass are to take action for damages if any, and/or to take out an injunction to prevent further or continuing trespass. A form of self-help is for the person in possession of the land forcibly to evict the trespasser who refuses to leave, but this option should be a last resort and exercised with great care.

A contractor carrying out work on a site is said to have a licence to be on the site for the purpose of carrying out the building. There may be an express licence, but it is more usual that the licence will be implied. A contractor who stays on the land after the work is complete or after determination of employment will be a trespasser. Trespassers, particularly children, can be a real problem on building sites and those in possession of the site have an especially strict duty to ensure that children do not suffer injury.[18]

An occupier owes a duty to trespassers by virtue of statute[19] if:

'he is aware of the danger or has reasonable grounds to believe that it exists; . . . he knows or has reasonable grounds to believe that the other is in (or may come into) the vicinity of danger . . . the risk is one against which in all the circumstances of the case, he may reasonably be expected to offer the other protection.'

The duty is to take such care as is reasonable in all the circumstances of the case to see that the entrant to the property does not suffer injury on the premises by reason of the danger concerned. This duty may be discharged by giving warning of the danger on an appropriately worded notice.

9.6.4 Nuisance

Nuisance has been mentioned briefly under trespass. It is another category of the law of tort. There are three types of nuisance:

- Public nuisance.
- Private nuisance.
- Statutory nuisance.

Public nuisance

An act or omission without lawful justification which causes damage, injury or inconvenience to the public at large. It is a crime as well as a tort. It must affect a reasonable-sized class of people or the nuisance cannot be categorized as public. An example is the obstruction of a highway. A private person has no remedy for public nuisance unless that person suffers from that nuisance over and above the damage suffered by the public at large.

Private nuisance

An unlawful interference with the use or enjoyment of land. The usual examples are smell, smoke, noise and tree roots. If a person wishes to sue for nuisance, damage must be proved. Remedies available are damages or an injunction. The suffering party may take action to abate the nuisance in wholly exceptional circumstances only. In some instances, building work can be held to be nuisance.[20] It is now rare for actions to be brought in this respect, however, because building operations are generally of quite short duration, it is usually reasonable use of property to permit or cause building works to be carried out from time to time, and there are statutory powers for the local authority to regulate building works to prevent excessive noise, dust, etc.[21] Nuisance is a complex subject and should any problem arise, the architect should advise the client to seek legal advice.

Statutory nuisance

Anything which is declared by statute to be a nuisance.[22] The local authority may serve an abatement notice to require the perpetrator to bring the nuisance to an end.

9.6.5 Rights of light

This right is sometimes called *ancient lights*. It is a negative easement (see section 9.6.6 below) which entitles an owner to prevent his neighbour from building so as to obstruct the flow of light through particular windows. The right is not acquired in respect of the whole building, unless it is entirely glazed, but only in respect of the window openings. For this reason, when considering the redevelopment of a property which has rights of light to certain windows, it is essential that a careful measured survey is carried out so that any new windows will be replaced exactly in the same positions as the original windows. The right is usually acquired under the Prescription Act 1832 which requires the right to be enjoyed for 20 years without interruption and without written consent.

The existence of a building with rights of light on adjoining land can put severe constraints on the development potential of a site. In order for an act to be considered as an interruption, it must continue for at least a year. At one time, it was necessary to erect a screen to block the light to prevent the right from being acquired. Since the Rights of Light Act 1959, the owner of land over which a right of light might be acquired may register as a land charge a notice identifying the properties and specifying the size and position of a notional screen. Parties likely to be affected must be given prior notice and the notice itself is in force for a year during which time an affected party may seek to have it varied or cancelled. In order to prevent the right from being acquired, it is necessary to re-register at least every 19 years.

If a party considers that another is infringing his or her right of light, the injured party must show that the light which remains is not sufficient for the comfortable use and enjoyment according to the ordinary notions of mankind.[23] Any action would be brought in nuisance (section 9.6.4 above) and a practical test which is often adopted is whether the light can flow into the window without interruption at an angle of 45° from the horizontal measured at the cill.

The nature and use of the building will determine the amount of light entitlement. Thus a greenhouse will need more light than a private house.[24]

9.6.6 Easements

This is a right held by one party to use the land belonging to another or to restrict the use of such land by another. Common examples are rights of way, and rights of drainage or for services. These are known as positive easements as compared to negative easements such as rights of light or right of support. An easement relates to land, not people. The land which enjoys the right is called the dominant tenement; the land on or against which the easement is exercised is called the servient tenement. It is essential that the two pieces of land have different owners.

There is often confusion with regard to right of support although the position is very clear. All land enjoys right of support from adjoining land. In the present state of the law, no successful action would be possible against a person excavating near a neighbour's boundary unless the excavation caused actual physical damage to the adjacent land. A neighbour could not successfully bring an action for the cost of building a retaining wall to prevent possible future slippage. That is simply economic loss and it is not recoverable in tort. There is no natural right of support for buildings.

If, however, the removal of support from land causes the collapse of that land and the building standing on it, the building owner would have the right to bring an action. The right of support when applied to a building is usually acquired by prescription, but it can also be acquired expressly. A fairly common situation is where a property has been in existence for some years when the adjoining owner builds next to, and taking support from, the original property. There may be an express agreement entered into before building or to regularize the position, or the owner of the original property may take no action for 20 years.

A profit a prendre is a right to remove something from another's land; turf, for example. Easements and profits may be created by Act of Parliament; by express grant, usually by deed; by express reservation, when land is sold; or by prescription (see section 9.6.5 above).

References

(1) *Blissett* v. *Marquis of Salisbury* (1989) *The Times* 9 September 1989.
(2) For example see the *Architects' Journal* and *Building*.

(3) DOE Circular 1/85 *The use of planning conditions in planning permissions* sets out the appropriate types and forms of conditions.

(4) Town and Country Planning Act 1990, Part VII, s. 172–182.

(5) Town and Country Planning Act 1990, Part VII, s. 183–187.

(6) DOE Circular 18/86, Appendix 1, sets out the form which the statements should take.

(7) Town and Country Planning (Inquiry Procedure) Rules 1988.

(8) Department of the Environment (1987) *Planning Appeals: A Guide.*

(9) Planning (Listed Buildings and Conservation Areas) Act 1990. This Act consolidates all listed building and conservation area legislation and covers such things as listing, getting listed building consent, appeals and enforcement.

(10) Planning (Listed Buildings and Conservation Areas) Act 1990, ss. 61 and 62.

(11) Planning (Listed Buildings and Conservation Areas) Act 1990, s. 69.

(12) Town and Country Planning General Development Order 1988, sch. 2 (termed article 1(5) land).

(13) Town and Country Planning Act 1990, s. 197–199, cover the requirement for local authorities to consider the protection and planting of trees and the making of tree preservation orders.

(14) Town and Country Planning Act 1990, s. 191–196.

(15) Town and Country Planning (Control of Advertisements) Regulations 1989.

(15) Town and Country Planning Act 1990, s. 106.

(16) Town and Country Planning Act 1990, s. 106.

(17) London Building Acts (Amendment) Acts 1939, s. 44–59.

(18) *Pannett* v. *McGuinness & Co.* [1972] 2 QB 599.

(19) Occupiers' Liability Act 1984, s. 1(3).

(20) *Andrea* v. *Selfridge & Co. Ltd* [1937] 3 All ER 255.

(21) Control of Pollution Act 1974.

(22) Public Health Act s. 91 and 92.

(23) *Colls* v. *Home & Colonial Stores* [1904] AC 185.

(24) *Allen* v. *Greenwood* [1979] 1 All ER 819.

Chapter 10

Stages E and F

10.1 Detailed design

This stage of the architect's work is essentially a completion of the design stage. The architect must collaborate with, and co-ordinate the work of, the design team. This is easy to say and less easy to do.

During this period, the architect must ensure, so far as possible, that all conflicts between consultants' work are ironed out. If any specialist sub-contractor design work is involved in the project, this must also be co-ordinated together with final details from statutory and other authorities. As a general rule, the use of sub-contractors in a design capacity is not to be advised, because it can cause complications and certainly requires the use of a form of collateral warranty to protect the client. In any event, the client must authorize such design delegation (Chapter 7, section 7.2). The contractor is entitled to receive correct information. It is not the contractor's responsibility to look for errors and inconsistencies.[1] Careful cost checks will be made by the quantity surveyor if the project is large enough to support one; otherwise the architect must carry out this exercise.

If the project is sufficiently large to support a design team, they will be carrying out specific functions during the period, culminating in a meeting of the full team under the chairmanship of the team leader. This may be a project manager especially appointed by the client, but it is still most likely to be the architect, because the architect is the only building professional who is trained to take on this task as part of his or her normal professional duties. The separate functions of the members of the design team will depend on the type of project, but as a general guide, they may be expected to be carrying out the following tasks.

Quantity surveyor

- Reviewing the cost plan in the light of the client's comments and decisions on the scheme design. The review highlights potential

additional cost areas and indicates scope for savings.
• Carrying out cost studies and cost checks as the design team finally shape their details. There must be a constant flow of information between the architect and the consultants, the architect and the quantity surveyor and the quantity surveyor and the architect (Figure 10.1 shows the principle).

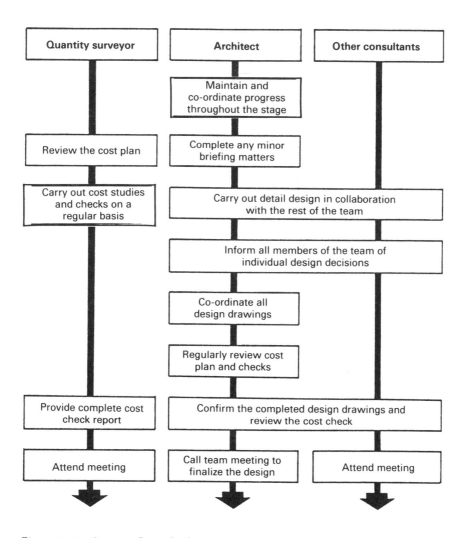

Figure 10.1   Stage E: flow of information.

Civil and structural engineers

- Collaborating in the cost plan review and cost checking procedures.
- Finalising all details in respect of dimensions, levels, loadings, concrete mixes, etc.
- Developing the specifications in detail.

Mechanical and electrical engineers

- Refining the design of all services to be incorporated in the building.
- Developing the specifications in detail.

Strenuous efforts must be made to obtain the client's decision on any outstanding items. If the client makes any change in the size, location, shape or cost of the scheme after this stage, there will be a cost penalty to pay for the re-doing of work already carried out. Ideally, there should be no changes at all in the design after this point but, in practice, it is impossible to eliminate all changes. Particularly in the case of some projects such as hospitals, the brief will be constantly evolving and the client just has to accept that there is a price to pay for changes. This difficulty may sometimes be eased by the choice of a particular procurement path and/or contract form, but it can never be removed entirely.

Stage E of the RIBA Plan of Work usually merges imperceptibly into Stage F (production information) and both stages amount to what would once have been termed 'working drawings'. To be precise, detailed design is probably composed of roughly equal parts of completion of design and commencement of working drawings. It does not matter. Indeed, it is perfectly proper that the process should not be divorced from the crucially important construction process.

The architect will continue the important twofold function of designer and manager throughout this and the next stage. It is likely that, in so far as the architect can ever be said to have reached a finite end to this stage, he or she will have a large collection of design studies in a final condition and covering every part of the project. This is the raw material from which the production information will take shape. There are several systems of setting out production information (see section 10.3 below), but in every case, the architect cannot simply start by drawing a foundation and work up or start with the roof and work down.

The architect must know the form of each part of the building; it is during this stage, more than any other, that the building takes shape as a whole. All parts must progress together so that the architect is aware, when considering the ducting details for example, what effect they have on the foundation designs, lift wells, room plans and so on. This is the most important stage in the architect's work on a project.

10.2 Building Regulations 1991

10.2.1 General

The Building Regulations in England and Wales are made by the Secretary of State under the Building Act 1984. Their purpose is to secure the health, safety, welfare and convenience of people in or about buildings and of others who may be affected by buildings or matters connected with buildings, to further the conservation of fuel and power and prevent waste, undue consumption, misuse or contamination of water.

Most cases of building or alteration to buildings must be notified to the local Building Control authority. The following building types, at present subject to certain conditions, are exempted from the Regulations, but are controlled under other legislation:

- Prison buildings and buildings for the detention of criminals.
- Buildings required for the purposes of any educational establishment erected to plans which are approved by the Secretary of State for Education and Science (other than houses, offices and showrooms).
- Buildings of Statutory Undertakers held and used for the purpose of their undertaking.
- Buildings subject to the Explosives Act 1875 and 1923.
- Buildings (other than dwellings, offices and canteens) on a site with a licence under the Nuclear Installations Act 1965 in force.
- Buildings subject to the Ancient Monuments and Archeological Areas Acts 1979.
- Buildings (other than dwellings, offices and showrooms) which are used in connection with any mine or quarry.
- Buildings into which people cannot or do not normally go, subject to siting.
- Detached buildings containing fixed plant or machinery to which people only go intermittently to inspect or maintain the plant or machinery.
- Greenhouses (unless used for retailing, packing or exhibiting).
- Any building used for agriculture, including fish farming, sited one and a half times its height from any point of a building containing

sleeping accommodation and having no point more than 30 m from an exit which may be used in the case of fire (unless the main purpose of the building is retailing, packing or exhibiting).

- Any building intended to remain erected for less than 28 days.
- Mobile homes subject to the Mobile Homes Act 1983.
- Any building on an estate used in connection with the sale of buildings or building plots, provided there is no sleeping accommodation.
- Any building used by people in connection with the erection, extension, alteration or repair of buildings and containing no sleeping accommodation.
- Small, detached single-storey buildings not exceeding 30 m² floor area containing no sleeping accommodation and either sited more than 1 m from the boundary of its curtilage or constructed substantially of non-combustible material.
- Nuclear, chemical or conventional weapon shelters not exceeding 30 m² and which do not affect the foundations of adjoining buildings.
- Any conservatory, porch, covered way or carport at least open on two sides extensions which has a floor area not exceeding 10 m², subject to glazing requirements.
- Certain temporary exhibition stands.
- Tents or marquees.
- Moveable dwellings under s.269 of the Public Health Act 1936.
- 'Static' mobile accommodation (e.g. caravans).
- Certain engineering structures (e.g. docks, tunnels).
- Tower masts not attached to a building (not chimneys).
- Plant or machinery.
- Storage racking (unless supporting a floor).
- Amusement or fairground equipment.
- Scaffolding or falsework.
- Street furniture.
- Fences, walls or gates.
- External storage tanks.

The Regulations are much shorter than previous editions, being expressed fairly simply in functional terms, but there is a set of Approved Documents which indicate ways in which compliance with the Building Regulations may be achieved. However, it is possible to show compliance with the Regulations by reference to other standards or by calculation. Important new features have been introduced allowing building control by local authorities and by private certification. The latter system operates under the Building (Approved

Inspectors, etc.) Regulations 1985. Control is operated through three procedures.

10.2.2 Notification

It is an offence to commence building operations without first depositing plans or a building notice giving at least two clear days' notice to the local authority. Note, however, that it is not necessary to await approval before commencing work. The notice procedures are:

Deposit of full plans

This is the traditional system. A full set of plans must be deposited with the local authority in duplicate together with completed forms which may vary in layout from authority to authority, but which all contain requests for the same basic information. Where Part B Fire Safety imposes a requirement, two further copies shall be deposited demonstrating compliance. It is now possible to request, at the time the plans are deposited, that the local authority issue a completion certificate in accordance with the regulations. A fee, calculated in accordance with the prescribed scale, must also be included.[2] The fee is in two parts: for the passing or rejection of plans, and for inspection of the work.

The drawings, each of which must be signed by the applicant or appointed agent, are generally expected to consist of the following.

- A block plan, not less than 1:1250 scale, showing the size and position of the building in relation to adjoining buildings, boundaries, position of all buildings within the curtilage, width of adjoining streets, lines of drainage, size depth and gradient of drains and means of access, position and level of drain outfall and sewer connection.

- Sufficient plans and sections to suitable scales (usually not less than 1:100) showing full details of the intended construction of the project including site and floor levels, number of storeys, foundations, construction of floors, walls and roof, windows, doors, barriers to moisture, fire safety, means of escape, insulation, ventilation and access for the disabled.

The local authority must give written notice of approval or rejection of the application within five weeks of the date of deposit of plans provided the requisite fee has been paid and a reasonable estimate of the cost of the work has been submitted. The period may be extended in writing to a total of not more than two months by agreement of both parties. If the authority fail to give written notice, it is in breach of its duty and a fee must be refunded. There is no deemed approval and indeed, even if there were such deemed approval, it would be of little value if there was any disconformity, in the face of the applicant's obligation to construct in accordance with the Building Regulations. If the application is rejected, the applicant may appeal to the Secretary of State.

Building notice

There is no approval of plans by the authority where this procedure is adopted and work can be commenced subject to the submission of notices (see above). A building notice is now valid for three years if work is not started and it cannot be given for a building which requires a means of escape and which is designated under the Fire Precautions Act 1971 or if so altered would become subject to the requirements of that Act. There is no prescribed form for the notice, but it must contain certain basic information: the name and address of the person intending to carry out the work, notice that it is given under regulation 11(1)(a) of the Building Regulations, and a description including the use of the building to which the application relates. In addition, appropriate drawings and the prescribed fee must be deposited.

The drawing, to a scale of not less than 1:1250, will usually show the size and position of the building, its relationship to adjoining buildings, boundaries, positions of all building within the curtilage, width of adjoining streets, numbers of storeys, building use, means of drainage and building over sewers. Details of insulation and hot water storage systems must be given in a detailed statement.

The authority may request the submission of whatever additional drawings or information they require to enable them to carry out their duties.

Initial notice

This procedure is used if private certification is to be employed, using an approved inspector (section 10.2.1 above). The notice must be in the prescribed form and must contain a description of the work, whether it is 'minor work' under the Building (Approval Inspectors, etc.) Regulations 1985, an undertaking to consult the fire authority, a statement of awareness of statutory obligations and a declaration that

---

The Building Act 1984, section 47, and the Building (Approved Inspectors, etc) Regulations 1985

INITIAL NOTICE

To: The Brudax Metropolitan District Council, Department of Planning (Building Control Section), Old Town Hall, Bruddax

1. This notice relates to the erection of a home for frail elderly persons, corner of Low Road and High Street, Bruddax

2. The approved inspector for the work is:
   Seymore Thanniew RIBA
   Canny Buildings
   Bruddax
   Tel: Bruddax 987

3. The person intending to carry out the work is:
   Hope Furthurbest
   Penury House
   Neely Spent
   Bruddax
   Tel: Bruddax 654

4. The following documents relating to the work are enclosed with this notice:
   A copy of the approved inspector's notice of approval.
   A scheme of insurance approved by the Secretary of State, issued on behalf of Yorisk Insurers plc relative to the work described.
   A plan to 1:1250 scale indicating site location, boundaries, drainage, connection and location of existing sewers.

5. The work is not minor work.

6. I, Seymore Thanniew, declare:

   a) that I have no professional or financial interest in the work; and
   b) that I will consult the fire authority before giving a plans certificate in accordance with section 50 of the Act or a final certificate in accordance with section 51 of the Act in respect of any of the work; and
   c) that I am aware of the obligations laid upon me by the Act and by regulation 10 of the 1985 Regulations.

Signed   Signed

Approved Inspector   Person intending to
                                              carry out the work
11 July 1992   11 July 1992

Figure 10.2 Example of an initial notice.

an approved insurance scheme is in operation. (Figure 10.2 is an example of such a notice.) The notice must be signed by the inspector and by the applicant. It must be accompanied by an appropriate drawing. The drawing must be a site plan to not less than 1:1250 scale showing the location of the site, boundaries, connections to sewers and any proposed work over a sewer.

The local authority have ten working days from the date of receipt of the notice to accept or reject it. If the notice is not rejected within this period, the authority are presumed to have accepted without conditions. The authority may impose various conditions when accepting the notice.

A local authority may reject a notice on the following grounds only:

- The notice is not in the prescribed form.
- The work is not within the area of the authority on which the notice has been served.
- The person signing as approved inspector is not an approved inspector.
- There is insufficient information about description, location or drainage.
- An initial notice is not accompanied by notice of the inspector's approval.
- There is no evidence of insurance cover.
- There is no undertaking to consult the fire authority (if applicable).
- The inspector has a professional or financial interest in the work (unless 'minor work' involved).
- Drainage proposals are unsatisfactory.
- The authority is not satisfied that it may consent to building over a public sewer (if applicable).
- Local legislation will not be complied with.
- There is an overlap with a still effective initial notice.

Upon acceptance, supervision of the work becomes the responsibility of the inspector and the authority's powers to enforce the Building Regulations are suspended until either the initial notice is cancelled by the inspector or it ceases to have effect on the lapse of certain defined periods.

10.2.3 Commencement, completion, etc.

Where full plans have been deposited in the traditional way, building works must be commenced within three years of the date of deposit of plans with the local authority. Once work has started, neither the Regulations nor the Act itself stipulate the speed at which the work must progress, probably because it would not be feasible to so specify. It is possible for the work to be carried out over a very protracted period without the applicant's incurring any penalty.

If the local authority is to supervise the work by means of its own inspectors, the Regulations require the applicant or the builder to give the following notices in writing. The authority may, and often does, inspect on the basis of a telephone call, where permitted by the Regulations, but it is preferable from every point of view if the proper written notices are served and that:

- Two days have elapsed before commencement of work on site.
- One day has elapsed before any excavation is covered.
- One day has elapsed before any foundation is covered.
- One day has elapsed before any damp-proof course is covered.
- One day has elapsed before any site concrete is covered.
- One day has elapsed before any drainage or sewer is covered.
- Not more than five days have elapsed after the covering of any drain or sewer.
- Not more than five days have elapsed after completion.
- Five days have elapsed before occupation, if the building is occupied before completion.

'Day' excludes any Saturday, Sunday, bank or public holiday.

Local authorities must now issue completion certificates in the following cases:

- When requested at the time of full plans submission.
- When due notification has been received that the building will be put to a designated use (Fire Precautions Act 1971).
- When notices have been received for completion or part occupation before completion.

Where an approved inspector is involved, the inspector must issue a final certificate when work is complete. The local authority are deemed to have accepted the certificate if they do not reject it within ten days of receipt.[3]

10.2.4 Dispensations and relaxations

The local authority has the power to dispense with or relax a Regulation. This is a power delegation from the Secretary of State.

The authority must be satisfied that the requirement would be unreasonable in a particular instance. Unless it concerns internal work only, a relaxation application normally must be advertised in a local newspaper by the authority at least 21 days before a decision is to be made. If the authority refuses the relaxation or because of failure to respond within two months it is deemed refused, the applicant has the right to appeal to the Secretary of State. The applicant must appeal within one month of refusal setting out the grounds for appeal and all relevant information.

The Secretary of State may also grant what is known as a *type relaxation* with or without any representations being made. Conditions may be attached to such relaxations or they may be made for a limited period only.

10.2.5 Contraventions

The local authority may require the removal or amendment of work which is carried out in contravention of the Regulations. This is normally done by service of a notice on the building owner. Failure to comply with such notice within 28 days entitles the authority to take action itself to correct the contravention and to charge such costs to the owners. Such notice may not be served after the expiry of 12 months from the date of completion of the work. Appeal from such notice is to a magistrates' court. An alternative is for the building owner to obtain a written report from a suitably qualified person in regard to the subject of the notice. The time for compliance with the notice is then extended to 70 days. On receipt of the report, the authority may withdraw the notice and may pay the building owner appropriate expenses.

10.2.6 The Fire Precautions Act 1971

Fire has proved to be a major hazard in buildings for centuries. The Building Regulations 1991, Schedule 1 Part B, Fire Safety, now contains five requirements:

B1   Means of escape from all buildings, including dwelling houses.
B2   Internal fire spread (linings).
B3   Internal fire spread (structure).
B4   External fire spread.
B5   Access and facilities for the fire service.

In large and complex schemes, the only viable and acceptable standard would be achieved by the fire engineering approach coupled with consultations with the local authority (building control) and the fire authority at every stage in any project.

The Fire Precautions Act 1971 is designed to ensure adequate means of escape and related fire precautions in premises, the use of which, broadly speaking, involves members of the public being present in any number. Its object is to protect life in the event of fire and it cannot be applied directly to the protection of buildings and their contents.

The Act is enforced by the fire authorities and it provides that a fire certificate shall be required for all premises put to designated uses. The fire certificate will be issued only after the fire authority for the area is satisfied that the means of escape and other fire precautions for the particular premises are such as may be reasonably required.

The classes of use which may be designated under the Act are:

- Use as sleeping accommodation.
- Use as an institution providing treatment or care.
- Use for entertainment, recreation or instruction, or for purposes of any club, society or association.
- Use for any teaching, training or research.
- Use for any purpose involving access to the premises by the public whether by payment or otherwise.
- Use as place of work (also covered by other legislation).

Application for a fire certificate must be made to the fire authority in the prescribed form and the applicant must be ready to supply such further information as the fire authority may require and within any time specified. The fire authority must have an inspection of the premises made. If the authority is not satisfied, it must serve a notice specifying what needs to be done within a specified time. The fire certificate when issued must specify:

- The use of the premises.
- Means of escape in case of fire.
- Means with which the building is provided (other than fire-fighting equipment) for securing that the means of escape is capable of being safely and effectively used at all material times.
- Type, number and location of all fire-fighting equipment.
- Type, number and location of means of giving warning in case of fire.

The certificate may impose such other requirements as the authority consider to be appropriate in the circumstances.

A person who is aggrieved by the contents of the certificate or by the authority's refusal to grant such certificate and other connected matters may appeal to the magistrates' court within 21 days.

This is an important piece of legislation which is closely linked to the Building Act 1984. Architects should be familiar with its provisions so as to be able to advise clients broadly concerning its application in particular instances.

10.3 *Production information*

10.3.1 General

This is Stage F of the RIBA Plan of Work. It has already been remarked that this stage merges imperceptibly with Stage E. However, this stage does mark the firming of all construction decisions and the completion of all information in readiness for the quantity surveyor to produce bills of quantities.

During this period, the architect prepares drawings, specifications and schedules. These are the instructions to the contractor to tell him what is to be built and the quality required. Although some architects leave the detailed specification to the quantity surveyors, this is thoroughly bad practice because the architect is ultimately responsible for the specification, and from every point of view it is best if the architect prepares it.

This is also the time for agreeing details of the contract with the client and for obtaining quotations from those who are to be nominated, named or listed sub-contractors. The architect must be in a position to inform the quantity surveyor of the nature and amounts of all prime cost and provisional sums which are to go into the bills of quantities.

10.3.2 Drawings

There are several different ways of producing the kind of drawings which make up the bulk of the production information. The design presentation drawings usually form the starting point for the preparation of working drawings. It has already been observed that by this stage the design drawings will be very detailed. Many offices now produce virtually all their drawings with the aid of computers (see

Chapter 15, section 15.8). With the right equipment, and architects who are practised in its operation, drawings can be produced quite quickly.

Under most standard forms of building contract, the responsibility for supplying the contractor with correct information lies with the architect.[4] Mistakes will always occur, but in view of the cost of rectifying a mistake on a drawing which no one has spotted until too late, it is of the utmost importance that the drawing system should be simple and capable of highlighting errors. Of course, there is no such foolproof system, but some methods are probably better than others.

Traditionally, architects worked on all aspects of the building at once, having half-finished drawings showing plans at each level, elevations, sections and rough sketch drawings of all the major details to a large scale. These *typical details* were often drawn on the same sheet as a plan or section which included the detail to a much smaller scale. The drawings were all brought to completion together and generally formed a well-integrated set. Such sets of drawings were characterized by very many more lines than strictly necessary to tell the story and an apparent desire on the part of the architect to leave no square millimetre of paper unused. Notes littered the drawing and they were often repetitive in nature.

This kind of drawing system is quite satisfactory, although expensive, if the building is relatively small and uncomplicated by special services. It is likely to be accurate because it is produced as a set and it has the advantage of having all the large-scale details on the same sheet as the small-scale information to which it relates. Moreover, the bricklayer can see what the carpenter has to do and the steel erector can readily appreciate the reason for any fine tolerances which have been specified. In fact, each part of the building can be understood in relation to every other part.

The problems with this kind of drawing system stem from the advantages. Although the system is fine for small buildings, it is very difficult to build a medium to large building from such drawings. One problem is the change in number of drawings from perhaps an optimum of two or three to perhaps 50 or more for a building only marginally larger and more complex than a large detached family house. The other problem is the unstructured way in which the information is presented. If details are drawn on the same sheet as small-scale drawings, finding such a detail will be difficult if there is more than one drawing showing the small-scale item, but the large detail is only on one. There is a rule, whose name escapes the authors at present, which states that whichever drawing the site agent picks up, the detail will be on another. The sheer complexity of such drawings, when multiplied for a large building, makes errors almost certain.

A drawing system which attempted to overcome the defects in what can be termed the traditional method was the elemental drawing. The idea of this is that each element of the building is given a special drawing or set of drawings. Each item of information is given just once, in the appropriate place and to an appropriate scale. Among other things, the alteration of a drawing is made easier than where a traditional drawing is involved. Thus there is a complete set of reinforced concrete drawings showing every detail of the concrete including dimensions, but nothing else. Similar sets are provided for brickwork and blockwork, plastering, joinery, plumbing etc. Further drawings in outline are provided to show the way in which the elements fit together.

This system was developed into a four-stage and more practical drawing method:

- Location drawings.
- Assembly drawings.
- Component drawings.
- Details/schedules.

Location drawings

These drawings are produced to a small scale, typically 1:100, but sometimes, for very large buildings, 1:200 is used. The purpose of the drawings is reflected in the content. They are intended to show the location of the building and other elements on the site, so as to enable the site agent to set them out properly, and to show the position of all the other major elements in the building itself. Thus there is a site plan, plans at each level, elevations, and sections through every difficult portion of the building. Such plans and sections are not intended to show how the building should fit together; they are principally to serve as an index or menu from which the site agent can get a reference number for the required drawing. Some additional information may be included, such as finished floor and foundation levels and setting-out and other dimensions, but the golden rule is that every line must be on the paper for a definite purpose. Very often, these drawings are produced on a standard grid basis to simplify location of walls, doors and windows.

Assembly drawings

These are the drawings which show how the components of the building fit together. They are the successors to the traditional 'half inch sections' although they may not be sections and the scales can be any standard scale from 1:50 to 1:10. These drawings tend to contain the information which is not found elsewhere.

Component drawings

These show how the parts of the building are to be manufactured, including such items as fitted joinery, windows, doors, stairs, screens, concrete products and standard panels. Generally, there is a separate drawing for each component. Components are often drawn full-size or to some other appropriate large scale.

Details/schedules

The final category of drawings includes large-scale details of specific items of construction not shown sufficiently clearly elsewhere. Special details of damp-proof courses, weatherings, eaves, junctions and external hard landscaping may be included. This category also includes schedules. Schedules are a very good way of presenting information for categories of building element. They also impose a good discipline on architects who learn a lot about their buildings in particular, and construction in general, by producing schedules. The architect who schedules everything possible will make a friend of the quantity surveyor. Common schedules include the following:

- Ironmongery.
- Sanitary fittings.
- Precast concrete.
- Doors.
- Windows.
- Floor, wall and ceiling finishes.
- Lighting.
- Glazing.
- Tiling.
- Colour.
- Inspection chambers and manholes.
- Lintels.

Some less obvious subjects for schedules, but ones which are well worth doing, include:

- Architraves.
- Skirtings.
- Casings.
- Pipe runs.
- Gulleys.
- Outdoor paving.

10.4 *Contract selection and implications*

If the architect is carrying out his or her normal duties in contract administration, it is the architect's duty to advise the client about the most suitable form of contract to use for the particular project. This is recognized by Architect's Appointment 1990 (see Chapter 7, section 7.2). No two projects are exactly the same, and therefore very careful thought must be given to the appropriate form. Architects do not have a good reputation in this field. In the rush of practice, it is all too easy to advise the client to use a contract form with which the architect is familiar. There are a considerable number of standard forms to suit varying situations. The forms used for building works are summarized in Figure 10.3 together with available supplements.

Ideally, the architect should have a thorough knowledge of each contract so as to be able properly to advise the client. It has been suggested that an architect who advises the use of the wrong form of contract which results in the client suffering loss would be negligent. We can see no good reason in principle to doubt that view although assembling the necessary proof might be a different matter. In any event, it is certain that an inappropriate choice of contract will make it very much more likely that problems will occur and that, when they do, the contractor will have a justifiable claim for additional money. There are various publications which can assist the architect.[5]

Sometimes, a client will insist that the company solicitor draws up a suitable contract. The task of drawing up a suitable form of contract would be daunting to say the least even if the solicitor is well experienced in building matters. In most cases, the result will be disastrous. It is always worth while the architect explaining to the client the basic advantages of using a standard form. They are as follows:

- It is comprehensive, covering most common building situations.

Joint Contracts Tribunal (JCT) Series

Standard Form of Building Contract 1980 (JCT 80)
   Private with quantities
   Private with approximate quantities
   Private without quantities
   Local authorities with quantities
   Local authorities with approximate quantities
   Local authorities without quantities

Intermediate Form of Building Contract (IFC 84)

Agreement for Minor Building Works (MW 80)

Standard Form of Building Contract With Contractor's Design (JCT 81)

Management Contract (JCT 87)

Fixed Fee Form of Prime Cost Contract (FF 76)

Measured Term Contract (MTC 89)

Jobbing Agreement (JA 90)

Principal supplements:
   Sectional completion for JCT 80 and IFC 84
   Phased completion for JCT 87
   Contractor's designed portion for JCT 80
   Fluctuation Clauses for JCT 80 and IFC 84

Scottish contracts are available to amend JCT 80, MW 80 and JCT 81

Association of Consulting Architects

Form of Building Agreement 1982 (ACA 2) 1990 revision.

BBF Form of Building Agreement 1984 (BPF/ACA) 1990 revision.

Architects and Surveyors Institute

Building Contract 1986 (ASI 86)

Small Works Contract (ASI SW)

Minor Works Contract (ASI MW)

Figure 10.3   Standard forms of building contract.

- It is drawn up and updated at regular intervals to take account of the most recent legal decisions.
- It is known to the contractor and widely accepted in the industry. The contractor will be aware of the advantages and shortcomings and thus there will be no necessity for the employment of specialist professionals to advise on the pitfalls. Thus there will be no inflation of the tender figure from this cause.

- Many of the standard forms have a range of related documents.
- Some of the standard forms and all the ones current in the JCT range are negotiated documents and will not normally be caught by the *contra proferentem* rule: the rule of interpretation of a contract which states that where there is an ambiguity in a document, the court may choose the meaning least favourable to the party seeking to rely on it.

The choice of contract should be the end of a sequence of activity on the part of the architect and the client. The contract should fit the procurement system (see Chapter 8, section 8.2).[6]

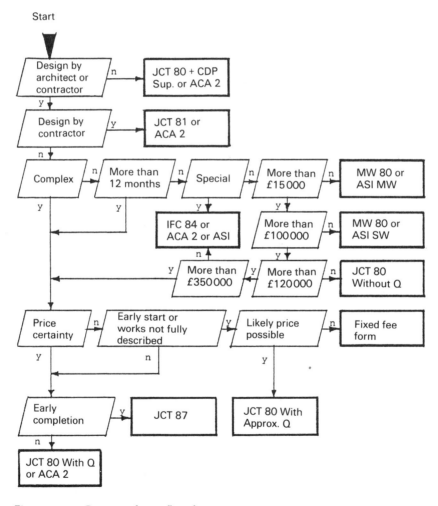

Figure 10.4   Contract choice flowchart.

Once a decision has been made in regard to the procurement system, the number of possible standard forms will be reduced. There will be some procurement systems which have no standard form. A current example is construction management which is commonly dealt with by the use of purpose-written forms or the use of unsuitable standard forms with amendments. Figure 10.4 shows a flowchart method of getting a rough idea of the appropriate form of contract.

It is not unusual to find that after a contract has been chosen as being most suitable, it still leaves a great deal to be desired in detail. It is possible to amend the standard forms, but five points should be noted:

- Any amendments must be kept to a minimum, because amendments often cause problems during the course of or at the end of a contract period.
- Amendments invariably lead to concomitant amendments being required elsewhere in the contract and it is easy to overlook them. (For instance, deletion of delay on the part of nominated sub-contractors as a ground for extension of time under the standard JCT 80 form of contract requires no less than 16 other amendments to be made.) Failure in this respect can have dire results.
- Amendments should be drafted by someone with specialist building contract expertise.
- Since many standard forms contain a clause giving the printed form priority over other documents, amendments should be made on the printed form itself or the clause should be struck out. If the amendment is simply made in the specification or the bills of quantities, it will be ineffective[7] (see Chapter 11, section 11.6).
- The *contra proferentem* rule may apply to amendments.

References

(1) *London Borough of Merton* v. *Stanley Hugh Leach Ltd* (1985) 32 BLR 51.
(2) The Building (Prescribed Fees, etc.) Regulations 1985.
(3) Powell-Smith, V. & Billington, M.J. (1992) *The Building Regulations Explained and Illustrated*, 9th edn, BSP Professional Books Ltd, Oxford.
(4) *London Borough of Merton* v. *Stanley Hugh Leach Ltd* (1985) 32 BLR 51.
(5) JCT Practice Note 20, *Deciding on the appropriate form of JCT Main Contract*, revised July 1988 (deals only with JCT forms).
(6) These factors, together with systems of contract choice, are explained in Chappell, D. (1991) *Which Form of Building Contract*, Longmans.
(7) *M.J. Gleeson, (Contractors) Ltd* v. *London Borough of Hillingdon* (1970) EGD 495.

Chapter 11

Stages G and H

11.1 Co-ordinated project information

One of the prime causes of disruption of building operations on site has been highlighted[1] as being shortcomings in drawn information together with a lack of compatibility in project information generally: i.e. the drawings, specifications and bills of quantities all say something different.

In order to improve the situation, the Co-Ordinating Committee for Project Information (CCPI) was set up by the major bodies in the construction industry and after consultation with all interested parties produced a *Common Arrangement of Work Sections for Building Works* (CAWS). They also produced Codes of Project Specification Writing and Production Drawings as well as working with the producers of the Standard Method of Measurement for Building Works (SMM7).

The purpose of CAWS, as set out in the introduction, is to define an efficient and generally acceptable identical arrangement for specification and bills of quantities.

The main advantages are:

- Easier distribution of information, particularly in the dissemination of information to sub-contractors. One of the prime objects in structuring the sections was to ensure that the requirements of the sub-contractors should not only be recognized but kept together in relatively small tight packages.

- More effective reading together of documents. Use of CAWS coding allows the specification to be directly linked to the bill of quantities descriptions, cutting down the descriptions in the latter whilst still giving all the information contained within the former.

- Greater consistency achieved by implementation of the above advantages. The site agent and clerk of works should be confident that when they compare the drawings with the bill of quantities they will no longer ask the question 'Which is right?'

CAWS is a system based on the concept of work sections. To avoid boundary problems between similar or related work sections, CAWS gives, for each section, a list of what is included and what is excluded, stating the appropriate sections where the excluded item can be found.

CAWS has an hierarchical arrangement in three levels. For instance:

- Level 1   R   Disposal systems
- Level 2   R1   Drainage
- Level 3   R10   Rainwater pipes/gutters.

There are 24 level 1 group headings, 150 work sections for building fabric and 120 work sections for services. Although very much dependent on size and complexity, no single project will need more than a fraction of this number: perhaps as a very general average 25–30%. Only level 1 and level 3 are normally used in specifications and bills of quantities. Level 2 indicates the structure, and helps with the management of the notation. New work sections can be inserted quite simply without the need for extensive re-numbering.

11.2 Bills of quantities

11.2.1 General

The work of quantity surveyors is described in Chapter 1 and was generally described as being to measure and value but as will have been seen today covers a much wider range of activities. The comments in this chapter are restricted to the preparation of bills of quantities, an important part of the measuring and valuation function.

11.2.2 Time for preparation of quantities

The quantity surveyors' work is the last stage before receipt of tenders, except estimating by the contractors. Consequently, there is a tendency for the cumulative result of delays during the earlier stages of a scheme to have its effect on the time allocated for preparation of quantities. With drawings completed and everything apparently cut and dried, it is sometimes difficult for clients to understand further delay, and the surveyor is accordingly pressed.

Surveyors can and will work at high pressure when necessary, but they cannot do so for everybody and all the time. They are, after all, preparing a contract document which will define the contract work precisely, and accuracy in the bill depends on a systematic checking of each stage, and a very careful reading through of the final draft. Excessive pressure can only result in work being done hurriedly or in part omitted, with dangerous results. Therefore no attempt should be made to reduce the period for taking out the quantities to compensate for earlier delays.

It is a great help in shortening the time required for preparation of a bill if the quantity surveyors have full and accurate warning of when the documents will be ready. All preparation of quantities being, with few exceptions, in a rush for some reason, surveyors may not always have staff available to take on an unexpected job, and cannot shelve it – at least not for long. They cannot keep a number of takers-off doing nothing, waiting for new work, so a job sent without warning is bound to disorganize plans, and consequently take longer. They may even not be able to do it at all.

If surveyors are approached at an early stage, they should be kept informed of the programme and advised of any slippages as they arise. When drawings are approaching the final stages they should be given a definite date which, when once given, will be adhered to. They will then be able to plan their work so that the job can be done in the minimum of time. If they are definitely anticipating drawings on a fixed date, this may make them refuse other work; so it is most important to adhere to promised dates. Moreover, if surveyors are expecting drawings they can do the work in, say, six weeks; the same period may not be sufficient if the drawings turn up a fortnight late, or if they come slowly in batches.

The period is fixed having regard to the work expected to be in hand at the time, and assuming that all particulars will be available together, unless otherwise arranged. The architect may be confident that surveyors, for their part, will do the work as quickly as possible, as it is in their interest to do so.

11.2.3 Procedure in the quantity surveyor's work

In order that the architect may appreciate the requirements of quantity surveyors in the way of drawings and particulars, it is necessary to give some idea of how they set about their work.

The building is divided into sections structurally, and each section is individually measured one section at a time. A list of sections in a typical building might be:

(1) Foundations up to damp-proof course
(2) Brickwork (superstructure)

  (3) External facings
  (4) Floors
  (5) Roofs
  (6) Staircases
  (7) Internal finishings
  (8) Windows and openings
  (9) Doors and openings
(10) Plain openings (no doors)
(11) Fittings
(12) Plumbing
(13) Heating, hot water etc.
(14) Electrical work
(15) Drains
(16) Paths, fences etc.

This list is obviously elastic, and a particular building might introduce additional sections, e.g. lifts, cooking equipment. The list is in a logical order, more or less following the construction of the building. The surveyors going through these sections see the erection of the building carried through in their mind's eye and must see every detail (even the fullest of drawings cannot show everything); they must decide for themselves what that detail is, for they cannot measure without something definite in mind.

Obviously it will be of great assistance to the surveyors if all the drawings are made available at one time but if certain drawings are delayed the surveyors will not necessarily be held up. It must be the right drawings which are kept back. Surveyors may be able to do without joinery fittings, or drains and not upset their organization; but if they are sent foundation drawings and are told by the architect 'You will have to wait for the depths', it is worse than useless.

Even if they are told 'It's all there except the bar reinforcement, I'm waiting on the engineer', surveyors are bound to lose time. They would normally measure reinforcement whilst the foundations are fresh in their mind. If they have to go over the whole again, there is much wasted effort. When complete drawings are not going to be available the surveyors should be consulted as to priorities.

11.2.4 Standard methods of measurement

Standard Methods of Measurement have been introduced over the years to ensure that all bills of quantities are prepared on the basis of a set of rules accepted and agreed by the industry.

The most common in use is the Standard Method of Measurement of Building Works agreed between the RICS and the BEC. This is currently in its seventh edition (SMM 7) and is a set of rules structured in CAWS which provides a uniform basis of measuring. Under the JCT forms of contract bills of quantities are deemed to have been measured using SMM 7 unless specifically stated to the contrary. SMM 7 is accompanied by a Code of Measurement Practice for use as a non-mandatory explanatory document.

For engineering works the ICE publish a Civil Engineering Standard Method of Measurement which like its counterpart in the building field provides a uniform basis for measuring. This method of measurement does not have the same contractual significance as SMM 7 in that it is not mandatory under the ICE form of contract.

Other standard methods of measurement available include a Method of Measurement intended for Work Overseas published by the RICS.

Deviation from a standard method of measurement is to be avoided unless there are very good reasons for doing so. If deviations are chosen it is essential that they are made clear to tendering contractors otherwise disputes are certain to arise.

11.2.5 PC and provisional sums

For various reasons it is not always possible to define finally, at design stage, everything necessary for the completion of the building. For instance it may be necessary for the architect to select certain articles such as sanitary appliances, ironmongery and the like in consultation with the client, and the details of these may very well not have been considered at the early stage when tenders are being sought. It is therefore not unusual to include *prime cost* (PC) sums for these items which the estimator will include in the tender for goods to be obtained from a supplier, but which are subject to adjustment against the actual costs of the articles selected. These suppliers are known as *nominated suppliers* (see Chapter 1). The contractor has to be given the opportunity in the tender to add profit for each of these items.

Further, it may be necessary to employ certain firms for jobs which contractors do not do in the normal course of their business, or which it is considered is better done by a specialist: for instance asphalting, electrical work, heating and hot water services and lift installations. If possible, estimates for these works will be obtained from specialist firms and PC sums will be included in a tender for work to be carried out by a *nominated sub-contractor* (see Chapter 1). Alternatively the chosen firm will be 'named' and the tendering contractor left to obtain a price to include in the tender. In the case of nominated sub-contractors under JCT 80 a combined system of tender, offer and nomination leading to a formal sub-contract is available. A similar system is available for named sub-contractors under JCT IFC 84.

Provisional sums are included for work for which there is insufficient information available for proper measurement and/or pricing. They may also be included to cover possible expenditure on items which may be required but for which there is no information available at tender stage. Provisional sums may either be for 'undefined' or 'defined' work: i.e. work which can be described fairly fully but not measured, perhaps because the extent is not known or some other finite detail inhibits full description. In respect of the latter the contractors are expected to have taken into account all their own costs and when the actual sum expended is ascertained for the final account no other adjustment to prices or time is made. On the other hand if the work is 'undefined' then other prices, such as plant items for example, may have to be adjusted when the work is valued for the final account and the contractor may be entitled to an extension of time and loss/or expense.

In most if not all building projects there are bound to be unknown matters arising such as changing ground conditions, new by-law requirements or problems emerging when an old building is opened up. In order to ensure that money is available to pay for these unexpected extras it is usual to include a sum of money known as a *contingency sum* to be used if required or if not omitted in whole or part as the case may be. It should be emphasized that a contingency sum, which of course is an undefined provisional sum, is there for the very purpose described and is not there to be spent because the architect has had a change of mind or has forgotten to include part of the client's brief.

11.2.6 Figured dimensions

Figured dimensions on drawings may be divided into three categories:

(1) Overall dimensions of the building.
(2) Subdivision of the last for setting out, showing spacing of structural openings for frames, windows and doors.
(3) Internal dimensions of rooms.

Quantity surveyors will require (1) and (3). They use (1) to calculate the girths of the walls, and a whole series of items are dependent on these girths: trench digging, concrete foundations, brickwork, damp-proof courses, facings, copings etc. They must have (3) to record the measurements of ceiling and floor finishes and to establish the girths of the rooms for wall plaster, skirtings etc.

Architects should ensure, therefore, that they give overall dimensions of all sides of the building and that the exact dimensions of every room in either direction can be seen at a glance. Where there is a range of rooms of similar dimensions, obviously the figuring need not be repeated for each, but otherwise the two dimensions should be clearly given on the plan. The dimensions of piers, recesses, cupboards, etc. should be clearly marked. The figuring of heights on sections must not be forgotten, with no doubt as to whether they are floor-to-floor or floor-to-ceiling heights.

Category (2) of the figured dimensions is not of interest to quantity surveyors but, of course, is absolutely necessary on drawings from which the building is to be built.

Contractors also require the overall dimensions (except where setting-out is for a steel frame) as they will be setting out the corners of the building before they have to think about the position of the window or door openings, etc. In the same way, the inside sizes of rooms will assist them in setting out the internal walls and partitions.

All figured dimensions on plans will normally be of the shell of the building, i.e. between wall faces before plastering. It should be made quite clear whether heights are to finished level or surface of the structure: the allowance to be made for thickness of finishings should be definitely given, so that the agent has figures to follow. Architects must, however, remember where there is any requirement of minimum height for rooms, that such minimum will be between finished surfaces, and they must make allowance accordingly.

It may be found convenient to mark floor levels on each floor in relation to some datum, particularly where they vary on a floor. It should be made clear by a note on the drawing whether these are finished or slab levels (usually the former).

11.2.7 Specification notes

Drawings need to be supplemented by descriptive information. This may be either a full specification such as would be used if there were no quantities, or in the form of notes expressing the architect's requirements and leaving the gaps to be filled in by the surveyor, who perhaps knows the architect's usual standard requirements (see also section 11.3 below). Where the Government Form of Contract (GC/

Works/1) is used the specification is a contract document, and is usually supplied to the quantity surveyor in full. In the JCT form, the specification is not a contract document and so need not be in so full a form.

Following the introduction of co-ordinated project information (CPI) referred to above the specification now plays a key role in tender documentation and whilst not itself a contract document, the relevant parts need to be incorporated in some way. The fuller the information given to quantity surveyors, the more will the bill represent the architect's requirements and the less trouble there will be in answering questions raised by the quantity surveyors. The surveyors, as already explained, have to pass the whole building before their mind's eye; they must decide every detail that is not shown on the drawings or included in the information. These must be ascertained by enquiry to the architect.

Specification notes are sometimes found written all over the drawings. If they are at all full, they hinder easy reading of the drawings, particularly if the same note is repeated in several places. For instance, a note '255 mm cavity wall' is sufficient, if the bricks are known to be 102.5 mm thick. Detail as to bond, ties, etc., is not necessary for the drawing but is, of course, essential for the specification.

11.2.8 Corrections to drawings

The very detailed analysis made by surveyors can be of great assistance to architects in that it will bring to their notice any errors or inconsistencies in the drawings or specification. Even if not definite errors, points raised by the surveyors may sometimes involve alteration. After the bills of quantities have been completed it will be found a good plan to ask the surveyor to lend a copy of the drawings marked with any amendments which have been discussed and agreed, so that the necessary corrections can be made to the architect's drawings before they are issued to the contractor.

The contract drawings must correspond with the bill of quantities and they must also be identical to the tender drawings, so if, as sometimes happens, alterations are discovered to be necessary after the bills have been prepared, and the surveyor is told to leave the alteration to be adjusted as a variation, it is most important that the drawings to be signed with the contract should not show the alteration. When it comes to signing the contract, if prints of the original drawing cannot be made, or if the architect, not realizing the discrepancy which arises, supplies the revised prints, inconsistency is caused between drawings and the contract bills of quantities and the employer may be put to some expense.

If, during the preparation of the bill of quantities, the architects propose to alter the drawings, they should give immediate warning to the quantity surveyor. Even a line altered or erased may involve substantial alterations to the dimensions. Such changes as reducing the length of a building by 250 mm or the pitch of a roof by 5° involve complications not apparent at first sight.

Alterations made during the progress of the measuring are not only a waste of valuable time, but mean that, when it comes to adjusting variations, it is necessary for the quantity surveyor to hunt in two or three places to find what is in the contract, and so the adjustment is complicated. If revised prints are to be sent to the quantity surveyors to correct drawings which they have, it is most useful if the architect circles the revision using a coloured pen, otherwise much time is spent searching for the alteration and there is no guarantee that minor alterations will not escape notice.

11.3 Specifications

11.3.1 General

In the context of tender and contract documentation the specification has always played a key role. With the introduction of CPI, as described above, the specification has become more important than ever. CCPI in their publications make it clear that the specification is the key document from which all other information, either for drawings or bills of quantities, will flow.

The writing and use of specifications is a subject in its own right and as such warrants separate study.[1] Suffice it therefore in this book to restrict comment to what a specification is for and the changes that have come about in recent years in the way that specifications are drafted.

11.3.2 What is a specification for?

The specification has three main purposes, in each case in conjunction with the drawings:

- To be read by the contractor's estimator as the only information available on which to prepare a competitive tender.

- To be read by the quantity surveyor to enable a bill of quantities to be prepared as a basis for such competitive tenders.
- To be read by the clerk of works and the contractor's agent during the progress of the contract as the architect's instructions for carrying out the work.

11.3.3 The specification as a basis for tenders

In smaller contracts, usually those under about £100 000 in value, contractors prepare their tenders from drawings and specifications only. Estimators take their own measurements of the work from the drawings and build up their estimates, relying on the specification for a full description of quality, materials and workmanship. Besides this, drawings and specifications, when read together, must indicate everything required to be included in the estimate. If anything is omitted, something that is required is not mentioned or shown, or very obviously necessary or implied, such work will not be part of the contract. If its carrying out is insisted upon the contractor will be entitled to extra payment.

The writer of a specification for this purpose will, therefore, realize the importance of the work necessary. Instructions must be crystal-clear and complete in detail. The specification will be one of the contract documents and it is not to be hurriedly thrown together. It must have all the preciseness of an agreement (in fact it will be part of such an agreement) conveying exactly to the contractor what is wanted and protecting the building owner from claims for extra payment which would arise from vagueness and uncertainty.

11.3.4 The specification for the quantity surveyor

For contracts where the value exceeds about £100 000 it is usual for a bill of quantities to be supplied to the contractor on behalf of the client if competitive tenders are being considered. The measuring work, which in the previous case would be done by all the tenderers, is in these circumstances done for them by the quantity surveyor who puts the facts before them, but each tenderer is left with the estimating, this being largely a matter of individual judgement.

In order that the quantity surveyor may prepare the bill, instructions must be given by the architect. While such instructions need not be as complete as those required by the contractors when taking their own measurements, they must be sufficient to ensure that all cost-significant matters are fully described. In this case the architect's full specification is not usually a contract document, although bearing in mind the dictum of CPI it may very well form an adjunct to the bill for cross-referencing purposes. It can however be less formal and convey the information in the form of notes either separately or on the drawings. For certain standard clauses reference may be made to similar clauses in other contracts.

While such a specification should be as complete as possible, omissions are not as vital as in the first case. The quantity surveyor will find the gaps, since in taking out the quantities every stage in the erection of the building has to be visualized and questions will arise whenever further information is required.

The specification preambles will be in CAWS order to facilitate easy reading with the measured items, which themselves will also be in CAWS order. These specification preambles must convey the specific information so that when read in conjunction with the measured items (the bills) they 'fully describe and accurately represent the quantity and quality of the work' as required by the SMM.

11.3.5 The specification for site agent and clerk of works

When erection of the building starts the work will be supervised on behalf of the contractor by the agent. On large projects a clerk of works will be employed as an inspector on behalf of the building owner, since constant inspection will be necessary and the architect is not expected to be continuously on the site. Both site agent and clerk of works require instructions and they take these, subject to any variations ordered by the architect, from the contract documents: i.e. drawings and specifications or drawings and bill of quantities. Where quantities have been prepared, the quantity surveyor will have incorporated the specification in the descriptions or in the bill preambles.

There is, however, certain information required by the site agent and clerk of works, which will have been excluded from the bill. The locations of items, for instance, will not usually be mentioned in the bill because they do not normally affect price; however, the site agent must have this information when it comes to erecting the building. Spacing of joists, colour schedules and fittings location are other matters which, while not included in a bill of quantities, need to be available to the site staff.

11.3.6 Drafting specifications

For many years it was common practice for specifications to be handwritten, albeit often using previous documentation suitably amended. Over the intervening years the practice of writing specifications fell into decline. On many occasions specifications became a matter of a few sheets of hastily drafted notes; more often it was a case of 'It's all on the drawings'.

Today, owing to the advances in computer technology, slowly at first but with gathering momentum, standard specifications have become the order of the day. Now architects and surveyors can enjoy the benefits of having the facility to call up mark-up copies of a standard specification to be adapted for each specific project.

11.3.7 National Building Specification

The National Building Specification (NBS) is not a standard specification, rather it is a large library of specification clauses all of which are optional; many are direct alternatives, and often require the insertion of additional information. NBS thus facilitates the production of specification text specific to each project, including all relevant matters and excluding text which does not apply.

NBS is available only as a subscription service, and in this way it is kept up to date by issue of new material several times a year for insertion into loose-leaf ringbinders. NBS is prepared in CAWS (section 11.1), matching SMM, and complies fully with the recommendations of the CPI Code of Procedure for Project Specifications (section 11.3.1). There are three versions of NBS, The Standard Version, an abridged Intermediate Version and a Minor Works Version.

11.4 Schedules of work

A schedule of work is a list of items of work required to be done and should not be confused with a specification. It is mainly used in works of alteration to spell out the items which are only covered in the specification in general terms. Recently schedules of work have started to appear as an adjunct to the specification but they have to be used with care.

A specification, like a bill of quantities, incorporates contract particulars, employer's requirements, contractor's liabilities as well as a full specification of the materials and workmanship. A specification, however, should never contain quantities; these are matters for the quantity surveyor where there are bills and the contractor when there are no bills.

To quote quantities in a specification is inviting trouble: the contractors will say 'We've priced the quantities we were given' whereas they should have priced everything that they considered necessary from their own measurements to arrive at a lump-sum price. Where the specification option is used in some standard forms of contract, the inclusion of quantities can lead to those items gaining priority over the drawings.

In the same way problems can arise when the description of the work is set out in schedule form following the materials and workmanship clauses. Old-fashioned specifications used to end up with words such as 'Carry out all the work shown on the drawings'. Today there is a tendency on the part of the employers to require the lump sum to be broken down into component parts, and schedules of work are appearing indicating specific packages – alterations, sub-structure, brickwork, roofing etc. – and a £ sign is appearing against each of these packages.

While this can be of some assistance in checking interim valuation applications, in giving the client a breakdown of the price and in some ways costing variations, the same problem exists: 'We only priced what was written down', whereas the intention was that they should have priced everything necessary. Because of these problems the same care must be taken in drafting these schedules of work as is taken in drafting the specification itself. It must be very clear to the estimator exactly what is wanted and nothing must be missed.

11.5 *Tendering*

11.5.1 Procedure in preparing a tender

The preparation of a contractor's estimate may be divided into two parts: the ascertaining of facts and the application of judgement. The facts are the nature and quality of the materials and the workmanship required, which must be set out in a form suitable for pricing. These are provided by a bill of quantities. Where no bill of quantities is supplied the tenderers must, with the guidance of the specification, prepare their own quantities from the drawings.

The deciding factor in the preparation of a tender when quantities are supplied is the tenderers' judgement on prices. They should not follow rule-of-thumb or price books (although some inexperienced firms have been known to do so) because every contractor's office has to take different circumstances into account.

Tenderers will in all probability have from their own records the actual cost on different jobs of the main components of a building, and these costs will help them as a basis for pricing new work. They may have particularly good workmen in some trade, or may have special opportunities of buying some materials advantageously. They must consider the particular location of the job in question, its distance from the office, its accessibility etc. and adjust their costs accordingly. An isolated site involving transport and travelling time for workmen can make a big difference to the real cost of an hour's work. There will be many items for which tenderers must obtain quotations for materials in order to build up suitable rates.

They may well adjust their tender according to their need for new work. If they are short of work they may be satisfied with a low level of profit and sometimes with no profit at all, although this can cause problems on all sides as the work progresses and the contractor is faced with unexpected costs. If they are busy they may not want the work unless they can get it at an advantageous price.

It is important to remember that in submitting competitive tenders a mistake may involve serious financial loss. Contractors do not enjoy the facility of correcting their mistakes as do architects, engineers and quantity surveyors. It is therefore most important that contractors should have all possible information available and every facility to acquire as full a knowledge as possible of the circumstances of the proposed work.

11.5.2 Documents for tendering

Where a bill of quantities is supplied, it will be accompanied by a copy of the general 1:100 or 1:50 scale drawings together with any component details required. The supply of this type of drawn information gives tenderers a better idea of the nature of the job and their probable commitments than does a hurried look in the architect's office. Where no quantities are supplied, each contractor must, of course, be given a complete set of all the drawings from which to prepare their estimate.

In the case of works of alteration, a set of drawings issued to each tenderer is almost indispensable. If, however, for some special reason each is not issued with a set, one should be made available on the premises to be altered; the difficulties of an estimator going round a building pricing spot items without a drawing must be appreciated. Where there are substantial alterations to be priced a set of drawings to be inspected at the architect's office is of no use.

In works of alteration, where rooms are divided or two or more are thrown into one, rooms should be given serial numbers on the drawings according to the existing plan. The specification and the bill of quantities should be similarly referenced. The numbers then have a clear meaning to the estimator walking around the building before any alterations have been made. If identification of the new rooms is required in a similar way, a series of letters can be used (or vice versa).

Where there are no quantities, a full specification will be supplied to each firm tendering, but not when quantities are provided: everything affecting a price should be in the bill of quantities.

11.5.3 Selection of contractors

The selection of contractors to tender for each project should be made having full regard to its size and nature. The architect should aim to have contractors of similar standing tendering in order to make tenders properly comparable. A small house will warrant a different list from that for a civic centre and contractors who may be suitable for a civic centre contract may not necessarily be suitable for a reinforced-concrete factory. Whereas many contractors could tackle a dozen houses in a housing scheme, the number in the locality who could undertake a contract for 200 houses is certainly more limited.

The nature of the work and the financial capacity of the prospective contractor must always be taken into consideration. Reference should be made to the Code of Procedure for Single Stage Selective Tendering (1989) and the similar Code of Procedure for the Two Stage Tendering (1983) both published by the NJCC.

In many lists of tenderers there are some who are ineffective. A firm will perhaps, agree to tender because they think (often quite wrongly) that they might offend the architects or prejudice future enquiries if they do not do so. They might feel that the work is not 'in their line', or though quite suitable, they may be so pressed with other work that they cannot undertake the job. The result is the practice 'of taking a price' from another tenderer: someone who has prepared a genuine tender gives a price somewhat higher than their own (known as a *cover price*) which, therefore, is certain to be rejected. The tender form is filled in accordingly and, if the priced bill of quantities is to be delivered sealed with the tender, it will often be found, if opened, to be blank.

Certain public authorities, by their standing orders, are required to advertise their contracts publicly. This can result in a mixed list, and many of the better firms, as long as they have plenty to do, will refrain from tendering in such circumstances. They have to compete with inexperienced firms, who may cut the price merely to get a start in the contracting business. As they are often unknown, tendering in this manner is the only way in which to make a start. The lowest price in those circumstances is not necessarily the best, or even the most economical in the end. If the authority could be persuaded to advertise that it will select a list from the applicants, there would probably be an actual saving in public money instead of an apparent saving which turns out to be illusory.

Where open invitations are issued it is not uncommon for the employer to require the successful contractor to provide a guarantee bond, and this may be obligatory to comply with the standing orders of some public authorities. The guarantor undertakes to meet any deficiency due to the failure of the contractor to carry out the contract, up to an agreed specified limit. The details of the bond are a matter for the employer's solicitor and are usually outside the province of the architect.

Public sector construction contracts over one million units of account (approximately £415 000) within the European Community must be invited and awarded in accordance with the procedures laid down in EEC Directive 71/105. The Directive provides for 'restricted tendering procedure' which permits the selection of technically and financially competent contractors following advertisement in the official journal of the European Community circulating throughout member states.

11.5.4 Time for tendering

With the object of ensuring that contractors have every opportunity of preparing a proper tender which they can safely stand by, the time allowed for tendering should be as long as possible. An excessively short period results in rushed work and inability to get estimates in proper time, and in consequence increases the risk of errors.

When a bill arrives in a contractor's office for pricing, the usual procedure is for the estimator to go through it and mark up those parts for which quotations are required, either for the supply of materials, or the subletting of work. The marked portions will then be copied with any adaptations necessary and these portions will be used for competitive enquiries. The bill will then be put aside because it cannot be priced until all replies have been received, as to do so piecemeal is a waste of time. When the replies are received they are sorted and examined and the most suitable used, with the necessary additions for profit and fixing if appropriate.

While it is always advisable to ask contractors in good time if they would like to tender, where time is short for some reason they should be given warning as to when documents will be sent out and the date for delivery of the tenders. The Codes of Procedure for Tendering already referred to make provision for such a preliminary invitation. Any firm that cannot tackle the job in the time will then be able to say so and last-minute requests for extensions of time will be avoided. Four weeks should be regarded as the minimum time for tender.

It is obvious that when contractors are tendering on a specification and drawings only they will need longer to tender than when a bill of quantities is supplied for a similar building, as they will have to prepare their own quantities.

11.5.5 Sending out documents

The architect will send to each firm tendering a copy of the specification and tender form and a complete set of drawings or, if a bill of quantities is used, that too with a selection of drawings (see below) under a covering letter which should state:

- Invitation to tender, if not already sent.
- List of enclosures.
- Date and place for delivery of tenders.
- Whether the site is open for inspection and if so what arrangements should be made to visit it.
- Request for acknowledgement.

Figure 11.1 illustrates a typical letter.

Tenders will usually be delivered to the architect, unless the employer particularly wants them to be delivered to them. In the case of public authorities both the sending out of documents and receipt of tenders will be handled by the clerk to the authority. A recommended form of tender is illustrated in Figure 11.2. The documents should be accompanied by a suitable envelope for delivery of the tender ready addressed and marked 'TENDER FOR . . .' on the face. These envelopes will on receipt be recognized as containing tenders and will be left unopened until the time stated for delivery has passed and a check has been made that all have been delivered. If this procedure is not

---

Dear Sir

[insert heading]

I refer to your letter of the [insert date] in which you expressed willingness to submit a tender for the above project. I now have pleasure in enclosing the following:

1. Two copies of the bills of quantities.
2. Two copies of each of drawings numbers [insert numbers] giving a general indication of the scope and character of the works. These will become the contract drawings.
3. Two copies of the form of tender.
4. An addressed envelope for the return of the tender and instructions relating thereto.

Please note the following:

(a) Drawings may be inspected at [insert place].
(b) The site may be inspected by arrangement with [insert person and telephone number].
(c) Tendering will be in accordance with the Code of Procedure for Single Stage Selective Tendering 1989.
(d) Examination and adjustment of priced bills: alternative 1/2 [delete as appropriate] of section 6 of the Code will apply.

The completed form of tender is to be sealed in the endorsed envelope provided and must arrive at [insert place] not later than [insert time] on [insert date].

Please acknowledge safe receipt of this letter together with the enclosures noted and confirm that you will submit a tender in accordance with these instructions.

Yours faithfully

Figure 11.1   Letter from architect to contractor: invitation to tender (assumes bills of quantities used).

scrupulously observed the employer may be liable for a tenderer's abortive expenditure.[2]

Where there is a bill of quantities much the same procedure is followed though the documents are usually (but not in the case of a public authority) sent out by the quantity surveyor on completion of the printed bills so saving a little time. There will be a selection of small-scale drawings with perhaps typical details and special drawings required by the SMM to accompany tenders, indicating broadly the scope and quality of the work and the covering letter will state where the remaining drawings can be seen if required (usually the office of the architect or surveyor).

If the bill is to be delivered with the tenders, as is often the case, the

Tender for   [describe works]
at   [insert location]

To   [insert name and address of employer]

I/We, having read the conditions of contract, articles of agreement, appendix and specification/schedules of work/bills of quantities [delete as appropriate] delivered to me/us and having examined the drawings referred to therein, do hereby offer to execute and complete the Works described in accordance with the terms therein for the sum of: _____

_____ (words) £ _____

In consideration of the sum of £1.00 receipt of which I/We hereby acknowledge I/We undertake to keep this offer open for a period of [insert period] days from the date of this tender.

I/We agree that

(a) The employer is not bound to accept the lowest or any tender.

(b) Persons tendering do so at their own cost.

(c) If errors in pricing or errors in arithmetic are discovered in the priced specification/schedules of work/bills of quantities [delete as appropriate] before acceptance of this offer, such errors will be dealt with in accordance with alternative 1/2 [delete as appropriate] of section 6 of the Code of Procedure for Single Stage Selective Tendering published in 1989.

(d) Unless and until a formal agreement is prepared and executed, this tender together with your written acceptance thereof shall constitute a binding contract between us.

Dated this .... day of .... 19 ....

Signed ....

in the capacity of ....

duly authorized to sign tenders for and on behalf of:

Name ....

Address ....

Figure 11.2 Form of tender.

documents must include a separate envelope of suitable size and strength to hold the bill, addressed in the same way as the envelope for the tender. The tenderers should be notified in the covering letter to put their name on the outside of the bill envelope so that only the bill accompanying the lowest tender is opened. The remaining bills should be returned unopened.

11.5.6 Opening of tenders

Before opening the tenders, it is important to see that they have all been delivered, and care is necessary if any tender is delivered late. After the time fixed for delivery there may be enquiries from one builder to another on the telephone as to figures, and one must accordingly be sure that no late tenderer has taken advantage of this.

If tenders are delivered to the architect's office they will be opened and a list prepared, arranged in order of price, for submission to the client. Any special conditions attached to the tender should be noted and entered against the tenderer's name in the list. If tenderers are required to state a contract period as well as a price, as is often the case, this too will be entered against each name. If the tenders are being opened by the clerk to a public authority (often in the presence of an elected member) the same procedure will be followed for submission of the result to the council or committee concerned.

11.5.7 Reporting of tenders

In considering tenders other factors than the price may be of importance. The time required to carry out the work, if stated on the form of tender, may be compared, as time may be very important financially to the client. The time stated by a reputable contractor may be taken as a reasonable estimate, having regard to the circumstances as known.

The architect having considered these matters in consultation with the quantity surveyor, or the clerk to a public authority will report the tenders to the client or committee concerned and if there is any doubt set out clearly for their consideration the arguments in favour of acceptance of one tender or another.

When tenders are invited from a selected list of contractors, the lowest, or potentially lowest, should be accepted. All go to a good deal of trouble and expense in preparing a tender, and the object of such tendering is to decide which amongst a number, all acceptable to the building owner, will do the work at the lowest price. Whether expressly disclaimed in the invitation or not, there is no legal obligation to accept the lowest or any tender.

However, when tenders are advertised and any builder who can raise the required deposit and surety may submit a tender, the circumstances are different. One can justly say 'I didn't ask you and I don't want you,' though even then, when the expenditure of public money is involved, there may be repercussions.

As soon as the lowest or any tender is accepted then all the tendering contractors should be notified (see section 11.5.10 below).

11.5.8 Examination of a priced bill

If the employer decides to proceed with the work, the tenderer whose offer is under consideration will be asked to supply a copy of the priced bill (if it has not already been submitted with the tender), either a blank copy being sent for the purpose or the contractor making a photocopy. This will be examined by the quantity surveyor who will make a mathematical check and will also look generally through the rates for any possible serious errors or omissions in the pricing. If there are no serious errors, and provided there are no other inhibiting circumstances, then the tender can be safely recommended for acceptance.

However, if mistakes are found the contractor must be notified. Then one of two things will happen according to the principles previously decided upon and notified to tendering contractors: the contractor will be invited either to stand by the tender price or withdraw, in which case a commercial decision will need to be taken. The mistake may be of such magnitude that withdrawal of the tender is the only option, in which case the next lowest bid is considered in the same way. However, the contractor may be prepared to stand by his tender and the contract sum will remain as the tender. It is not usually good policy to press a contractor who has made such an error to stand by the tender. The inevitable effort to recover the position is fairly certain to give trouble.

While the contract sum will remain as the tender sum, correction of any material errors should be made in the body of the text solely for the purpose of providing a fair schedule of rates for the adjustment of variations. The principle to be followed is that the total of the bill must be unchanged and must agree with the contract sum: the adjustment due to correction of errors will be treated as a rebate or as a plusage on the whole of the prices (except prime cost and provisional sums) and appear immediately before the final total on the summary by way of a percentage.

However, if it was made clear at the time of tendering that genuine errors would be corrected then the corrections are made and a revised tender sum is established. If the resultant figure shows that the revised tender is now in excess of the next lowest tender then it is the next lowest tender which comes into contention and is subject to a similar examination. The way in which corrections of errors found in tenders are to be treated is set out in the NJCC Code of Procedure for Single Stage Selective Tendering previously referred to.

11.5.9 Reductions

It is unfortunately not uncommon for tenders to be higher than expected, sometimes due to too optimistic an attitude of architect and quantity surveyor at the approximate estimate stage or, more probably, because a full cost-planning exercise has not been carried out. If employers are not prepared to meet the higher cost, ways and means have to be found to get down to their figure, and at the same time meet their requirements as to accommodation etc.

The architect will have to re-examine the drawings and specification with this in view. Here the help of the quantity surveyors can be useful as they may be able to suggest, from the analysis which the priced bill has provided, where the architect's requirements are expensive and might be cut down. A list of possible reductions will be prepared and valued in consultation with the quantity surveyors. They will prepare a bill of omissions and any counterbalancing additions, from which the tender sum can be adjusted.

For what sounds quite a simple reduction, adjustment on a bill of quantities may be lengthy. To take 150 mm off the length of a building (which may only mean a few broken lines and figured dimensions on the architect's drawings) affects a large number of items through many sections in the bill of quantities, from stripping surface soil to the paint on the walls and ceilings.

There is one cause of excessive tenders and consequent reductions which should be avoided: the inclusion of something which the architect wants, in the hope that the clients can be persuaded to want it, when they discover that it is included in the tender. The architect may feel that it is easier to cut out such an item when tenders come in than to add it afterwards, but unless there is a reasonable hope of keeping within the client's price, it should be cut out in the first instance. Reductions in a tender only make additional, unnecessary and unremunerative work for architects and quantity surveyors in altering drawings and specifications and preparing reduction bills and, moreover, involve the client in additional fees and expenses.

11.5.10 Informing tenderers

Preparation of competitive tenders is today a very expensive activity. Much time and effort and consequently money are expended and it is only reasonable that tendering contractors should be made aware of the result. The winner will want to know 'how much they left on the table': i.e. what margin there was between their bid and the next lowest. The losers in their turn will need to know, for future pricing and policy purposes, just where they stood.

Much is made of the need for confidentiality in competitive tendering and it is sometimes argued that publication of tender results breaches that confidentiality. Actual confidentiality is perhaps questionable; there are too many common contact points by way of suppliers, ready-mix concrete firms etc. whereby it is not unknown for a tender list to become public knowledge. Once tenders are submitted it is quite common practice for tender amounts to be exchanged by the competing contractors.

However, none of this alters the architect's duty to publish the list and, with the confidentiality referred to above in mind, this can best be done by publishing a list of amounts without the firms' names being given. Each tendering firm will recognize their price and see where they came. If in addition they are able to put names to sums that is their business. The architect's conscience is clear; it was not they that published the names.

11.5.11 Negotiated tenders

All that has gone before in this chapter assumes that competitive tendering procedures are being adopted. However, perhaps the contractors are known to both employer and architect for whom they have performed well in the past; or it is a further stage of a contract upon which the contractor has already worked or is still working; or perhaps an advantage of gaining time is being sought. For any of these or similar reasons a decision is taken to negotiate a tender.

The procedures that are to be gone through are similar to those required for competitive tendering except that before the final tender is submitted it will have been examined by the quantity surveyors, who may have been involved in the pricing themselves, and the tender prices will have, if necessary, been negotiated. Such negotiations can lead to several advantages referred to above, and although the price can be shown to be the right price it can never be proved to be the cheapest. If the cheapest price is the criterion for letting the contract then negotiation has no place.

11.6 *Preparing the contract documents*

The duty of preparing the contract by completing the various blanks in the articles of agreement usually falls on the architect although the quantity surveyor is sometimes asked to do it. It may be necessary to add special clauses to the conditions of contract and to amend other clauses; if so, they must be written in, and the insertion or alteration must be initialled by both parties at the time of signature. Any portions to be deleted must be ruled through and similarly initialled. All other documents contained in the contract (each drawing and the bill of quantities) should be marked for identification and signed by the parties, e.g.

	This is one of the drawings		
or	This is the bill of quantities		
	referred to in the contract		
	signed by us this	day of	19

In the case of the bill of quantities this identification should be on the front cover or on the last page and the number of pages can be stated. If the standard form is used (with quantities) the specification as such is not part of the contract, and will not be signed by the parties. Where there are no quantities the full specification is a contract document and must be signed accordingly. All the signed documents must be construed together as the contract for the project.

Contracts are either signed under hand, when the limitation period is six years or, when 12 years is required, are completed as a deed (formerly under seal). In the latter case it is important to ensure that this is duly recognized, as failure to do so could have serious implications.[3]

Case law exists that illustrates the importance of ensuring that all the contract documents are in agreement with each other. There was a discrepancy between completion dates set out in the contract bills and the completion date in the appendix to the JCT form of contract. Delays had occurred, and the question was which date was to be taken in calculating liquidated damges. The court held[4] that under the relevant clause of the standard form in use at that time (JCT63 clause 12(1)) the date in the appendix prevailed, but the litigation would not have occurred if all the contract documents had been checked for inconsistencies.

References

(1) Willis, C.J. and Willis, J.A. (1991) *Specification Writing for Architects and Surveyors*, BSP Professional Books, Oxford.
(2) *Blackpool & Fylde Aero Club* v. *Blackpool Borough Council* (1990) CILL 587.
(3) The Companies Act 1989 and the Law of Property (Miscellaneous Provisions) Act 1989 state the requirements for companies and individuals respectively (see Chapter 7, section 7.2).
(4) *M.J. Gleeson (Contractors)* v. *London Borough of Hillingdon* (1970) EGD 495.

Chapter 12

Stages J and K

12.1 Contractor's programme

The value of a programme is that it will enable the contractor to plan ahead, give early and precise notice to sub-contractors, avoid the risk of overlooking the ordering of materials or fittings in good time, and enable adequate steps to be taken to reinforce or reduce the labour force as the occasion demands. Finally it is a constant pointer to contractor, agent, clerk of works, architect and client as to whether or not the work is proceeding at a satisfactory rate.

On large contracts it is customary for the contractor to include in the programme the dates by which full details are required of the various sections of work from the architect or engineer, and also instructions with regard to the expenditure of prime cost and provisional sums. As the contract proceeds it may be necessary to expand the progress schedule to show in more detail the co-ordinated installation and commissioning of complex engineering services.

Clause 5.3.1.2 of JCT 80 contains an optional requirement for a master programme. This is not a contract document as such, but the clause gives the architect the right to see the contractor's programme or schedule. The clause also requires the contractor to update the programme whenever the contract programme is extended for whatever reason.

This master programme or progress schedule is usually drawn up by the contractor at an early stage of the work, probably before the first site meeting, and kept up to date week by week. It should be prepared so that all the information can be clearly tabulated and should be placed in a prominent position in the site office. It must not be too complicated, but should at the same time give a precise indication of the progress planned by the trades each week, together with the actual progress maintained.

The most common programme is the *Gantt* or *bar chart* upon which proposed and actual progress can be indicated. A line is drawn in black (or any other colour chosen) against each trade or operation, commencing at the week in which the particular work is due to start and continuing through the number of weeks that it is expected to proceed. This may not, of course, be a continuous line, as it may be necessary to suspend the particular work while some other operation is proceeding and then return for a second spell. The actual progress should be recorded by a line or lines in a different colour.

Other forms of programmes include network analysis, precedence diagrams and line of balance. These are for 'mega' projects and show the planning of the work in great, and sometimes over-complicated, detail. In the case of a critical path network analysis the facility becomes available to plan alternatives and variants to the critical, or chosen, path when for some reason or other there has to be a change to the planned path.

As an architect is not authorized under the terms of the JCT contract to give instructions regarding the contractor's programme, the requirement to provide a programme, or critical path network in a more complex project, should be made in the bill of quantities or in the specification if there is no bill of quantities. Though co-operation in preparing such a schedule or programme may be valuable, responsibility for progress is the contractor's. Any comment by the architect can only be advisory.

The position under GC/Works/1 is somewhat different. Here condition 33 requires the contractor to submit a programme with the tender and as such it is taken into account when evaluating the tenders received. The programme in this case is required to show the whole period for completion and the sequence that the contractor proposes to adopt highlighting events which are considered critical to satisfactory completion of the works. While not specifically listed as a contract document the programme has considerably more contractual significance than under the JCT form because the following condition 34 requires the contractor to proceed with diligence and 'in accordance with the programme'.

The question is often asked: should an architect be required to provide information in accordance with the contractor's programme, which may well show a completion date earlier than that fixed in the contract? Alternatively, is the only requirement to be to suit the contract completion date? Case law[1] shows that in the court's view the information had to be provided relative to the contract date not the contractor's date: i.e. there was no implied term in the contract that the architect was under any obligation to supply information to suit a contractor's programme which indicated an early completion date.

12.2 *Meetings*

Every architect will be involved in meetings.[2] There really is no escaping meetings although most people claim to consider them a waste of time. A meeting *will* be a waste of time unless there is a clear purpose and unless the participants are carefully selected and relevant to the purpose. It is useful to work on the basis that if the most effective meeting consists of two people, every extra person reduces the effectiveness in inverse ratio to the numbers attending. The meetings in which architects may be involved can be roughly divided as follows:

- Staff meetings.
- Client meetings.
- Design team meetings.
- Site meetings.
- Meetings for special purposes.

12.2.1 Staff meetings

This is the kind of meeting at which all members of staff attend to talk about pensions, office reorganizations, expansion, contraction, etc. and to discuss strategy. Many offices make a practice of having a regular staff meeting every month or two months to discuss points of interest to the whole office. It is also a good way to air problems. How successful such meetings are depends on the maturity of the participants. In some offices, staff meetings may be called rarely to deal with major concerns, and contributions 'from the floor' may be discouraged. How staff meetings are used, indeed whether they are used effectively at all, depends on the management styles of the partners responsible.

12.2.2 Client meetings

The best meetings are one to one. A client meeting may involve one person other than the architect, or the client may be a board of directors or local government committee. Meetings between the architect and a board of directors should be few. It is only really necessary when the commission is being set up and possibly when the architect is demonstrating the initial design proposals. At other times, the board should nominate someone with authority to deal with the architect on the board's behalf; otherwise, progress will be slow. Generally, the architect will initiate client meetings to make decisions, receive reports, view proposals and so on. Occasionally, there may be other professionals present. These may be the client's legal and financial advisers or the other members of the design team.

12.2.3 Design team meetings

In planning this kind of meeting, the architect should be guided by, but should not slavishly follow, the RIBA Plan of work.[3] Depending upon the size of the project, the personalities of the participants and the stage of the work, the client may be present at these meetings. In any event, all the consultants should be present. This meeting is necessary in order to co-ordinate the effort of the team and to create the right sort of enthusiasm which is essential for the success of any major job. Normally, these meetings are called at key points in the scheme rather than, say, 'every month just to make sure that everything is proceeding smoothly'. Such meetings are usually counter-productive.

The general rule about numbers is equally valid with reference to team meetings and the architect will often find it easier to work on a one-to-one basis with consultants with the key meetings mentioned above. In practice, it is common to find that the necessity for full design team meetings ends at tender stage. After that, one-to-one meetings are the norm.

12.2.4 Site meetings

Architects commonly have regular fortnightly or monthly site meetings, although one school of thought considers that there is little to commend them. The purpose of site meetings is presumably:

- To measure actual against predicted progress.
- To answer queries.
- To provide information.

Progress is in the hands of the contractor. His best interests will be served by a quick and workmanlike conclusion to the contract. The architect's principal role in assisting progress is to ensure that all necessary production information is provided at the proper time. The clerk of works, if appointed, can be asked to submit a weekly progress report in any format and incorporating whatever information the architect may desire. The contractor can be asked to submit a separate weekly report. Any problems with the progress of the project can be taken up directly between the architect and the contractor, in person, by telephone or, best of all, by correspondence.

The site meeting is not the correct forum for answering queries. Most queries arise between meetings and they should be answered immediately. In any event, it is best to answer queries and provide information by letter so that there is a proper record. Site meeting minutes are notorious as vehicles for what the architect wished had been said! Site meetings are always preceded by a site inspection, but an inspection can be carried out without a meeting.

A final point against regular site meetings is the number of expensive man-hours which are swallowed up. At every meeting there are many people in attendance who have an interest in only a small part of the proceedings. Indeed, in some cases, a professional may be there 'just in case', rather than for a specific purpose. This may be an excessively strict view.

Obviously, there must be a meeting for all interested parties before the project commences on site. This is usually erroneously called the 'pre-contract' meeting rather than the more accurate 'pre-start' meeting. After the first meeting to sort out procedures and deal with the many preliminary matters which must be resolved before work can actually start, site meetings should be reserved for specific purposes. Then the meeting becomes an important occasion, not to be taken lightly. Before arranging a site meeting (or any meeting for that matter) it is useful to ask what the meeting can achieve which cannot be achieved in some other way, more effectively and at less cost.

12.2.5 Meetings for special purposes

There will always be the kind of meeting which cannot be properly categorized except under this heading. Meetings with local government officers, members of an amenity society or ministry officials fall into this group.

It should go without saying that every meeting must have a purpose. So also, a good meeting will be the result, among other things, of careful preparation. It is usual to prepare an agenda and to circulate it to participants together with any papers which should be read before the meeting. Provided that the date of the meeting has been agreed in advance, it is best to circulate the agenda and supporting papers no more than a week before. This gives people the time to read the information, but does not really allow time for it to be

Shops, Offices and Garage Development, High Street, Bruddersfax, South Yorkshire

Agenda for Pre-Start Meeting

To be held on 3 September 1999 at 11.00 am in the site accommodation

1. Personnel

2. Production information
   (a) Prepared
   (b) To be prepared

3. Contractor's copy of contract documents

4. Insurances
   (a) By Employer
   (b) By Contractor

5. Bond

6. Sub-contractors

7. Employer's licensees

8. Architect's instructions

9. Clerk of works directions

10. Oral instructions

11. Queries and information requests

12. Further meetings and participants

13. Contractor's programme, form and updating

14. Progress reporting

15. Role of the clerk of works

16. Samples

17. Covering up work

18. Setting out

19. Services

20. Signboard

21. Consultants and their roles

22. Procedural matters not otherwise covered.

23. Any other business

24. Date, time and place of next meeting if appropriate

Figure 12.1   Example of a pre-start meeting agenda.

put on one side. The generally accepted format for any kind of meeting is:

- Record of those present including status.
- Apologies for absence.
- Agreement to minutes of the last meeting.
- Any matters arising from the minutes of the last meeting.
- Items for discussion.
- Any other business.
- Date and time of next meeting.

An example of an agenda for a pre-start meeting is shown in Figure 12.1. That is only the merest outline of course. Architects should not assume that the pre-start meeting is an opportunity to put restrictions on the contractor. By this time, the contractor should be in contract with the employer on clear terms. The architect has no power to vary those terms, and if variations of work or materials are instructed during the meeting, there will be a price to be paid. The meeting is to give everyone the opportunity to meet and, hopefully, form the beginnings of a team and to remind everyone of the important points about the project. There will also be a certain amount of business to be carried on regarding insurance policies, bonds and the like unless these have been dealt with already.

It is usual, and desirable, for architects to chair their own meetings. This is a difficult task to do properly. The chairman must lead the discussion and be prepared to silence the talkative. Minutes should be brief, recording decisions, not the perhaps endless discussion leading to the decision. Minutes should be circulated within 24 hours to everyone attending the meeting or who has an interest in the results of the meeting. Anyone receiving the minutes of a meeting should read them immediately and carefully to check for mistakes, omissions and sometimes insertions which should be reported by letter to the author of the minutes without delay. Such a letter should also be sent to all those people noted on the circulation list. It is fatal to wait until the next meeting to attempt to rectify a mistake; memories will have faded by then.

12.3 *Site inspections*

'Inspection' and 'supervision' are often confused. Architects are commonly referred to as being responsible for 'design and supervision'. That, of course, is quite wrong. Inspection involves looking and noting, possibly even carrying out tests. Supervision, however, not only covers inspection, but also the issuing of detailed directions regarding the execution of the works. Supervision can only be carried out by someone with the requisite authority to ensure that the work is carried out in a particular way. That is the prerogative of the contractor.

Inspection is not something to be carried out lightly.[4] Many architects simply wander on to the site with no very clear idea of what they expect to find nor indeed what they should be looking for. Before commencing an inspection of the works, the architect must have a plan of campaign as follows:

- Inspections should have a definite purpose. They should coincide with particular stages in the works. It is sensible for the architect to sit down beforehand and draw up a list of parts of the construction which must be inspected on that particular visit together with items of secondary importance to be inspected if possible.[5] The composition of the list and the frequency of inspections will depend on factors such as the employment of a clerk of works, the size and the complexity of the project. Comments can be made against the checklist as the inspection progresses. The list and the comments are for the architect's own files, not for distribution. Although an architect's inspection duties are quite onerous, he or she will be better able to defend themselves in court against an allegation of negligent inspection if they can show, by reference to contemporary notes, that inspections were carried out in an organized manner.[6]
- Times of inspections should be varied so that a devious contractor cannot rely upon getting poor work covered up between inspections.
- The architect should always finish an inspection by spending a few minutes inspecting at random.
- Action should be taken immediately the architect returns to the office, whether or not any defects have already been pointed out to the site manager. It is wise to put in writing all comments regarding defective work.
- During site inspections, the architect is bound to be asked to answer queries. It is prudent to give answers on return to the office when it is possible to sit down calmly and assess the situation. Many decisions made on site are either amended or regretted later.

12.4 Safety

The health and safety of those employed on a building site is governed by Act of Parliament and subsidiary regulations. The principal Acts are:

- The Health and Safety at Work Act 1974.
- The Factories Act 1961.
- The Offices, Shops and Railway Premises Act 1963.

    Some of the regulations under the Factories Act are:

- The Construction (General Provisions) Regulations 1961.
- The Construction (Lifting Operations) Regulations 1961.
- The Construction (Health and Welfare) Regulations 1966.
- The Construction (Working Places) Regulations 1966.
- The Notification of Accidents and Dangerous Occurrences Regulations 1980.

    The architect should have a reasonable knowledge of safety regulations and be on the look-out for any infringement on site. The architect should take basic precautions such as reporting to the site manager immediately on arrival, wearing a hard hat and other protective clothing as appropriate and conforming with all reasonable safety rules set up by the site management. Every office should have its own safety policy which should be clearly set out to all members of staff besides, of course, conforming to statutory safety regulations.[7]

12.5 Architect's instructions and variations

Building contracts generally give architects wide powers to issue instructions and they must adopt a systematic method for documenting all variations to the contract. In the past many architects have used standard forms for this purpose which were called 'variation orders' (usually abbreviated to VOs). The term 'variation order' itself does not appear in the JCT form of contract and its use is to be discouraged. The RIBA standard form is entitled 'Architect's Instructions' (Figure 12.2).

    JCT forms of contract require that all variations must be the subject of architect's instructions which are contractually defined. A letter or memorandum signed by the architect is actually sufficient authority for an instruction, but a form has the advantage of keeping the

Issued by:
address:

**Architect's
Instruction**

Employer:
address:

Job reference:

Instruction no:

Contractor:
address:

Issue date:

Sheet: of

Works:
situated at:

Contract dated:

Under the terms of the above-mentioned Contract, I/we issue the following instructions:

	Office use: Approx costs	
	£ omit	£ add

To be signed by or for
the issuer named
above

Signed _____

Amount of Contract Sum	£
± Approximate value of previous Instructions	£
± Approximate value of this Instruction	£
Approximate adjusted total	£

Distribution   Original to: Copies to:

☐ Contractor   ☐ Employer   ☐ Quantity Surveyor   ☐ Clerk of Works

☐ Nominated   ☐ Consultants   ☐ File
Sub-Contractors

F809 for JCT 80/IFC 84/MW 80   © RIBA Publications Ltd 1991

Figure 12.2 RIBA Architect's Instruction (courtesy RIBA Publications Ltd).

information complete and orderly for every instruction throughout the job. It will appear distinct from other correspondence and forms, especially if a tinted paper is used and all copies are filed separately. The following information should be on every architect's instruction:

- Name of project.
- Name of contractor.
- Date of instruction.
- Serial number, each project starting with the figure 1.
- Subject matter of the instruction or instructions.
- Architect's signature.

This last requirement is very important. Each instruction must be signed by the architect. It is also useful to indicate the distribution of all copies on the instruction. On the architect's and quantity surveyor's copies may be put the approximate cost of the variation and, if desired, a summary of the balance remaining from the contingency sum. It is not advisable to put any value on the contractor's copy, as such value for an extra will tend to be treated by the contractor as a minimum whereas in fact, if the quantity surveyor has been prudent, it will be a maximum and complications could arise when it comes to agreeing the final account.

Where an instruction involves something quite different from the original requirements a definite estimate may, of course, be obtained from the contractor and accepted by the architect on behalf of the employer as a firm price. In such cases it is, however, advisable to consult the quantity surveyor who, before acceptance, will examine the detailed build-up of the estimate and ensure that proper credit has been given for balancing any omissions that there may be.

When instructing variations it is wise to mark each clearly whether they are omissions or additions to the contract and to give each item a subsidiary number within the overall instruction. A variation can be described in one of two forms: for example, either

1. For softwood door to Entrance Hall substitute oak to detail.
2. OMIT Softwood door to Entrance Hall
   ADD   Oak door to detail

It is not advisable to quote item reference numbers from the bill of quantities to define a variation nor to mention prices except when a definite quotation is being accepted. The architect will not be fully aware of what bill items other than those noted might be affected. It is better to specify the variation in normal terms and leave it to the quantity surveyor to look up the dimensions and see which items need to be adjusted.

Architects cannot generally delegate their powers or duties under the contract other than the customary delegation within a practice, and not even that without the client's permission if the architect has been appointed on a personal basis. Accordingly an instruction signed by a clerk of works cannot constitute a variation within the meaning of JCT 80. As has been said earlier, duties of a clerk of works are solely that of an inspector. While certain inspection duties may be delegated, instructions to vary the contract must be given by the architect.

Some contractors keep a 'variation order' book on the site, into which the agent enters all instructions purported to have been given and the architect may be asked to sign them when visiting the site, afterwards receiving a copy. Remember that if a contractor confirms a verbal instruction to the architect in writing, perhaps on a form titled 'Confirmation of Architect's Instruction', then this constitutes a formal notification under clause 4.3.2 of JCT 80 and, unless dissented from in writing by the architect within seven days of receipt, it will take effect as an architect's instruction.

With the sub-contract procedures set out in JCT 80, as amended 1991, notification of a nomination must be made by way of the issue of NSC/N which confirms all the negotiations completed under the tender documentation NSC/T and gives to the contractor all the information necessary for the completion of the sub-contract NSC/A. In these circumstances the issue of written covering instructions as well, while not out of order, could lead to confusion.

One copy of all architect's instructions and revised or supplementary drawings should be sent to the quantity surveyor if one is employed.

12.6　*Variations and their valuation*

12.6.1　General

Most building contracts include provision for changes in both design and construction if these are found to be required either for reasons of a change of mind by the architect or employer or because of the exigencies arising from construction. These changes are better known as 'variations'. Variations in their nature can be very expensive matters and architects need to think very carefully before authorizing them. They must in particular adhere strictly to the terms of the contract and ensure that they do not act outside their powers.

The variation procedures under the JCT forms of contract are covered in the main by clause 13 of JCT 80 and clauses 3.6 and 3.7 of IFC 84. The procedures under the new Government form, GC/Works/1 Edition 3, are somewhat different in that facility is provided for the pre-costing of variations and there is a much closer relationship with loss and expense.

The JCT contracts draw a clear distinction between valuing variations (usually tied to rates in the contract bills or in the schedule of rates) and ascertaining loss and expense which may arise over and above the value of the actual variation. As mentioned above this is not the case with the Government form whereby loss and expense for prolongation and disturbance are required to be included in the costing of variations; only such loss or expense which arises from events other than variations is treated separately.

The line between the two is not always easy to draw in practice and, even if it were, there is the problem of reconciling costs which differ considerably from the rates in the contract. Clearly the latter apply to variations but the question arises should the employer have to pay costs which may greatly exceed rates simply because they rank as a loss and expense rather than an item to be valued. This dilemma can be partly resolved by listing the reasons that can give rise to such differences:

- Underestimate in the rate.
- Remedial work.
- Inefficiency and default.
- Inflation.
- Non-reimbursable costs (e.g. those caused by nominated and domestic sub-contractors).
- Disruption caused by act, omission or default of the employer or his agent.

12.6.2 Definition of a variation

A variation is defined as the alteration or modification of the design, quantity or quality of the works as shown upon the contract drawings and described by or referred to in the contract bills (or specification if there are no quantities). The addition, alteration or omission of certain of the obligations or restrictions imposed by the employer also fall within the definition of a variation. In the case of the standard forms this includes:

- The addition, omission or substitution of any work.
- Alteration of the kind or standard of any of the materials or goods to be used in the works.

- Removal from the site of work or materials.
- Changes to access to the site or part thereof.
- Limitations in working space or hours.
- Changes to the order of the works.

It excludes nomination of a sub-contractor.

12.6.3 Valuing variations

Items to be dealt with by valuing under JCT 80 clause 13 and IFC 84 clause 3.7 are:

- Variations.
- Provisional sums both defined and undefined.
- The effect of variations on the remainder of the work.

Items to be excluded from valuation under JCT 80 clause 13 are:

- Variations the price of which is agreed between the employer and the contractor.
- Disruption to regular progress and any items to which clause 26 (JCT 80) and clause 4.11 (IFC 84), the loss and expense clauses, apply.

Factors relating to work which can properly be valued by measurement and which is varied by addition or substitution can be summarized as follows:

Character	Conditions	Quantity	Basis of valuation
(1) Similar	Similar	No significant change	The rates and prices in the contract bills
(2) Similar	Similar	Significant change	As last but make due allowance for the change
(3) Similar	Not similar	No significant change	Ditto
(4) Not similar	—	—	Fair rates and prices

Other matters which need to be considered in the valuing of variations include the following:

- Work which cannot properly be valued by measurement is valued by reference to daywork. Daywork sheets must be delivered for verification within detailed timetables (JCT 80 clause 13.5.4; GC/Works/1 condition 42 (10)).
- Omitted work is valued at rates in the contract bills.
- Work that is not varied *per se* but is affected by a variation (including an omission) is valued as if it were the subject of a variation.
- Where work is valued by reference to bill rates allowance must be made for:
  (a) measuring to the same rules (SMM) as applied to the contract bills;
  (b) any percentage or lump sum in the contract bills;
  (c) adjustment of preliminaries.

As bill rates form the key to the valuation of variations it is important that any errors and/or inconsistencies are removed before the contract is signed. Alternative rules for achieving this are laid down in the NJCC Code of Procedure for Single Stage Selective Tendering (Chapter 11, section 11.5.3).

The above procedure for pricing variations could be described as the traditional route and applies to the valuation of variations under the Government form when it applies to other variations or variation instructions where a lump sum quotation has not been called for. Under condition 42 the project manager, as has been stated above, has the right if so wished to call for a lump sum quotation. These quotations must include the cost of the work and the cost of prolongation and disturbance (if any), each to be separately identified. A strict timetable is laid down for submission of the quotation and, if called for, supporting documentation and for the subsequent acceptance or non-acceptance of the quotation. In the event of non-acceptance then the traditional route is reverted to.

The question often arises as to how work should be priced where there is an obvious inconsistency or downright mistake in the original pricing. Practice suggests that the fair solution is to hold the contractor to the wrong rate for the original quantity but to apply a corrected rate for any additional quantity. There is however case law[8] which lays down that a contractor can be held to the original rate irrespective of quantity. This was something of a special judgment and it is questionable if it would stand today.

It is often the case that the quantity surveyor, on behalf of the architect, agrees a final account with the contractor and thereafter has to resist attempts by the employer and/or the auditors, be they local or central government finance officers or (in the case of private clients) their professional accountants, to amend or challenge this. These attempts have to be resisted as these matters are decisions of the architect whose powers are expressly laid down in the contract. The remedy for an aggrieved employer lies elsewhere in arbitration or, if necessary, through the courts.

12.7 *Controlling costs*

Possibly the most common criticism that is made by clients of their architects (and quite often quantity surveyors as well) is that they never keep them informed of how their money is being spent. They have in most cases signed what has been described to them as a 'lump sum firm price' contract and they have the greatest of difficulty in understanding why they are now being asked to pay a lot more money.

For this reason architects have a particular duty to watch the expenditure of their clients' money. When clients want changes made not only must they be advised whether or not such changes are feasible but also what the cost is likely to be both in terms of time and money. Equally well they must be kept so informed when unavoidable changes have to be made for matters such as changed ground conditions or unexpected problems arising when an existing building is opened up. Finally of course architects must resist the temptation to change to suit their revised thoughts. If such architects' changes are envisaged then the clients must be consulted and again advised of any financial effect on the total budget. If the financial effects are of any magnitude the chances of the clients' concurring in the changes being made are slim.

A running record of cost can be kept by having a valuation of each variation recorded and totals of omissions and additions to the contract sum made from time to time. Prime cost sums must be adjusted against specialists' estimates as these are accepted, if formal written architect's instructions are not issued to cover them. Such a record depends very much for its accuracy on the prompt issue of written instructions. Obviously if they are neglected figures will be of little value. Price adjustment increases and payments made for loss and expense must also be taken into account.

Ideally a statement of the financial position should accompany each interim certificate so that clients when paying the contractors have in front of them a financial picture of the job. A specimen of such a

---

SHOPS AND OFFICES, WILLOW CENTRE, ANYTOWN
FOR
WILLOW DEVELOPMENTS LTD

FINANCIAL REPORT 6

Smith & Jones	Date	8.9.90
Chartered Architects	Contract week	27
	Date for possession	6.3.90
	Date for completion	1.3.92

	£	£
Approved contract sum		4,268,750
Less Contingencies/daywork		85,000
Estimates for instructions issued	£	£4,183,750
Architect's instructions 1–16 as report 5	28,640	
A:I.17 Revolving doors	285	
18 Redesign of balustrades	(2,500)	
19 Additional fire officer's requirement	1,170	
		27,595
Estimates for instructions to be issued	£	
Lift	2,500	
Atrium paving	6,000	
		8,500
Ascertained claims		—
Estimated final total (excluding contingencies)		£4,219,845
Current approved sum		4,268,250
Balance of contingencies		£ 48,405

NOTES

3 weeks extension of time granted. Contract completion date now 22.3.92. Anticipated actual completion date 14.4.92, i.e. contractor estimated to be in 3 weeks culpable delay.
Loss and expense claim received in the amount of £26,500. Sum not ascertained or certified – not included above.
All figures exclusive of VAT and professional fees.

Figure 12.3   Specimen financial report.

statement is shown in Figure 12.3. It is very important that the figures contained in such statements should be, if not accurate, then on the pessimistic side. There is nothing worse for clients than to be lulled into a sense of false security only to receive a bombshell at the end of the contract.

12.8 *Workmanship and materials*

Workmanship and materials are the very essence of a building and they should be specified by the architect in accordance with the design. Materials are inextricably bound up with the appearance and use of the building and specification of the wrong materials can ruin the concept and possibly leave the architect open to an action from the client for failing to take proper care. Examples would be if the architect specified an unsuitable roof covering which subsequently let in water, or a floor finish which was inappropriate to the expected traffic and became badly marked or worn.

The specification of workmanship is less obvious and less clearly defined, yet just as detrimental to the building as a whole. If poor workmanship is applied to the task of erecting the finest materials, the result will be worse than if less expensive materials had been erected with first-class workmanship. Good workmanship is difficult to define, but easy to recognize. The specification of workmanship is more difficult than the specification of materials. Certain aspects of good workmanship can be described, such as the way in which bricks are to be laid, but generally good workmanship is described by the result expected. Thus materials are the basic building elements; workmanship is the process which puts the elements together.

It is one of the architect's functions, and of the clerk of works if appointed, to check that the correct materials have been used by the building contractor and that the workmanship of the building is in accordance with the specification. Depending upon the size of the project, a clerk of works may spend a great deal of time checking materials and, for example, taking samples of concrete for testing in the laboratory. Under most standard forms of contract, the architect has wide powers to reject materials or work not in accordance with the contract. Under JCT 80, for example, the contractor must provide materials in accordance with the contract so far as they are procurable. That is a valuable protection for the contractor whose obligation seems to come to an end if the materials are truly not procurable. Of course, not procurable at a price or at a date the contractor considers reasonable does not fall within the meaning of this provision. Workmanship is to be to the standards described in the bills of quantity or specification if there are no bills. If no standards are described, the workmanship is to be to a standard 'appropriate to the works'. That is fairly broad, but probably as good a standard as any in the absence of precise specification.

It is always open, and provided for in the contract, for the architect to specify materials or workmanship to be to his or her satisfaction, in which case the contract stipulates that they are to be to the architect's reasonable satisfaction. This is obviously intended to prevent the architect from insisting upon an inappropriately high standard. Whether the standard is inappropriate or not is something which, in the last resort, must be settled by arbitration if the parties cannot agree. Clause 8.2.2 requires the architect to express dissatisfaction within a reasonable time of the execution of work which is to be to the architect's satisfaction. No doubt, some architects may be tempted to advise their clients to delete this particular clause as being a potential cause of trouble.

JCT 80 has elaborate provisions, in clause 8.4, to allow the architect to order the removal from site of work or materials which are not in accordance with the contract. The architect may also or alternatively allow the work to remain and make an appropriate deduction from the contract sum; or issue reasonably necessary instructions requiring a variation at no additional cost, no extension of time and no loss and/or expense; or require the contractor to open up or test the work to establish whether there is the likelihood of similar failure at no additional cost, but with an extension of time if the work examined is found to be in accordance with the contract.

There are certain conditions which have to be satisfied and the architect should become familiar with them. The Intermediate Form IFC 84 has provisions which are less far-reaching, but to similar overall effect. Both JCT 80 and IFC 84, in clauses 8.3 and 3.12 respectively, give the architect power to order opening up and/or testing of work or materials. If the work or material is found to be in accordance with the contract, the contractor is entitled to an extension of time, if appropriate, and whatever direct loss and/or expense can be shown to have been suffered.

12.9 Certificates and payments

12.9.1 Responsibility for certificates

It usually falls on the architect under a building contract to certify from time to time the amount of instalments on account to be paid to the contractor and to certify the total of the final account. It is generally provided that certificates shall include the value of work properly executed and unfixed materials on site, less a specified percentage to be retained which is known as the retention sum or reserve.

While the quantity surveyor will usually make valuations and recommend to the architect the amount to be certified, the architect is

Valuation

Quantity Surveyor

Valuation No:
Date of issue:
QS Reference:

To Architect/Contract Administrator

Employer

Contractor

Contract sum £

Works

I/we have made, under the terms of the Contract, an Interim Valuation

as at   * and I/we report as follows:—

Gross Valuation
(excluding any work or material notified to me/us by the Architect/The Contract Administrator in
writing, as not being in accordance with the Contract).   £

Less total amount of Retention, as attached Statement.   £

                                                                                                     £

Less total amount stated as due in Interim Certificates previously issued by the
Architect/The Contract Administrator up to and including Interim Certificate No.............   £

Balance (in words)   £

Signature: Quantity Surveyor

Notes:
(i)   * All the above amounts are exclusive of V.A.T.
(ii) The balance stated is subject to any statutory deductions which the Employer may be obliged to make under the provisions of
      the Finance (No. 2) Act 1975 where the Employer is classed as a 'Contractor' for the purposes of the Act.
(iii) It is assumed that the Architect/The Contract Administrator will:—
      (a) satisfy himself that there is no further work or material which is not in accordance with the Contract.
      (b) notify Nominated Sub-Contractors of payments directed for them and of Retention held therein by the Employer.
      (c) satisfy himself that the previous payments directed for Nominated Sub-Contractors have been discharged.
* (iv) The Architect's/The Contract Administrator Interim Certificate should be issued within seven days of the date indicated thus
(v)   Action by the Contractor should be taken on the basis of figures in, or attached to, the Architect's/The Contract
      Administrator Interim Certificate.

© 1980 RICS

Figure 12.4 Standard valuation form (courtesy The Royal Institution of Chartered Surveyors).

nevertheless responsible for the issue of the certificate,[9] the survey-or's recommendation being possibly affected by deductions for unsatisfactory work, delays in payment to sub-contractors etc. A standard valuation form is published by the RICS for completion by the quantity surveyor. Public authorities often have their own form for this purpose.

On smaller contracts architects should quite easily be able to make their own assessment. Where there are no bills of quantities the contract schedule of works (if priced) can be used, or the contractor may ask for the original estimate to be used as a guide to the sub-division of the contract sum. Clause 5.3.1.3 of JCT 80 without quantities only asks for a schedule of rates which because it contains no quantities or pricing-out cannot serve this purpose. Provision can be made in the contract for the contractor to provide a detailed statement with each application which can then be checked.

12.9.2 Method of valuation

How architects make their valuations will depend on the size and complexity of the project. In the case of repetitive housing it may be possible to fix values per house at each of half a dozen stages, say:

* Damp-proof course level.
* First floor joists fixed.
* Roof plate level.
* Roof completed.
* Plastering completed.
* Second fixing and decoration completed.

To this would have to be added the proportion of drainage and external works completed plus an allowance for the preliminary costs. As a valuation this would only be approximate but would be sufficient for the purpose.

In contracts for larger buildings the architect, if without the help of the quantity surveyor, will have to go through the bill of quantities and, taking one work section at a time, pick out in a general way (without bothering too much about minor items) the work which has been done and its value. A total will thus be built up. Again a suitable proportion of the preliminary bill would be included together with any percentage addition made pro rata and any sums for insurances etc. shown in the summary.

Architects should beware that if they carry out work normally undertaken by quantity surveyors they could find themselves without appropriate insurance cover (see Chapter 17, section 17.4).

Another variant is payment in accordance with a predetermined stage payment chart or table, either provided as a tender document or submitted by the contractor at the time of tender. Payments will then be made at regular intervals based on the stated percentage. Allowances can be made to amend these percentages either up or down according to whether the contractor is ahead or behind the programme.

12.9.3 Unfixed materials

Most forms of contract provide for interim payments to include the value of unfixed materials properly brought on to the site. The contractor should be asked to prepare a priced list of these at the date of the valuation, which can be checked by the clerk of works (if any) or by the architect. If verification of cost of any of the items is required this can be asked for and at the same time assurances sought regarding retention of title to ensure that they are the property of the contractor and can safely be passed to the employer.

When these materials are paid for they become the property of the employer. Being the property of the employer, they must not, of course, be removed without permission, and in the event of the contractor's bankruptcy they would not be an asset vesting in the trustee, but could be removed or, as is more likely, used by the employer.

A matter that needs careful consideration is the inclusion in a valuation of the costs of unfixed materials that are not on the site and so outside the physical control of the employer and agents (JCT 80 clause 30.3). There may be circumstances where, with a contractor of sound financial standing, the architect might well agree to include in an interim valuation the value of materials not on site, but if there is any doubt as to financial stability, the request should be refused. The employer's right to ownership confirmed by a court six or twelve months later would be of little use when the materials are wanted immediately so that the work can proceed with another contractor.

If payment is to be made for materials off site the contract requires that:

- Proof of ownership can be shown, also of adequate insurance.
- The materials shall be complete in all respects ready for inclusion in the works.

Statement of Retention and of Nominated Sub-Contractors' Values

Quantity Surveyor

Works

This Statement relates to:

Valuation No:
Date of issue:
QS Reference:

| | Gross Valuation | Amount subject to: | | | Amount of Retention | Net Valuation | Amount Previously Certified | Balance |
		Full Retention of %	Half Retention of %	No Retention				
	£	£	£	£	£	£	£	£
Main Contractor								
Nominated Sub-Contractors:-								
TOTAL								

© 1980 RICS

No account has been taken of any discounts for cash to which the Contractor may be entitled if discharging the balance within 17 days of the issue of the Architect/S.O.s Certificate.
The sums stated are exclusive of V.A.T

Figure 12.5   Statement of retention and of nominated sub-contractors' values (courtesy The Royal Institution of Chartered Surveyors).

Issued by:
address:

Employer:
address:

Contractor:
address:

Works:
situated at:

Contract dated:

Interim Certificate and Direction

Serial no: **C 526307**

Job reference:

Certificate no:

Issue date:

Valuation date:

Contract sum:

Original to Employer

This Interim Certificate is issued under the terms of the above-mentioned Contract.

Gross valuation inclusive of the value of works by Nominated Sub-Contractors .... £

Less Retention which may be retained by the Employer as detailed on the Statement of Retention .... £

Sub-total £

Less total amount stated as due in Interim Certificates previously issued up to and including Interim Certificate no: _____ .... £

Net amount for payment .... £

I/We hereby certify that the **amount for payment** by the Employer to the Contractor on this Certificate is (in words)

I/We hereby direct the Contractor that this amount includes interim or final payments to Nominated Sub-Contractors as listed in the attached *Statement of Retention and of Nominated Sub-Contractors' Values*, which are to be discharged to those named in accordance with the Sub-Contract.

All amounts are exclusive of VAT

To be signed by or for
the issuer named
above

Signed _____

[1] Relevant only if
clause 1A of the VAT
Agreement applies.
Delete if not
applicable.

[1] The Contractor has given notice that the rate of VAT chargeable on the supply of goods and services to which the Contract relates is _____ %

[1] _____ % of the amount certified above is .... £

[1] Total of net amount and VAT amount (for information) .... £

This is not a Tax Invoice

F801　for JCT 80

©RIBA Publications Ltd 1990

Figure 12.6　Interim certificate (courtesy RIBA Publications Ltd).

• The materials are set apart and clearly marked as to ownership and ultimate destination.

12.9.4 Nominated sub-contractors

Architects when issuing certificates must notify the contractor of the amounts included for nominated sub-contractors. A form is published by the RICS for use by the quantity surveyor which sets out these details (Figure 12.5) and provision is made in the RIBA certificate form for the information to be included (Figure 12.6). The RIBA also publishes a form for individual notification to each sub-contractor (Notification to Nominated Sub-contractors). It is only by notifying these amounts and asking for the contractor to produce proof of payment that the architect can enforce the authority given under clause 35.13 of JCT 80 to certify payments of the accounts of nominated sub-contractors direct by the employer.

12.9.5 Price adjustment

Where provision is made for price adjustment on account of fluctuations in cost of labour and materials, this must be taken into account in the valuation under the relevant contract clause.

Before any increased cost is included under the price adjustment clauses, the contractor should submit a statement showing the price adjustment formula computations for checking; if the adjustment is to be by way of wages and materials increases, the necessary information (backed up by time sheets, invoices, vouchers etc.) must be produced. Increased costs (or in rare cases decreased costs) cannot be taken into account in interim certificates until they have been incurred and no profit is added (or deducted).

12.9.6 Nominated suppliers

Nominated suppliers fall into the same category as ordinary merchants supplying materials to the industry; the only difference is that they are nominated by the architect. The protection given to nominated sub-contractors under clause 35 of JCT 80 is not available to nominated suppliers under clause 36. Furthermore there is no obligation for the architect to notify the amounts due to each or the power to certify direct payments.

12.9.7 Retention sum

In preparing valuations architects have to take into account the sum to be retained under the contract. If the quantity surveyors have submitted a statement, the amount retained will be shown. The retention sums outstanding on various contracts constitute a substantial part of a contractor's capital. While they are part of the financing which is expected of contractors they should not be expected to do more than the contract requires of them. The architects should therefore see that, so far as they are concerned, there is no delay in releasing balances at 'practical completion' and at the end of the defects liability period. To this end they should be prompt in making their final inspection and in giving notice to the contractor of defects to be remedied.

The retention provisions of JCT 80 are set out in clauses 30.4 and 30.5 and the appendix makes provision for stating the percentage of the value of the work done and materials supplied that is to be retained. The footnote suggests figures which are commonly adopted. In calculating the amount of retention to be held at any one time the total value of the contractor's work and of the nominated sub-contractor's work together with the value of materials on site (and sometimes off site: see section 12.9.3 above) must be taken into account when applying the percentage. Amounts notified are gross and the contractor will deduct the relevant retention monies together with discount before paying the sub-contractor.

Clause 30.2 of JCT 80 indicates which work is subject to retention and which is not. The first category includes the value of work done, the materials on and off site and fluctuations computed under the price adjustment formula; the second category includes loss and expense claims and fluctuations adjusted on the rise and fall of labour rates and material prices. The requirements of the Government form in this respect are slightly different.

The employer's interest in the retention sum is fiduciary as trustee for the contractor; under the private edition of JCT 80 the employer is required, if asked, to set the money aside in a separate account in the joint names of the employer and the contractor. This means that in the event of default or bankruptcy of the employer the money is available to pay off the contractor and it is not lost in the general funds which may or may not remain. When the employer is a local authority the same circumstances apply but there is no requirement for a separate bank account although it seems that a contractor could insist.[10]

12.9.8 Final check

When the certificate has been completed a careful check should be made to ensure that the figure shown as already certified is correct as a slip here can cause a serious error in the valuation.

12.9.9 Release of part of retention

It is usually provided that half, or some other part, of the retention shall be released when the work is complete, the balance being retained until the end of the defects liability period. Clause 30.4.1 of JCT 80 provides for this release on 'practical completion' of the works, the architect being required to issue a certificate of practical completion under clause 17.1. It is not, therefore, necessary for the contractor to have completed his contract (see Chapter 13, section 13.2).

Under JCT 80 nominated sub-contracts are now treated as contracts in their own right and the rules for ascertaining and releasing retention are the same as for the main contract. When the valuation has been prepared by the quantity surveyor and the standard form of valuation has been used (Figures 12.4 and 12.5) the second sheet is of particular importance. An examination will show that the recommendation is in three parts:

- Works still going on: subject to full retention.
- Work which has reached practical completion but for which defects have not been cleared: subject to half retention.
- Work completed and cleared of defects: no retention.

These categories are shown for both main and sub-contractors and this sheet will be particularly important as it shows at a glance what the financial position of the job is at each interim valuation.

12.9.10 Release of final balance

Under clauses 17.4 and 30.6 of JCT 80 the whole of the balance of the retention sum is to be released forthwith on the issue of the certificate that making good of defects has been completed. Provision is made for adjustment later of any balance (either way) when the total of the final account is known. Release of the final balance may be delayed because the accounts are not complete. If variations are reasonable, the final figure should be available by the end of the defects liability period.

12.9.11 Form of certificate

Certificates are usually issued in a standard form such as that published and sold in pads by the RIBA (Figure 12.6). Each certificate form in such pads is in quadruplicate, the distribution being employer, contractor, quantity surveyor and file. Certificates need not be in any prescribed form, but they should use the words 'I (or we) certify . . .', stating the name of the contract, names of contractor and employer, the amount certified as due and the date, and they must bear the signature of the architect. It is an obvious advantage if they are given a serial number. As referred to above provision is available for the amounts due to nominated sub-contractors to be identified.[11]

Under the JCT forms (of all kinds) as indicated above the certificate is issued to the employer with a copy to the contractor. It is now no longer necessary for the contractor to present the certificate to the employer in order to receive payment.

12.9.12 Need for promptness

Finance is an important factor in the running of any business and contractors are no exception; like all businessmen they naturally want to reduce to the minimum the amount of capital they have tied up. The intervals at which interim certificates will be issued is usually dictated by the contract, and architects should see that they give prompt attention to the matter at the specified intervals. If the architect is slow, delays visits for valuations and does not deal with the matter promptly on return to the office, particulars given by the contractor quickly become obsolete, and the time-lag between valuation and payment increases.

While it may seem that a delay of a week or two in payments of what may be relatively small sums of money may not be very important, the aggregate of such outstanding amounts can be substantial. Where the contractor has no very great margin, delays in payment may cause financial difficulties from which the employer may come to suffer. Quite apart from anything else, the architect would be in breach of contract for which the employer would be liable.[12]

12.10 Delays and extensions of time

Contracts entered into between employers and contractors usually take the form of an agreement that the works will be constructed for a certain sum of money, or at least specify the way in which that sum will be computed. In addition many contracts include an agreement as to the length of time that the works will take to complete. Accordingly either starting and completing dates are stated or a set period is given. In either case an end or *contract completion date* is established.

In many cases, for various reasons, a job often overruns and finishes on a date later than that originally set. This later date is termed the *actual contract completion date*. The fact that contractors have to spend longer on site than they contracted for means that unless the contract completion date is amended they become liable to pay liquidated, that is ascertained, damages for late completion. Most contracts provide for architects to have the power to extend the original contract completion date if they are satisfied that the reasons for the overrun were outside the control of the contractor.

Certain contracts, the Standard Forms in particular, set out very clearly the duties of contractors and architects in this respect. The contractor has to give notice as soon as it becomes apparent that delay has or is likely to arise, to state the reasons and give an estimate of the length of delay. Architects in their turn have, within prescribed periods, to decide first whether or not in their opinion delay actually is going to occur and second what the true reasons are for the delay. To assist in the second of these requirements what are known as *relevant events* are set out in the contract. In the case of JCT 80 the relevant events contained within clause 25 are as follows:

- *Force majeure.*
- Exceptionally adverse weather conditions.
- Loss or damage from a specified peril or perils.
- Civil commotion, strikes etc.
- Architect's instructions.
- Late instructions.
- Delay by nominated sub-contractors.
- Work by employer's own employees.
- Act or statutory power by Government.
- Inability to obtain labour and/or materials.
- Delay by local authority/statutory undertaking.
- Failure by employer to give ingress to site etc.
- Deferment of possession.
- Approximate quantities not an accurate forecast.

It will be seen that these 'relevant events' fall into two categories: those which are neutral, i.e. neither the fault of the employer nor of the contractor; and those for which the employer or his or her agent is responsible.

Once architects are satisfied that the delay is due to one or more of these relevant events then they are empowered to fix a new contract completion date and the threat to the contractor of the implementation of damages is lifted for that period. While an architect has to state the grounds upon which the decision was based there is no requirement to give separate time allocation. In the event of the full overrun not being awarded as an extension of time then the contractor is in what is known as a *period of culpable delay* and remains liable for the specified damages.

Other JCT contracts have similar clauses but contain significant variations. For instance the JCT Intermediate Form, because it does not recognize nominated sub-contractors as such, does not include delay by such firms as a ground for an extension of time. Equally the effect of an Act or statutory power of the government is also excluded. Under GC/Works/1 the project manager has the power to grant extensions of time for any matter which is considered applicable, with the notable exception of weather conditions, which are specifically excluded.

When questions of extensions of time arise architects must study carefully the particular contract clause and act accordingly. Certain basic facts have to be borne in mind.

- Unless the contract includes an acceleration clause the original contract completion date cannot be improved upon: i.e. there is no facility to shorten a contract.
- A contractor has a duty to make every endeavour to prevent delay arising short of expenditure of large sums of money. The obligation is to continue to work regularly and diligently. However, once delay has arisen there is no requirement that time lost must be recovered.
- Extensions of time provisions are to put the contractor back into contract and provide relief from the damages provisions. They can also be, as pointed out below, of benefit to the employer.
- No question of additional costs being paid arises at all.[13] These are matters dealt with elsewhere in the contract (see section 12.11 below).

Extension-of-time provisions are inserted in building contracts for the benefit of the employer as much for that of the contractor. As far as employers are concerned they protect their right to receive liquidated damages. If such provisions were not included and the contractor was caused delay by the employers or any of their agents then the right to recover damages would be forfeited and the contract would become (as the lawyers say) *at large*: i.e. the only obligation on the part of the contractor would be to complete within a reasonable time.

12.11 *Financial claims*

The word 'claim' as such is not used in the JCT forms of contract at all. What have come to be known under the generic head of claims are in fact an entitlement to reimbursement of direct loss and/or expense, to use the exact terminology of the contracts. Before considering claims at all it is necessary to define the differences between the two types of claim that the law recognizes: common law claims and contractual claims.

Common law claims are claims for breach of contract when the claimant needs to prove a breach of contract and is then entitled to recover damages calculated on common law principles. These claims have to be pursued by way of litigation or arbitration and the architect has no authority to deal with them unless expressly authorized to do so by the employer.

Contractual claims arise because some provision in the contract entitles the contractor to payment for 'loss' or 'expense', made and settled under machinery provided by the contract itself. In some cases events which give rise to such a claim will also be breaches of contract and as such will give rise to a common law claim. In other cases they will not: for example, the issue of a variation order may give rise to a loss and expense claim even though it is authorized by the contract itself. In both cases the burden of proof lies with the claimant.

Before considering claims at all it is also necessary to define what the phrase 'direct loss and/or expense' means. Perhaps it is easier to say what it does not mean. It is not the difference between what the contractor thought the costs would be and what they actually were. This is a commonly held fallacy believed by some contractors; it overlooks the possibility that the initial estimate might have been optimistic. It is what it says it is: direct loss and expense. The word 'direct' in this context means 'close to' or 'appertaining to the event causing the disruption'. 'Expense' means 'actual disbursements'. 'Ascertainment' means 'find out': not, as many claimants appear to think, 'work out'. In several cases, when considering JCT contracts, the courts have held that loss and/or expense is subject to the same principles as are applied to common-law damages.

Claims, to use the generic term, in the building industry fall into two categories: extensions of time, and loss and/or expense for disruption to the regular progress of the works. Claims for extensions of time are covered in section 12.10 above. Claims for loss and expense can be sub-divided into prolongation and disruption elements, and while the JCT forms of contract do not recognize any distinction (each being treated as part of the whole), it is necessary to consider the difference when it comes to the computation of a claim.

A *prolongation claim* arises from delay in completion of the contract works beyond the date when they would otherwise have been completed. Such a claim is sometimes erroneously called an extension of time claim.

A *disruption claim* is one that arises from the effect of an event upon the contract works which does not in itself necessarily involve a delay in the completion of the works. A popular misconception is that there cannot be disruption without prolongation. This supposition is quite false and it is no defence for an architect to say that no extension of time has been granted and therefore there can be no claim for loss and/ or expense; there certainly can be.

The subject of financial claims and their ascertainment warrants textbooks on its own, and indeed a variety of such books exist for further reading.[14] Suffice it to say that architects will from time to time have to make judgments by way of ascertainment and occasionally have to be judge and jury on their own misdemeanours.

In making these decisions architects must bear in mind two main principles:

- Can any wording of the contract, though not specifically mentioning it, be reasonably applied to the point?
- The value of the claim should not affect a decision on the principle. If the claim is very small, however, whichever party is concerned might be persuaded to waive it, or it may be eliminated by a bit of 'give and take'.

Some claims may be due simply to misfortune which neither party could have foreseen, and it may be reasonable for the employer to meet the claim *ex gratia* to a greater or lesser extent.

References

(1) *Glenlion Construction Ltd* v. *The Guinness Trust* (1987) 39 BLR 89.
(2) Chappell, D. (1987) *The Architect in Employment*, Architectural Press, London.

(3) Beaven, L., Cox, S., Dry, D and Males, R (1988) *Architect's Job Book*, 5th edn, RIBA Publications Ltd, London.

(4) Watts, J.W. (1980) *The Supervision of Construction: A guide to site inspection*, Batsford.

(5) Useful basic checklists are contained in: Aqua Group (1990) *Contract Administration for the Building Team*, BSP Professional Books, Oxford; and in Green, R. (1986) *The Architect's Guide to Running a Job*, 4th edn, Architectural Press.

(6) *East Ham Corporation* v. *Bernard Sunley & Sons Ltd* [1965] 3 All ER 619.

(7) *Guide to Metricated Construction Regulations*, Building Advisory Service. *Guide to the Construction Regulations* (1985) BEC & FCEC. A selection of useful booklets from the Health and Safety Executive and the Royal Society for the Prevention of Accidents (RoSPA).

(8) *Dudley Corporation* v. *Parsons & Morrin* (1967) unreported.

(9) *R.M. Burden Ltd* v. *Swansea Corporation* [1957] 3 All ER 243.

(10) *Rayack Construction Ltd* v. *Lampeter Meat Co. Ltd* (1979) 12 BLR 30.

(11) Three helpful guides to completion of all kinds of contract administration forms and other useful hints are published by RIBA Publications (1991) in respect of JCT 80, IFC 84 and MW 80. They are each entitled 'Contract Administration Guide'.

(12) *Croudace Construction Ltd* v. *London Borough of Lambeth* (1984) 1 Con LR 12.

(13) *H. Fairweather Ltd* v. *London Borough of Wandsworth* (1987) 39 BLR 106.

(14) Powell-Smith, V. & Sims, J. (1990) *Building Contract Claims*, 2nd edn, BSP Professional Books, Oxford. Trickey, G.E. (1983) *The Presentation and Settlement of Contractors' Claims*, E. & F.N. Spon.

Chapter 13

Stages L and M

13.1 Determination

Most forms of building contract provide that either party can bring the contractor's employment to an end on the occurrence of certain events. The contract itself is not ended, because it is important that the contract continues in existence to govern the situation after determination. There are some forms of contract which make no provision for contractors to determine their own employment, e.g. GC/Works/1. The act of bringing the contractor's employment to an end must never be taken lightly by either employer or contractor. The provisions are intended to be used as a last resort, which indeed they are so far as those contractual parties are concerned.

If there were no determination provisions in building contracts, determination could only be achieved under the general law. In that case, the contract itself would come to an end. There are four ways in which a contract can be ended:

- By performance.
- By agreement.
- By frustration.
- By breach.

13.1.1 Performance

Most contracts end in this way, when both parties have carried out their obligations properly. The contract then ceases to have a purpose and comes to an end.

13.1.2 Agreement

It is open to the parties to a contract to agree at any time that the contract should be ended. In theory, all that is necessary is for both parties to agree to walk away. In practice, because human nature is sometimes frail, it is wise to record the agreement in writing. For the agreement to have a binding effect, it must either contain consideration from both parties (i.e. both must gain and/or lose something) or it must be completed as a deed (see Chapter 7, section 7.2).

13.1.3 Frustration

This is a term with a specific legal meaning in relation to contracts. When an event completely outside the control of the parties results in the contract's becoming fundamentally different from that contemplated by the parties at the time it was made, the contract is said to have been frustrated. It is not sufficient simply that the contract has become more expensive to carry out than the contractor intended.[1] A good example of frustration would be if a contractor was unable to carry out a refurbishment contract because the building had burned down before the date for possession. There are less extreme examples such as a government order which restricts the work.

13.1.4 Breach

This is an unjustified failure to carry out contractual obligations. If it is a serious breach, it may entitle the other party to treat the contract as ended. The breach itself does not discharge the contract; this has to be accepted by the other party. The terms of a contract are either conditions or warranties. A breach of a warranty entitles the innocent party to sue for damages. A condition is an important term, breach of which entitles the innocent party either to treat the contract as ended and sue for damages or to treat the contract as continuing and sue for damages. Such a breach is known as *repudiatory*, because it is a repudiation of the contract.

The difficulty is knowing whether a term is a condition or a warranty. If a party wrongly accepted a breach as repudiatory and refused to continue with the contract, that party would then be the one in breach. As a general guide, a breach will be repudiatory if it is clear that, by the breach, a party demonstrates an intention not to be bound by the terms of the contract. Great care must be taken, however, because it has been held that where a contractor in breach of contract suspended work, that was not a repudiatory breach. Far from indicating an intention not to continue with the contract, the word 'suspension' indicated only a temporary cessation of activities.[2]

The conditions which have to be satisfied before the contractor's employment can be brought to an end under the contractual machinery can be far less onerous than those required under the general law. Typical grounds for determination by the employer are:

- If the contractor completely abandons the works.
- If the contractor fails to proceed regularly and diligently. This concept has caused some trouble in the past. It really has to be clear and unambiguous.(3)
- If the contractor refuses or neglects to rectify defective work and the works are seriously affected as a result. There are usually other more suitable contractual remedies.
- If the contractor does not observe the provisions of the assignment and sub-letting clauses.

Since determination is such a draconian step, the courts are likely to look very closely at the procedure. The party wishing to determine must comply strictly with the contractual terms governing determination. If the contract stipulates that notice must be given by registered post or recorded delivery, delivery by hand may not suffice.(4) In JCT 80, for example, although the architect is to give the prior notice of default, the actual notice of determination (if given) must be issued by the employer. There is no substitute for carefully reading the particular contract being used.

Where the contract requires that a certain number of days' notice must be given before determination, the determination will not be valid if attempted even one day early. In such a case, the contractor may be able to sue for damages for repudiation. The architect, as the person charged with administering the contract, has important duties to administer the provisions carefully after determination. The best-drafted contracts expressly provide that the contractor must give up possession of the site after determination. Although it may seem obvious that the contractor must leave the site, there have been problems where the contractor has disputed the determination.(5)

Most standard form contracts provide that the employer has the right to make use of the contractor's plant and engage others to finish the works, taking over contracts for the supply of work and/or materials. Generally, the employer will not be obliged to make any further payment until the works are complete. It will then fall to the architect and to the quantity surveyor to take all the expenditure into account including additional professional fees (some contracts include provision for the employer to throw his or her loss and damage into the calculation) and certify a final payment of the balance either to employer or to contractor.

If the contractor determines, the situation will be very serious, not to say catastrophic, for the employer. The architect should make every effort to prevent such an occurrence. Many contracts provide that a contractor who determines may claim the loss of the profit which would have been made had the contract continued.[6] Quite apart from that, the employer will have to shoulder the burden of completing the works using another contractor at increased cost of building and fees and in an extended time scale. There are two danger areas which cause problems:

- The employer's failure to pay certified sums within the period stated in the contract.
- Actions, inactions or defaults by the employer or the architect causing suspension of the works for a protracted period.

Most contracts provide for determination by either party for such things as prolonged suspension of the works due to causes outside the control of either party. Normally, the consequences are simply that the contractor is paid up to date and the parties have no further liabilities to each other. Of course, the employer still has the problem of paying extra and waiting longer to complete the works.

A contractor has nothing to gain and everything to lose by determining employment as a result of suspension. However, the contractor cannot wait for ever, and the architect should attempt to obtain some agreement if it seems that suspension will last long enough to allow determination to take place. A most important provision is that the determination notice must not be given unreasonably or vexatiously. That provision must be interpreted in the ordinary common-sense way.[7]

13.2 Practical completion

'Practical completion' is a term used in the JCT series of contracts. The ACA Form of Building Contract (ACA 2) uses the phrase 'fit and ready for taking over'. There are conflicting views regarding the meaning of practical completion. It is certainly not when the building is totally complete:

'I take these words to mean completion for all practical purposes, that is to say for the purpose of allowing the employer to take possession of the works and use them as intended. If completion in [the possession and completion clause] meant completion down to the last detail, however trivial and unimportant, then [the liquidated damages clause] would be a penalty clause and as such unenforcable.[8]

There is much sound common sense in that view.

It has also been said that the architect may certify practical completion when the architect is satisfied that the works are reasonably in accord with the contract even though there are some minor defects.[9] The architect would certainly find it hard to justify withholding a certificate of practical completion and, in theory at any rate, exposing the contractor to the risk of liquidated damages if the employer had occupied and was using the works. Although practical completion is something which the contract generally leaves to the opinion of the architect, in reality the architect has very little discretion. Practical completion is very largely a question of fact in each case.

The contractor will be anxious to see the certificate because it marks a very significant date. In most contracts it marks the date at which:

- The contractor's liability for damage to the works and goods intended for the work ends.
- The contractor's insurance liability ends.
- Liability for liquidated damages ends.
- Half the retention must be released.
- Liability for subsequent frost damage ends.
- Any reference to arbitration can be opened.

Most contractors will notify the architect when practical completion is about to be achieved although most contracts have no provision to that effect. A contractor will often serve notice prematurely. Architects must be on guard against this tactic which is possibly designed to suggest that the architect is being very unreasonable. The contractor may well write to the effect that it is two months since practical completion was achieved and still the architect refuses to issue a certificate. Such manoeuvres are highly reprehensible of course, but it must be said that some architects can be slow to certify.

The architect should inspect the building and, if it is not complete, write a very firm letter to the contractor pointing out that, at present rate of progress, it seems to be . . . weeks from practical completion and that practical completion had not been achieved on the date suggested by the contractor.

Certificate of

**Practical
Completion**

Issued by:
address:

Employer:
address:

Job reference:

Certificate no:

Contractor:
address:

Issue date:

Works:
situated at:

Contract dated:

Under the terms of the above-mentioned Contract,

I/we hereby certify that Practical Completion of

*Delete as
appropriate

*1. the Works

*2. Section No. _____ of the Works

was achieved on

_____ 19 _____

To be signed by or for
the issuer named
above

Signed _____

Distribution	Original to:	Duplicate to:	Copies to:	
	☐ Employer	☐ Contractor	☐ Quantity Surveyor	☐ Clerk of Works
			☐ Consultants	☐ File

F853   for JCT 80/IFC 84/MW 80

© RIBA Publications Ltd 1991

Figure 13.1   Certificate of practical completion (courtesy RIBA Publications Ltd).

There is nothing wrong and much to be said for architects who point out defects to the contractor. They should not be persuaded to carry out detailed inspections of every part of the building and prepare long lists for the contractor: the so-called 'snagging lists' beloved of clerks of works. A danger with such lists is that the contractor will rely on the architect and clerk of works to do what the contractor's site supervisory staff should be doing. Another danger is that the contractor will frequently consider that when the listed defects are rectified, practical completion will be certified. In fact, the architect may well carry out another inspection two days later and add further items to the list. The architect is perfectly entitled to do so, but it does not make for good relations with the contractor. Far better to get the facts straight at the beginning: i.e. it is the contractor's obligation under the terms of the contract to construct the building strictly in accordance with the contract; the architect has no duty to point out defects. Figure 13.1 shows an example of a form of certificate of practical completion.

Sometimes, the employer will try to persuade the architect to certify practical completion before it has really been achieved so that the employer can move into the building. Of course, as one of the parties to the building contract, it is open to the employer to agree with the contractor to take over the building at any time. However, the architect is not obliged, and it would be very unwise, to issue the certificate before practical completion has actually been achieved. If the employer takes the building before practical completion, the architect's duty depends on the form of contract. Under the provisions of JCT 80, if the employer takes possession of any part or parts of the works, the architect must issue a written statement identifying the part taken into possession and the date.

Many contracts have provision for such partial possession. The idea is that where there is just one date for completion in the contract, but during the progress of the works the employer wishes to take possession of some part of it before practical completion of the whole, this can be achieved provided that the contractor agrees. The provision does not enable sectional completion to be achieved. Where it is known at time of tender that sectional or phased completion is desired, care should be taken that the appropriate form of contract is used. Some contract forms have sectional completion supplements.

It is not usually sufficient to put a list of hand-over dates in the specification or bills of quantities if there is only one completion date in the contract form. In such circumstances, the architect will be unable to insist on sectional completion. He will be unable to give extensions of time to individual sections of the work, and the liquidated damages clause might well be a penalty and unenforceable.

13.3 *Defects liability period*

Most forms of building contract provide for a period of time after the practical completion of the works during which the contractor will be liable to make good defects which appear during that period. The usual period is six months, but twelve months is commonly specified in respect of mechanical services to allow the system to be exposed to the full yearly cycle. Twelve months is also becoming common for the defects liability period for the building as a whole for the same reason.

The reason for the period is often misunderstood. During the contract period, the contractor is said to have a licence to be on the site (the employer's property) for the purpose of carrying out the works. It is generally accepted that the licence allows the contractor to remain on the site until the works are completed. If the contractor were to stay on site or allow equipment to remain on site beyond that point, it would amount to trespass for which the employer could mount an action for whatever damages could be proven. The defects liability period allows defects to appear and provides for the architect to give a schedule to the contractor with a requirement to rectify them. The contract gives the contractor a licence to enter upon the site again to make good the notified defects. The contractor, therefore, has a right under the contract to rectify those defects.

Were it not for this clause, the employer would be entitled to engage another contractor to carry out the work and charge the cost to the original contractor (after due notice and time to inspect). This is a very valuable right to the contractor because the cost to the contractor for doing the remedial work will be very much less than the cost to the employer of getting in another contractor to do the same work. Some contracts allow the employer to decide not to allow the contractor to make good the defects and to make 'an appropriate deduction' from the contract sum. This sum is not the cost of engaging another contractor, but what it would have cost the original contractor to do the work.[10]

Another misconception is that at the end of the defects liability period, the contractor has no further liability for defects. Would life were so simple as that. The contractor is liable for all defects (i.e. work not in accordance with the contract) until the expiry of the limitation period (see Chapter 7, section 7.2). Thus if it was discovered three years after the end of the defects liability period that a contractor had omitted a number of wall ties specified to be used in the cavity walls, that contractor could be successfully sued for the cost of making the defect good. Technically, a contractor is liable beyond that period, but the Limitation Act operates to allow a contractor faced with an action in respect of breach of contract to escape the consequences after a period of six years from the date of the breach (or 12 years if the contract is a deed).

Most forms of contract provide for the architect to issue a certificate to the contractor when all the listed defects have been made good, and in some standard forms there is then provision for the second half of the retention to be released. The retention acts as a safeguard to the employer if the contractor fails to make good the defects. The contractor should make good the defects within a reasonable time after notification by the architect. What is a 'reasonable time' will depend on many factors. It is not possible to fix a period which applies to all circumstances. The criteria to be taken into account include the complexity of the work, the size of the project, the number and type of defects and the difficulty of making good.

If the architect is of the opinion that the contractor is not attending to the contractual obligations with reasonable expedition and does not respond to pressure, the architect should seriously consider giving notice on behalf of the employer that if the making good is not commenced/completed within 14 days or whatever is appropriate in the circumstances, the employer will engage others to do the work and charge the full cost to the contractor. That would normally amount to making a deduction from the retention fund.

Some contractors and even some forms of contract refer to the 'maintenance period'. The term is quite misleading and should never be used, because it suggests an obligation to keep the works in pristine condition rather than an obligation to correct defects. The only kind of defects which most forms of contract require the contractor to make good are those which are due to the work not being in accordance with the contract or to frost occurring before practical completion. Clearly, ordinary wear and tear is excluded as are the consequences of inadequate specification.

13.4 *Adjustment of contract sum*

It seems to be the fashion for architects to leave the calculation of the final account entirely in the hands of the quantity surveyor. In most instances, the result will be no less than satisfactory. Architects should remember, however, that they are the contract administrators and that when the final certificate is issued it will be conclusive (under most JCT contracts) that all the clauses which provide for adjustment of the contract sum have been correctly operated. The consequences of a failure in this regard could be quite serious. The only safe process is to check through the contract and make sure. To take the JCT Standard Form of Building Contract 1980 as an example, it contains no less than 26 different clauses which permit or require adjustment of the contract sum. They are indicated in Figure 13.2. Each clause should be

Clause Adjustments	
2.2.2.2	Errors in the contract bills
2.3	Discrepancy in contract documents
3	Contract sum adjustments
6.1.3	Divergence between contract documents and statutory requirements
6.1.4.3	Emergency in complying with statutory requirements
6.2	Fees legally demandable under Act of Parliament
7	Levels and setting out
8.3	Opening up the works and testing
9.2	Royalties and patent rights
13	Variations
17.2, 17.3	Defects, shrinkages and other faults
21.2.3	Insurance payments under clause 21.2 by the contractor
22B.2	Contractor insuring if employer defaults
22C.3	Contractor insuring if employer defaults
26.5	Loss and/or expense
28.2.2.2	Work begun but not completed at date of determination
30.6	Final adjustment of contract sum
32.3	Works required after outbreak of hostilities
33.1.4	Removal of debris and protective work after war damage
34.3.3	Loss and/or expense due to antiquities
35.24.7	Renomination of sub-contractor
36.3.2	Expense in obtaining goods from a nominated supplier
38, 39, 40	Fluctuations

Figure 13.2   Adjustment of the contract sum under JCT Standard Form of Building Contract 1980.

carefully considered and a positive decision should be made that the matters referred to in the clause have been dealt with.[11]

Architects should not leave everything to the quantity surveyor; they should check through the material provided by the contractor. Although it is probably inappropriate for architects to attempt the kind of financial reconciliations which are in the province of the quantity surveyor, architects can usefully see what sort of information has been sent by the contractor and the work categories concerned. Architects who do this may spot errors which the quantity surveyor has missed because the quantity surveyor was not so closely involved with the carrying out of the work. Needless to say, the quantity surveyor must have a full set of all the instructions issued by the architect during the course of the project. Included should be not only the standard architect's instruction forms, but also any instruction given by the architect in any other way.

If the contract is small and no quantity surveyor has been engaged, the architect will be responsible for checking the account in detail. All invoices of sub-contractors and suppliers should be requested and they should be checked against entries in the account and the amounts allowed in the contract. All extra items should be authorized by architect's instructions, and where there is no contractually precise method of valuation set down, care should be taken that prices are reasonable. The mathematics of the account must be finally checked.

When the final account has been sent to the contractor, and hopefully agreed, it should be sent to the employer. It is usually best to do this in a simplified version. The employer, of course, has the right to see the full final account and any other papers, but unless the employer has some professional expertise, a simple version will be appreciated. It is appropriate for the architect to prepare the simple version. It should not miss out anything important nor attempt to whitewash over difficulties. An example is shown in Figure 13.3. Where architects are dealing with local authorities or companies who have their own technical staff, they will almost certainly require the full accounts to be submitted and they will equally certainly have a great many queries which must be answered.

The architect should have kept the employer up to date throughout the contract with the assistance of the quantity surveyor. It should have been made clear that changes from the agreed scheme will inevitably result in extra cost. Any instructions from the employer to the architect should be confirmed in writing by the architect so that at final account stage there is no doubt about which costs have been incurred by the employer. Architects should never give instructions to the contractor which involve variations and extra cost unless so

Contract sum	£
Deduct contingencies	
Add sundry additional works (brief details)	
Deduct [or *Add*] adjustment of PC and provisional sums	
Deduct [or *Add*] adjustment of measured work	
Add fluctuations	
Add amount ascertained for loss and expense	
Final amount	

Figure 13.3   Statement of final account to client.

instructed by the employer. It sometimes happens that, towards the end of the contract, the architect may make savings which could usefully be spent on improving some aspect of the building. In such instances, the architect may never instruct the contractor without first seeking appropriate authorization from the employer.

Architects should always keep in mind that no matter how experienced the employer nor how firm his or her views, it is for the architect alone, assisted by the quantity surveyor, to carry out the function of settling the final account. It is helpful if the contractor agrees the figure, but if not and if the architect and quantity surveyor are of one mind on the matter, they should simply inform the employer that there has been no agreement with the contractor. It is always open to the employer to come to some special agreement with the contractor as two parties to the contract. This has nothing to do with the architect and the quantity surveyor.

13.5 *Final certificate*

There is a great deal of mythology about the final certificate. At one time, when the architect issued the final certificate, it was a statement that the whole of the works were free from patent (readily apparent) defects and complete in all respects in accordance with the contract. It is many years since that was the case under the provisions of any building contract but the idea still persists, sadly among many architects who ought to know better.

The only thing which can be said of the final certificate under all building contracts is that after the architect has issued the final certificate, he or she has no further powers under the contract. The architect, for example, cannot then issue further extensions of time.[12]

Some forms of contract make the issue of the final certificate conclusive about certain things. Other forms state that it is conclusive about nothing, not even the amount finally due. The final certificate under the JCT Agreement for Minor Building Works (MW 80) is an example of the latter category. At the other extreme, JCT 80 makes the final certificate conclusive in four instances. JCT 81 (With Contractor's Design), JCT 87 (Management Contract) and IFC 84 (Intermediate Form) have similar wordings. When the final certificate is said to be 'conclusive' what is meant is that if neither party has entered into litigation or arbitration before the issue of the certificate nor so enters within a stipulated period (usually 28 days) after its issue, the certificate is conclusive (i.e. unchallengeable) evidence in any such proceedings in regard to stipulated matters. Thus, if a final certificate is said to be conclusive in regard to the amount of the final sum certified, it will not prevent an aggrieved party from seeking satisfaction through the courts or by way of arbitration if the sum is considered to be wrong.[13] However, in court, the other party has simply to produce the final certificate for the matter to be at an end. Certificates under JCT 80, JCT 81, JCT 87 and IFC 84 are conclusive in respect of the following.

- *That where the quality of materials and standards of workmanship are to be to the reasonable satisfaction of the architect, the architect is so satisfied.* This refers back to an early clause (2.1 in JCT 80) stating the contractor's obligations, and it is a failure to realize what this means which has given rise to many misconceptions. Part of the contractor's obligations is to ensure that if the architect has stated that certain things are to be to the architect's satisfaction, such things *are* to his or her satisfaction. Note that the architect must first have stated (presumably in the specification or in the bills of quantity) that certain things are to be to the architect's satisfaction. This may have been done by stating that specified items must be 'approved' or 'to the architect's satisfaction' or some other form of words to the same effect. The danger is that when the final certificate is issued, it is conclusive evidence that the architect is satisfied with any matters which are so specified whether or not the architect has in fact specifically expressed approval or even looked at the item in question. It will readily be appreciated that to insert some such phrase as 'All workmanship and material unless otherwise stated, must be to the architect's satisfaction' is opening the door to the blanket conclusivity of the final certificate again. It should be noted that, at the time of writing some doubt has been thrown on this view by the case of *Colbart v. Kumar* (1992)[14] which has been before the courts. Although concerned with IFC 84, much of the basis of the decision appears to apply equally to JCT 80 (but not JCT 81). The court held that reference was not simply to specific materials and workmanship noted in the contract, but applied to all such materials and workmanship where approval was something inherently for the opinion of the architect. Prudent architects will act as if all matters are to be to their reasonable satisfaction.

- *All the provisions of the contract requiring adjustment of the contract sum have been complied with.* The mechanics of this were covered in section 13.4, but the final certificate is conclusive evidence that all necessary adjustments have been properly carried out. Claims by the contractor, after the appropriate period has elapsed from issue of the certificate, that the figures are wrong will be fruitless. The only exceptions are if there has been accidental inclusion or omission of work or materials or if there is an obvious arithmetical error.

- *All due extensions of time have been given.* This is to prevent the contractor raising the question after the final certificate when the employer may have deducted liquidated damages and all financial matters appear to have been settled.

- *That reimbursement of loss and/or expense is in final settlement of all contractor's claims in respect of clause 26 matters whether the claims are for breach of contract, duty of care, statutory duty or otherwise.* This is a very widely drawn clause intended principally, like the previous clause, to ensure that the final certificate really does spell the end of the financial road. The conclusivity is effective only in respect of the clause 26 matters. It will not operate to prevent the contractor from making claims in regard to breaches of contract outside this parameter.

It was common, in former times, for architects to be so concerned about the conclusiveness of the final certificate that they often neglected to issue a final certificate at all, leaving a minute sum of money outstanding in the knowledge that the contractor would not seek arbitration in respect of such a small amount. Something of the same attitude is not uncommon even today. Certainly, under JCT forms, it is misconceived. It will be seen from the list above that, provided the architect has not left anything to his or her satisfaction, the employer has much to gain from the issue of the final certificate which will effectively end most arguments about sums due. Contractors must either issue notice of arbitration or a writ within the

Issued by: address:		**Final Certificate**
Employer: address:	Serial no:	A 071340
	Job reference:	
Contractor: address:	Issue date:	
	Contract sum:	
Works: situated at:		

Contract dated:

> Original to Employer

This Final Certificate is issued under the terms of the above-mentioned Contract.

The Contract Sum adjusted as necessary is . . . . £

The total amount previously certified for payment to the Contractor is . . . . £

The difference between the above-stated amounts is . . . . £

I/We hereby certify the sum of (in words)

_____

_____

_____

as a **balance due:**

*Delete as appropriate

*to the Contractor from the Employer.

*to the Employer from the Contractor.

All amounts are exclusive of VAT

To be signed by or for the issuer named above

Signed _____

The terms of the Contract provide that, subject to any amounts properly deductible by the Employer, the said balance shall be a debt payable from the one to the other as from the

[1] Delete as appropriate. See cover notes for provision in particular contract.

[1] 14th / 21st / 28th day after the date of this Certificate.

[2] Relevant only if clause 1A of JCT 80 VAT Agreement, clause A1-1 of IFC 84 Supplemental Conditions or clause B1-1 of MW 80 Supplementary Memorandum applies. Delete if not applicable.

[2] The Contractor has given notice that the rate of VAT chargeable on the supply of goods and services to which the Contract relates is _____ %

[2] _____ % of the amount certified above is . . . . £

[2] Total of balance due and VAT amount (for information) . . . . £

This is not a Tax Invoice

F852 for JCT 80 / IFC 84 / MW 80

© RIBA Publications Ltd 1990

Figure 13.4 Final certificate (courtesy RIBA Publications Ltd).

stipulated time if they disagree. An example of a final certificate is shown in Figure 13.4.

13.6 Feedback

This is a most important stage of the building process. One of the most valuable references is an architect's own experience. Memory grows dim, however, and often it confuses facts. Records of projects become increasingly valuable as the numbers of projects completed increase.

At the end of each project a routine should be established to extract the maximum amount of useful information. Ideally, records should be building up during the running of the project. In practice, everyone connected with the project will be so busy during the construction process that they will put off doing anything which does not seem to be urgent. An architect does not simply come to a conclusion on one scheme and then the following day start work on another. The reality is that work on one project overlaps work on another. Depending on size, an architect may well be working on several different schemes at once. Finding time to carry out a feedback and appraisal exercise is not usually a priority. It has to be done, however, if the practice is to develop.

If all parties can be gathered around the table for an appraisal session at the end so much the better. Theoretically, all parties are terribly frank with each other and the contractor takes part. There is no doubt that such a session would be very useful, but the chances of achieving it are remote. By the end of the project, all parties probably know what they think of each other. They may not be on speaking terms at that stage and quite possibly, though regrettably, arbitration or litigation may be in the air.

Architects can produce quite a lot of useful feedback information simply by consulting the files and by spending an afternoon going through a prepared agenda and discussing among the design team within the architects' office just what was done and whether it could have been done in a more effective way. It is important that the discussion is carefully structured or it will achieve nothing. The first thing in preparation is to record the key dates and other information. Some suggested items, but by no means an exhaustive list, may be as follows:

- Dates of commencement of each Plan of Work stage: when was the first contact with the client? When were outline proposals started? When were they finished?

- Projected and actual dates for commencement and completion of the contract on site.
- The cost history. Estimates of cost from inception until tender stage, then accepted tender price, contract sum and final certificate figure.
- Project type, construction system, services.
- Procurement method and form of contract, amendments.

This is a useful starting point for discussion which should attempt to answer the question why? in relation to each item. Other matters which should be examined are:

- Drawings preparation and issue.
- Architect's instructions, content, pricing, reasons for issue.
- Site meetings and minutes.
- Cost control.
- Claims.
- Communications within the design team, to the client and to the contractor.
- Client's brief compared to finished building compared to building in use.
- Appropriateness of materials including reviews at set time periods.
- Appropriateness of details including reviews at set time periods.
- Areas where improvements can be made.

Some architects consider that the client should be involved in the process and a questionnaire can be sent inviting comment on specific issues. Others think that to do so would be inviting trouble, rather like asking the client to consider whether it is appropriate to serve a writ. That is perhaps to take a rather gloomy view. The client should appreciate that the architect is simply concerned to give a good service and always anxious to improve. Whether the client is involved or not, it is certain that architects will get much out of a thorough feedback exercise. Among other things, it promotes the questioning of long-established but possibly ineffectual practices. Many architects would be astounded to realize just how many times they have issued revised versions of certain drawings, just how long it took them to provide the answer to certain queries from the contractor, and just how many people-hours were spent on site meetings.

One final point: the feedback exercise is intended to help all concerned. It is not intended to be a witch-hunt to discover the culprit behind failed details or exceeded cost targets. If it is used as a method of apportioning blame by an office, there will only ever be the one exercise.

References

(1) *Davis Contractors Ltd* v. *Fareham UDC* [1956] 2 All ER 145.
(2) *F. Treliving & Co. Ltd* v. *Simplex Time Recorder Co. (UK) Ltd* (1981) Unreported.
(3) See the courts' views in *London Borough of Hounslow* v. *Twickenham Garden Developments Ltd* (1970) 7 BLR 81 and *Greater London Council* v. *Cleveland Bridge & Engineering Co. Ltd* (1986) 8 Con LR 30.
(4) *J.M. Hill and Sons Ltd.* v. *London Borough of Camden* (1980) 18 BLR 31.
(5) *London Borough of Hounslow* v. *Twickenham Garden Developments Ltd* (1970) 7 BLR 81.
(6) *Wraight Ltd* v. *P.H. & T. (Holdings) Ltd* (1968) 13 BLR 26.
(7) For a full discussion of determination see Powell-Smith, V. & Sims, J. (1985) *Determination and Suspension of Construction Contracts*, Collins.
(8) Lord Justice Salmon, *Westminster Corporation* v. *J. Jarvis & Sons Ltd* (1970) 7 BLR 64.
(9) *H.M. Neville (Sunblest) Ltd* v. *Wm. Press & Son Ltd* (1981) 20 BLR 78.
(10) *William Tomkinson and Sons Ltd* v. *The Parochial Church Council of St Michael's and Others* (1990) 6 Const LJ 319.
(11) For further lists of this kind relating to JCT 80 and other standard forms of contract reference can be made to Powell-Smith, V. and Chappell, D. (1990) *Building Contracts Compared and Tabulated*, 2nd edn, Legal Studies & Services (Publishing) Ltd.
(12) *A. Bell & Son (Paddington) Ltd* v. *CBF Residential Care and Housing Association* (1989) 46 BLR 102.
(13) *P. & M. Kay Ltd* v. *Hosier & Dickinson Ltd* (1972) 10 BLR 126.
(14) Unreported.

Part 3

General Office Matters

Chapter 14

Management Principles

14.1 Objectives

There are two kinds of objectives: the objectives of the firm and the objectives of the individual. As a rough guide, the most successful firms are those in which the objectives of the firm and its employees most nearly correspond, because they can all go forward together without jostling for advantage.

The objectives of an architectural practice might well be to enjoy and to produce fine architecture, contribute to the environment, and make a reasonable profit. The architects in the practice will have joined because they have similar objectives and they are also, perhaps, looking for career advancement. A good manager will ensure that these personal goals are capable of satisfaction within the overall framework of the practice objectives.

Many large organizations have problems, because the members of staff have rather different objectives from those of the organization. It is not uncommon to encounter the kind of individual who considers that his or her objective is achieved if the pile of papers in the 'in' tray can be transferred to the 'out' tray by the end of the day. In the context of that company, the objective may be valid, but everyone should ask the question, 'Is what I am doing assisting in achieving the objectives of the organization?' Sometimes it is difficult to see how particular tasks are helping to achieve objectives. In such cases, the employee should ask the manager for an explanation (see section 14.5 below).

Objectives, of course, both for individuals and for organizations are both long- and short-term. A short-term objective for a practice might be to complete a particular object. In the shorter term, completing a stage, such as the client's acceptance of outline proposals, may be crucial. Longer-term objectives are probably associated with such things as expansion, specialization, or movement to better premises. The longer-term objectives can only be achieved if the shorter-term objectives are secured first. Personal objectives have similar structures.

Achieving objectives can involve admitting mistakes – indeed must do so. Whoever first decided that it was a weakness to admit mistakes was very misguided. Everyone makes mistakes and it is only by acknowledging a mistake that progress can be made. For example, it is essential to know how to put a cost on a project so that appropriate fees can be charged (see Chapter 16, section 16.4). In order to achieve this objective, careful historical records must be kept to indicate just how well the practice's own cost and time targets are achieved. Staff time sheets are an essential part of these records. It is not unknown, however, for some architects to put down a proportion of their time to other work when they begin to see that they are in danger of exceeding the budgeted figures. The only clear result is that the practice builds up a set of unreliable records and it will continue to underestimate time periods, project after project, until the laying-off of time against other projects ceases.

Every practice should have a policy of admitting mistakes, including those of the partners, so that something can be done about them. Once a mistake is admitted, there should be commiserations all round; then the mistake should be forgotten and the concentration should be on objectives. Every architect should learn to take decisions on the basis of the practice objectives; if a mistake is made, an admission will save much time and files of internal memos. Architectural practices who try this approach experience teamwork, often for the first time. There really is no place for a practice with an infallible sole principal and six frightened assistants. Common objectives eliminate this problem.

Even if the objectives are clear, the best route towards them may be difficult to find. However, if the objectives are not defined, everyone will be setting off in different directions.

14.2 *Leadership*

Architects are called upon to practice leadership in different ways. In a small way, it is required in chairing a meeting. A principal, partner or director has to exercise leadership. If the office is large enough, a group leader is aptly named.

In the long run, the best leaders are low profile. There is much inconsequential verbiage written about leadership. A good leader really has only two functions:

- To decide objectives for those being led.
- To set the pace.

The importance of objectives has already been discussed. Deciding objectives is a clear function, if difficult to carry out. Setting the pace is more complex. How a leader sets the pace depends on many factors including the objective to be achieved, the circumstances, the personalities of others and, not least, the personality of the leader. This is what is sometimes referred to as *leadership style*. Some architects, with large outgoing personalities, like to lead from the front, building up an office image which is essentially their own image. This is not necessarily or even usually, effective. It results in a practice which is essentially one person plus helpers.

The real art of leadership is to appear to be following: hence the phrase 'leading from behind'. A good partner will ensure that everything is in place to make it as easy as possible for project architects to carry out their tasks. A good leader must also be a good facilitator, prepared to do the things which would distract the architects from their essential tasks. Good leaders put forward their ideas in such a way that the project architects think the ideas are their own. The true measure of successful leadership is the performance of the leader's staff.

14.3 Communications

Communication is the most vital aspect of management. Ineffective communication will render the most splendid ideas useless. Communication is a two-way process. Many of the problems associated with building contracts result from failure on both sides. The general principle is that if a message is misunderstood, it is the fault of the originator. It is in the nature of the profession that architects can only get their concepts realized if they communicate them effectively. So architects must be excellent communicators. Good communication involves:

- Clarity.
- Certainty.
- Brevity.
- Comprehensiveness.

14.3.1 Clarity

Architects should look at their drawings, specifications, reports and letters as though they were the recipients. Many architectural drawings seem to need second sight to decipher. Preparing production information (see Chapter 10, section 10.1) requires the application of a mind which, having analysed the problem, can synthesize the solution to produce easily digestible information. It is not easy. Eccentric and flamboyant drawing styles do not help matters.

14.3.2 Certainty

This quality goes arm in arm with clarity although there is a distinction. When the architect communicates with the contractor there should be only one interpretation possible. Very often, a message which may be a model of clarity in itself may be capable of two meanings when read in context with other messages or with the project as a whole. The architect should take care, therefore, that any communication, drawn, written or spoken, is incapable of misinterpretation. The message may be uncertain in itself, of course, as in such phrases as 'as soon as possible', 'when convenient', or 'good quality'. Even if a time period is specified uncertainty may still exist, as in 'You have only seven days to respond'. Does that mean seven days from the date, or from the receipt of the letter, or seven days from some other date which may be implied when the phrase is read in context with the rest of the letter?

14.3.3 Brevity

It is difficult to be brief. Extra words are added to a sentence or clause and extra lines are added to a drawing to make the meaning clearer. Often, they make the meaning more obscure. This is partly because it is more difficult to read. To be brief in a written document involves writing out the message as clearly, certainly and briefly as possible, then carefully editing out the superfluous, doing some re-arranging, then writing it out again. It will take the architect longer to prepare the document, but it should save time in the long term, because the contractor should be able to act on the document without any, or too many, questions.

14.3.4 Comprehensiveness

It is very common to assume that a recipient knows more than is actually the case. The golden rule is to assume that the recipient knows very little and proceed accordingly. This will involve more time in preparation, but again it should save questioning time and it is also useful when drawings or other documents have to be consulted long after they were produced. Brief messages in the style of 'Got your message, and agree your suggestion' are unfortunately quite common. Their only merit is that they encapsulate an ignorance of three of these principles, thus turning the fourth (brevity) into another fault. Messages of this kind are not the hallmark of the busy executive architect, but careless almost to the point of negligence.

These principles hold good not only between architect and contractor, but between architect and fellow consultants and between the project architect and the other architects in a particular group. Regrettably, architects' drawings are not always good examples of communication documents. The eminent architect Sir Edwin Lutyens once said that a drawing should be like a letter to the builder telling him exactly what is required, not a pretty picture to impress an idiotic client. Not very complimentary to his clients, but very true for all that.

14.4 *Delegation*

It is common to hear architects say that the architect above them in seniority does not know how to delegate. Grumbles of this sort usually indicate that the architect in question insists on keeping an eye very firmly on everything that is going on. That architect, however, will probably say that since he or she takes the responsibility in the end, such close supervision is justified. This kind of response puts the cart before the horse. Delegation is a key function of management and the art of delegation is to know what to delegate, when and to whom. Of course the senior takes overall responsibility; that is one of the reasons for the larger salary cheque.

The rule is to delegate work to the least qualified/paid person who is capable of doing the work. It is important to understand the principle properly. It does not mean that work should always be delegated to the least paid or least qualified. The important criterion is that the person should be capable of doing the work. Therefore, if the quality required is of a very high order, it might well be that the person capable is actually the best qualified and highest paid. If there are three people who can do the work, the least qualified and least paid should be chosen. To do otherwise is to squander talent and money.

Delegation encourages people to take responsibility. Architects in control of staff may be reluctant to delegate because they think that the task will not be carried out properly. What they really mean is that it will not be carried out precisely in the way they would have tackled it. In fact it could be carried out with greater efficiency.

An example will make this clear. There may be a meeting scheduled at which an important client will meet the contractor to settle some crucial matters relating to a large contract. The senior architect may well feel an obligation to attend even though there is a very competent project architect dealing with that contract. The truth is that if the senior architect delegates the attendance at that meeting, the preparation for it and report after the meeting will receive the kind of attention the senior architect is unlikely to be able to give it. The senior architect should delegate attendance to the project architect (with reasonable notice) with the message that whatever he or she agrees will be backed. The project architect will appreciate the confidence and will spend long hours (not all of them office hours) in preparation to make sure of achieving the best possible outcome. The senior architect will be freed to do non-delegatable work.

An important rule is not to delegate work and then interfere. A manager who does that has lost his nerve. Architects in a position to delegate work should pick the right person and then demonstrate total confidence in the delegation. They will rarely be disappointed. If they are, it will usually reflect their bad judgement.

14.5 *Motivation*

Motivation is in two parts: motivation of self and motivation of others. Self-motivation is very complex. It may depend on the solving of a problem or the desire to improve an already satisfactory situation. The desire for such things as status, money, power, social position, security, happiness, acknowledgement and service falls in either or both of these categories. Without a strong motive, little is achieved. The current term for a person with a strong motivation is 'self-starter'. It describes the situation very well. Most professional activity is motivating for the participant: possibly none more so than architecture. It offers challenge and the opportunity to rise to the occasion.

An unmotivated architect will probably stay in the same office for the whole of a working life, maybe doing unrewarding work and progressing slowly, if at all, at the whim of others. If such a person changes offices or progresses more quickly, it will be as a reaction to some external pressure. To that kind of person, the professional challenges which motivate others may simply be depressing, particularly if they are beyond that architect's capabilities.

A self-starter will determine his or her goals in life, long- and short-term, and create the appropriate internal pressure required to attain the goals. In fact, the unmotivated architect noted above is not really unmotivated. It is just that the motive is not the accepted kind. It may be to drift along to retirement with the minimum of fuss because the architect in question has some extra-office activity to which work is just a necessary interruption. Self-motivation in this context, however, is generally taken to mean the ability of an individual to drive him or herself without the necessity for any external pressure.

The motivation of others is very difficult. The secret is to discover what the individual goals of team members are. The key motivating factors are generally seen as achievement, recognition and advancement. Whether an individual acts in particular circumstances depends largely upon whether the action is seen as resulting in the desired outcome. The art of motivation, therefore, is to let the individuals see that their actions are achieving the desired end. The carrot is more effective than the stick. The golden rule for motivating others can be summarized as follows:

- Find out what they want.
- Show them how to get it by doing what you want.
- Ensure they are not disappointed due to your fault.

Chapter 15

General Office Practice

15.1 Introduction

There are certain basic skills which every architect should have in addition to specific professional skills. This chapter addresses the basic office skills which are essential to everyone who works in the office environment. Architects are usually left to acquire these skills as part of the practice experience. That is not the best way of learning. All architects should have a thorough understanding of good office practice before they enter the office in which they are to work and in which very bad office practice may be the order of the day. What follows is simply an outline of the key areas in which the architect should be proficient in the office. Some are relevant only to architects; some are of wider application.

15.2 Telephone and facsimile (fax)

A telephone or a share of one is essential. If the architect is allowed the use of someone else's telephone, an extra entry of the user's name can be made in the telephone directory on payment of the appropriate fee. With the sophisticated telephone equipment available today it is now possible to choose any installation appropriate to the office ranging from a single line to any number of separate lines incorporating facilities for inter-office communication, two- or more-way conversations, recording machines for times when the telephone operator is not available, and a variety of other combinations.

Telephone calls should be made and answered promptly and should be kept as brief as possible. Lengthy conversations can prevent outside callers from communicating with the office and, besides causing delay and annoyance, may have unfortunate consequences. A competent telephone operator is a boon to any office, and can create a good impression with outside callers. Basic rules for good telephone management include never keeping anyone waiting, and keeping a record of all incoming calls and messages to be passed on to the persons unable for any reason to take the call. The advent of car and portable 'phones has helped to ensure that contacts are made as quickly as possible.

While the telephone has for many years provided a means of transmitting the spoken word, facsimile equipment now available provides a means of transmitting the written word or drawing. This latest aid to office practice should be used for urgent matters and not, as is so often the case, for transmitting letters or documents which could quite well have waited to be posted. Facsimile transmissions are now, under certain circumstances, accepted as legal documents[1] but it is usual, some would say essential, that they be followed up by the original copy sent by post or by hand for confirmation. Facsimile is particularly useful for transmitting site instructions and drawn information so that an immediate response can be made to enquiries emanating from the site. Again the temptation arising from the ease of use should be resisted.

15.3 *Letter writing*

The object of writing is to convey the ideas of one person to the mind of another, who is not present to be addressed orally, and at the same time to make a permanent record of the communication. Owing to the lack of expression of the face and inflexion of the voice, the writer must convey by his words alone the emphasis he requires and the tone in which he is writing. Words and phrases must therefore be carefully chosen.

Without going fully into the subject a few suggestions may be made:

- Be sure that the points made are clear.
- Be as brief and simple as possible. Do not use two words where one will do. Avoid long words and roundabout phraseology.
- Start a new paragraph with each new point but do not split up the point into more than one paragraph.
- If a long letter develops, consider whether it is not better to put the matter in the form of a schedule or a report, with a short covering letter only.
- Be sure to write with the reader in mind. Do not use technical terms when writing to a non-technical client when a little thought would show that such terms would not be understood.
- Avoid commercial clichés, journalese, Americanisms and slang.
- Avoid spelling mistakes and bad grammar. They give a poor impression to the reader.

- Avoid the impersonal. 'It is regretted' means nothing. Regret is a personal sentiment; if regret is felt, say 'I regret' or 'We regret'. It may or may not be prudent to say 'the Minister, the Board, the Directors regret'.
- Be definite. Do not say 'this appears to be correct'. If satisfied that it is correct, say so.
- Standard reference books are available which can prove useful in ensuring that well-written letters are sent out.[2]

Some care should be taken over forms of address. Traditionally gentlemen have been addressed as Esquire and ladies as Mrs or Miss. Today the mode of address is more often Mr, Mrs, Miss or Ms. Whatever form is adopted qualifications and decorations should not be forgotten. When opening a letter the usual form is 'Dear Sir' or 'Madam' and the ending 'Yours faithfully'. Depending how well the parties know each other these may become less formal but in a business letter it is unwise to go beyond Mr, Mrs or Miss. Remember that letters sometimes end up in court and too much familiarity may come to be regretted.

15.4 *Reports*

The architect may be specifically asked to write a report, or may decide to do so when a letter looks like becoming long-winded. The art of report writing is a subject on its own but a few words of guidance are offered by way of assistance.

- Remember who is going to read the report. If it is to be a technical person then technical phraseology is quite acceptable; the reader will understand what is being said. If the reader is to be a non-technical person or a lay committee, they will be completely at sea unless the report is written in language they can understand.

- Plan the structure of the report. There is nothing worse than a report which is clearly the thoughts of the author just as they have arisen, put down on paper without any thought as to a logical order.

- A report should start with an Introduction setting out the subject matter and, if appropriate, who the writer is and his or her qualifications. Then follows the body of the report: it is most logical and effective to note the facts first before going on to matters of opinion. The report ends with a conclusion. Do not forget to sign and date (including the year) the document.

- Adopt a consistent and simple system of numbering. For example

1.00 *Introduction*
1.01 My name is . . . etc., etc.
1.02 I am asked to report on . . . etc., etc.

2.00 *Extensions of time*
2.01 Extensions of time have been granted as follows:

- Take care with the English, the punctuation and the spelling. A good report reads well; bad English, poor punctuation and a plethora of wrongly spelled words give the worst possible impression.

- Report on that which has been asked for. Cut out all unnecessary verbiage; it may add to the bulk of the report, but it adds little or nothing to the content. Better a short, pithy report than a long rambling version, which runs the risk of boring the reader and never being read.

- Read over the final version very carefully; much may hinge on your efforts.

There are several useful books available on the subject of report writing.[3]

15.5 *Filing*

15.5.1 Correspondence and reports

Once the letters and reports have been written, the office copies together with letters, reports, facsimiles etc received have to be filed.

The secret of good filing is to ensure that any document can be found quickly. Much time and cost to say nothing of frustration and temper can be expended in trying to trace a wrongly filed document.

The complexity of the filing will depend largely on the complexity of the project. A simple project will probably warrant a single file. More complicated ones may require a series of files for, say, client, contractor, quantity surveyor, engineer etc. Other files will be required for special matters such as partners' personal file, insurances and professional bodies.

As well as letters, the files can contain such things as reports, telephone messages, and internal memos. These will help to complete the history of the project and may prove invaluable later on, particularly in legal matters where the side with the best records is going to be at a great advantage.

Typical files for a medium- to large-sized project might be:

- Correspondence: Client, funder etc.
- Correspondence: Statutory authorities, planning, building control.
- Correspondence: Consultant quantity surveyor.
- Correspondence: Contractor.
- Correspondence: Prospective nominated sub-contractors.
- Correspondence: Suppliers, manufacturers.
- Heating and ventilating.
- Electricity.
- Structural.
- Landscaping.
- Clerk of works' reports.
- Site meetings.
- Architect's instructions.
- Certificates, valuations, financial reports.

15.5.2 Drawings

Drawings in current use should be filed flat in plan-chests or vertically in cabinets.[4] They should not be folded or rolled. Negatives, office prints and specialists' drawings should, if possible, be kept separate. Rough sketches which are probably prepared on pieces of paper of various size can, however, be folded and kept in large paper envelopes or box files.

When a drawing has been revised, the out-of-date print should be clearly marked 'superseded' and filed separately or else destroyed. Large paper envelopes can be procured for filing such drawings which can, of course, be folded if necessary. All drawings, cabinets, box files or envelopes which are used for storing drawings should be marked with the appropriate job number or reference.

Drawings which are removed from the plan-chest should be returned as soon as possible, and in a large office it will be necessary to devise a form of register in which a record can be kept of any drawings which have been taken out with the names of the borrowers. In some large local authority and government offices the filing and registration of drawings are undertaken by a clerk who is solely responsible for ordering prints, loaning drawings and keeping them in safe custody.

For convenience, except in a very large office, the drawing cabinets will be kept in the drawing offices, so that quick reference can be made to drawings of current jobs. It should be part of the daily routine to put all drawings away at night; they should not be used as dust-sheets or for rough sketches.

When a job is finished the drawings should be brought up to date, removed from the drawing office and suitably filed. Unless a large amount of storage accommodation is available, only the negatives need be retained, as it will be more convenient to order new prints if they are subsequently required. Old prints can probably serve a more useful purpose as backing sheets or scrap paper!

Traditionally old negatives were best filed in metal tubes which were stacked in racks. A tube 150 mm in diameter will store about 200 drawings. An alternative method of storage was in large paper envelopes which have the advantage of storing the drawings flat. These envelopes can be stacked vertically or clamped with wooden strips on one edge and slung from a bar rather like a coat-hanger on a rail. An index should, of course, be kept of all old drawings in store.

However, with today's technology even the smallest business can easily microfilm important information. Saving as it does tremendous space and being easily catalogued and retrieved, microfilm is probably the best method for storage of architectural records.

15.5.3 Trade literature

See Chapter 5, section 5.2.1.

15.6 Office-based meetings

See Chapter 12, section 12.2.

15.7 Drawing office practice

Although many architects now produce drawings, if not exclusively at least mainly with the aid of computers (see section 15.8 below), most practices rely on hand drawing. Every architect should study the relevant British Standard on drawing practice.[5] Where, as in the building industry, clear communication is all important, there is no room for an architect who employs exceptionally personalized drawing techniques. Many of the mistakes which occur on a building site undoubtedly stem from a misreading of drawings, and any attempt to co-ordinate symbols, hatching and representational methods of all kinds is to be welcomed. In some cases, an exception may be made for drawings which are purely for the purpose of explaining the proposals to a client. It is not proposed to dwell especially on this type of drawing, because this is one thing which architects quickly learn to do very well.

Certain basic information must be included on every drawing:

- Firm's name.
- Address and telephone number.
- Project title.
- Drawing title.
- Drawing number with revision number and description if appropriate.
- Scale.
- Date drawn and dates of revisions if appropriate.
- Name or initials of draughtsman.
- North point on plans.

It is common for a practice to have a set of standard-sized drawing sheets pre-printed with the basic information and firm's logo if applicable. Where grid lines are used to position structural elements or for modular purposes, they should be carefully referenced. It is usual to use numbers along one axis and letters along the other. Vertical positioning is best done by levels referenced to a datum. Such horizontal and vertical references must be used consistently, not only by architects, but by consultants also.

If all parties creating or using the drawings stick to this system of referencing, the chance of errors due to ambiguous descriptions will be minimized and time will be saved. Thus the vague 'wall next to splayed abutment opposite general office on second floor' becomes more simply and accurately 'wall between refs R4 and 5 on floor level 10.600'. The 'general office' will be unidentifiable during building operations (and perhaps after practical completion) and what constitutes a 'splayed abutment' is anyone's guess.

Time and clarity are served if symbols are used to show such items as WCs, washbasins and kitchen units, rather than having them drawn out in meticulous detail.

Some offices adopt the practice of using standard details. This can be very useful for items which recur, such as access panels, cills, lintels, eaves, door frames and casings, windows and skirtings. Although the same standard details will not be suitable for every project, architects should resist the temptation to design a totally fresh detail for everything on every project, bearing in mind that standard details should evolve over the years to represent the very best detail for a particular situation which that office can produce.

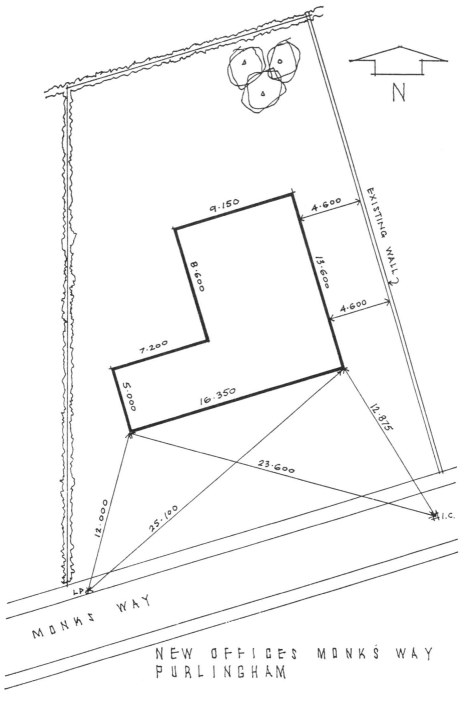

Figure 15.1 Setting-out plan. Original was drawn to scale of 1:200.

15.7.1 Dimensions

Dimensions form one of the most important items of instruction to the quantity surveyor and, later, to the contractor. Incorrect dimensions are a constant source of problems on site.

A block plan must give the overall dimensions of the building and the setting-out dimensions for all foundations and walls, together with their thicknesses. In practice, many architects do not understand what information a contractor needs in order to be able to set out properly on the site, yet most standard form contracts make the architect responsible for producing that information and probably such responsibility would be implied even if not expressed. The contractor needs to be able to locate at least one, and preferably two, base lines on site. To do that each point at the end of the base line must be securely fixed, by triangulation, from an already established known point (see Figure 15.1).

If a building has a steel or reinforced concrete frame, the setting out of the centre lines of stanchions should be shown on the foundation plan. The contours of the site should be shown and the levels of foundation bottoms, with positions of steps indicated. Levels should be referenced to an established datum. A key on the drawing should make clear the difference between existing and proposed levels. A simple system is to put each existing level in a small box.

Floor plans should show levels, detailed dimensions of rooms, corridors, thicknesses of walls and partitions, and widths of openings. Care must be taken that dimension lines are not capable of confusion with lines representing part of the building. It is usual to show the extremities of each dimension by a clear arrowhead, cross, dot or other symbol. Figures must be clearly written, particularly the stop separating the metres from decimal parts.

In a new building, the quantity surveyor and the contractor should have no doubt about the exact heights of and dimensions between walls in both directions of all rooms, including all recesses, cupboards formed by partitions, and passages. Where working between existing walls, it may be necessary to leave one of a series of dimensions to be verified on site, but all others should be given.

The finished floor and roof levels should be shown on the plans as well as on the sections, and it should be clear what allowance the contractor is to make for the difference between structural and finished surfaces. All doors and windows must be referenced so that they can be easily found in appropriate schedules.

Sections should be drawn through portions of the building where floor or roof levels vary, at the intersection of parts of the building, through staircases and any other places which are not shown elsewhere. To explain really difficult parts of the construction, isometric and planometric drawings should be used. The position at which sections are taken should be clearly marked on all floor plans. Floor levels and heights of rooms should be shown, and on 1:20 scale sections it is a good idea to incorporate a brick/block scale, so that the levels of lintel, cill, wallplate and floor bearings can be properly related to courses. It is also helpful if the materials in the larger sections are indicated by appropriate cross-hatching.

The elevations indicate the external appearance of the building, the different materials used and the finished ground levels against the building. They should also show the floor and basement levels dotted on and dimensioned, the levels of damp-proof courses, the opening portions of windows, external flashings and weatherings, vent pipes, rainwater pipes and the stepping to foundations. Windows and doors can be numbered on elevations as well. The common practice of never showing anything on an elevation that can be found elsewhere may save a little time, but it sacrifices the very useful extra check provided by the inclusion of such details.

It is sensible to include a note on each drawing that figured dimensions are to be followed in preference to scaled measurements. The need for figured dimensions can be reduced considerably if grids are used to represent, not only locations, but also standard dimensions. 300 mm is a common grid measurement.

15.7.2 Lettering

Neatness and clarity in lettering are essential; to achieve the best results, the letters should not be too large and should be evenly spaced out. The lettering should be kept as simple as possible and individual styling should be eschewed. Italic script, for example, can be very attractive in a letter and when carefully executed, but in the hands of many hard-pressed architects it can become neat but unreadable. Stencils can be used, but they are never so quick as good hand lettering. Another option is the typed adhesive strip (the typescript must be dense) or the rub-down transfers which can be used for other parts of the drawings as well as lettering.

15.7.3 Negatives

Drawings are prepared on translucent material, so that several copies can be obtained for distribution. They used to be prepared on linen; the authors have heard of the occasional practice where linen is still sometimes used, but its use is almost defunct. Nowadays tracing-paper or plastic film are normally used.

There are various grades of tracing paper, the thinner qualities generally being used for sketching and scribbling. It is worth while using a good stout quality of paper: not only will it stand up to frequent handling much better, but will also allow a lot of ink erasing without falling to pieces. Different types of plastic sheet are available which have a very good ink surface, are more transparent than stout tracing paper and better able to stand handling and erasing.

Negative prints can easily be obtained from the original negative. This process enables architects to have basic information reproduced on a number of additional negatives to allow working up into various forms. For example, the basic floor plans may be copied before notes and additional information are added so that separate drawings can be provided: e.g. for heating and electrical layouts, floor and ceiling designs and duct layouts.

A frequent problem is that when the contract documents are to be prepared, the architect finds that alterations and updatings have been made to the drawings on which the contractors tendered and which must therefore, or with agreed amendments, become the contract drawings. Problems of this kind can be avoided if a set of negatives is taken at tender stage especially for the purpose of preparing the contract documents in due course.

15.7.4 Reproduction

Drawings are still commonly reproduced by dyeline prints. Light-sensitive paper is used and the image turns black. Many practices have their own print machines which require relatively little skill to produce acceptable prints. In large urban areas, specialist printers will provide a service. Small drawings are often printed by photocopier which tends to give a clearer, crisper image than dyeline printing.

15.8 *Computer-aided design*

The number of offices using computers to assist in design is increasing, but there are few offices in which computers are the only design tool. The reason is probably because all computer-aided design (CAD) takes time and application to master. Even when mastered (and some systems are easier than others) it can be a relatively slow process.

The only way to learn to use CAD and to understand the possibilities is to sit at the computer and experiment after the initial period of instruction in the particular system. In the current state of the art, computers are not capable of thinking for themselves. The old adage 'rubbish in, rubbish out' is still true. The computer will only do what the operator instructs. It is unlikely that computers will replace the pencil-and-paper approach of the designing architect for some time to come. But computers are very useful for testing a design once produced. They can reveal the design in three dimensions from any chosen viewpoint, and they can be programmed to produce an impression of a walk through the building if sufficient data are input into the system.

If basic design information is put into the computer at an early stage, it can eventually form the basis of computer-draughted production information. Computer images can be combined with programs which allow investigation of acoustics, heating, daylighting levels and so on. There is also the benefit of being able to plot all services and reproduce perspective views to identify possible conflict areas.

CAD is moving forward very quickly and highly sophisticated software enables full interrogation of designs at an early stage. No architect can afford to ignore these developments.

15.9 Presentation

The way in which architects choose to present proposals to clients is largely a matter of personal choice. The truth is that whatever works is right. A client's capability to understand a scheme should never be overestimated. Many otherwise highly intelligent people find difficulty in understanding plans, sections and elevations, which is why models and perspectives are so popular. It is useful for architects to get into the habit of producing working models. Models which clearly explain the scheme at the stage it has reached are worth any number of drawings to a client.

When making a presentation to a client, a model should be the basis so that the client can quickly get an idea of the scheme. Then plans can be used to elaborate, and freely drawn perspectives used to show what it will actually look like. Sections and elevations are little use to a client. A building never looks like its elevations, and sections are too complex for the average client to understand. It is easier to make a quick sectional model to explain any complex parts of the building, and many times more effective.

Plans should be clearly drawn with the room name printed in each room. The use of a key at the side of the drawing together with a number in each room can be irritating. It is helpful to include a drawn scale on the drawing and also one or two dimensions. Any part of the building which is especially important or which needs particular consideration should be drawn out to a larger scale and a separate model prepared if possible.

Some architects produce highly intricate drawings and involved renderings to impress the client. The client may well be impressed, but also confused. If the client fails to understand the drawing, approval may be given for something which may be a source of disappointment and aggravation when built.

15.10 *Work programming*

Programming of any kind is a difficult business. Programming a project in an office is complex because there are so many imponderables. Yet there is a need to programme such work, otherwise when the client asks, 'Will it be ready to go out to tender in two months?' the architect has no way of answering.

The basis for planning any project should be the RIBA Plan of Work. The stages usefully split up the work to be done. The next step is probably to decide whether the project deserves one, two or more people working on it for any or all of the stages. For example, it is quite possible that a project may need only one person in the early stages and expand to require more people at stage E: but how many people, and for how long?

The only safe way of getting to this answer is to consult historical records and look at the fees. In most cases, the fee will depend on how long the architect estimates involvement. Every office should have time sheets for this very purpose. Only by looking at the time needed to carry out a comparable project can an estimate of future time requirements be formulated after adjustment to take account of any differences. Work programming is a serious matter; failure can result in disaster for the practice. All members of staff, including partners, must realize that the accurate completion of current time sheets is essential.

References

(1) *Hastie & Jenkerson* v. *McMahon* (1990) *The Times* 3 April 1990.
(2) *Concise Oxford Dictionary* (1990) 8th edn, Oxford University Press.

Gowers, E. (1986) *The Complete Plain Words*, 3rd edn (rev. S. Greenbaum & J. Whitcut), HMSO, London.

Fowler (1983) *Dictionary of Modern English Usage*, 2 edn, Oxford University Press.

Black, A. & C. (1981) *Titles and Forms of Address*, 19th edn.

Chappell, D. (1989) *Contractual Correspondence for Architects*, 2nd edn, Legal Studies & Services (Publishing).

(3) Sidney, E. (1969) *Business Report Writing*, London Business Publishers.

Hamilton, A. (1989) *Writing Matters*, RIBA Publications Ltd.

Chappell, D. (1989) *Report Writing for Architects*, 2nd edn, Legal Studies & Services (Publishing) Ltd.

(4) BS 3437: *Equipment for filing drawings*.

(5) BS 1192 (1987) *Construction drawing practice*.

Chapter 16

Finance

16.1 Introduction

Though the subject of bookkeeping is no longer taught as a subject generally, it has been re-introduced on a much wider basis under the heading of finance and accountancy, and is now part of most undergraduate courses. It is a practical form of economics and as such is important to the architect in general. A prospective principal in private practice will need at least an elementary understanding of the subject in order to keep accounts properly. An accountant will be needed for the annual audit, and at the same time can advise on taxation matters and any difficulties which are being experienced. Textbooks on the subject are apt to concern themselves with the accounts of trading firms and their purchases and sales, rather than with those of a professional man (see Additional reading).

16.2 Accountancy

Accountancy is a service which gathers together all of the data and facts about a company and presents them in financial terms. The methods used for preparation and interpretation of these accounts can be broadly described as financial analysis. The use to which the data is put is financial management.

The primary purpose of keeping accounts is to provide a record of all the financial transactions of the firm or company concerned, and to establish whether or not the firm is working at a profit. These records include:

- Details of the firm's or company's assets.
- The liabilities of the firm or company (the difference between this and the assets is its capital position).
- Increases or decreases in the capital, which can then readily be assessed.

These accounts can then be used:

- When the firm or company requires a loan from the bank.
- Where someone is interested in purchasing the business.
- As a proof of financial stability where extended credit is required from a supplier.

16.3 *Capital*

An architect starting in business must find the capital necessary to purchase furniture and stationery, pay rents and other expenses, as well as be able to draw something to live on. If already employing staff then there will be salaries to be paid somewhat ahead of receiving the fees for work completed. There may already be savings in the bank or ability to mortgage (or more likely remortgage) a house or other securities, or the assistance may be sought from relatives. These may be able to supply that much-needed commodity of cash or act as guarantors at the bank. The bank will normally acquiesce if security is available, but otherwise it may not be quite so ready to oblige. If a suggestion on the last matter may be made, it is that boldness and confidence, when backed by honesty, will pay.

In a properly run business, capital is always represented by assets. The money is not borrowed to spend, but to use. Starting with, say, £16 000 capital, after six months there may be only £5 000 in the bank. The position is now as follows:

Payments		*Receipts and assets*	
Furniture	6 000	Fees received	22 000
Salaries etc.	20 000	Fees due	8 000
Consumables	2 000	Work in hand: proportion	
Rent	4 000	of fees due	4 000
	32 000	Value of furniture	3,000
Balance	5 000		£37 000
	£37 000		

The initial capital injection of £16 000 which was available is excluded. If the business ceased it would show a £5 000 gross profit, and the amount of cash now left in the bank is £6 000 (£22 000 fees + £16 000 capital –£32 000 expenditure). The reduction in value of the furniture is due to depreciation and will be explained later. As the fees are received the bank balance will be increased, but further payments for salaries, etc., will drain it again. The case is rather like the problems that used to occur in arithmetic examinations about a bath being filled at so many gallons and being emptied at so many gallons per hour. The architect must for his or her own comfort see that there is plenty of water in the bath, and that it does not run away when no one is looking.

The amount of capital required must, of course, depend upon the prospective volume of work and the consequent number of staff. There are several ways in which a firm can supplement its finances, both in the long and short term. The most common way is by borrowing from a bank on an overdraft facility. The interest rate charged will usually be 2–4% above the bank rate, i.e. the rate at which the Bank of England will lend money for short periods of time to high-security customers.

The lender of short-term finance is interested both in the security of the capital and the interest to be paid, both of which may be at risk. Finance may be required to smooth out the strains on cash flow resulting perhaps from rapid fluctuations in workload and the payment for professional services.

It is unlikely that a professional practice will have need for a long-term loan, other than perhaps for a mortage on some premises. The purchase of 'machinery' such as photocopiers, word processors or computers is more likely to be a short-term proposition. Repayment of short-term loans is generally required within two years. The practice may, however, choose further to supplement its short-term financial needs by one or more of the following:

- *Hire purchase.* Under this system the company is able to enjoy the full use of the goods or equipment, without paying the full amount on delivery. This of course must be weighed against the higher total costs of these items.
- *Leasing.* The decision to buy or lease assets will depend on the overall planning and the projected cash flow. It has taxation advantages, and also the supplier or manufacter is prepared to maintain the goods or equipment for the full term of the lease. Sale and lease-back is a common form of freeing cash from fixed assets. Under this method the company who owns an asset can sell it to a financial institution and then lease it back at an agreed rate.

16.4 *Cash forecasting and budgeting*

The architect will need to have some expectations of how well the practice will do in financial terms and will need to prepare some sort of budget based upon projected income and expenditure. As the practice begins to grow, future projections can be based on previous established costs. If there is the intention to borrow money from a bank, then they are likely to insist upon a cash flow forecast for the ensuing six or twelve months. This laborious procedure is simplified if a computer spreadsheet is used, which allows for automatic reworkings of all subsequent numbers following an adjustment or correction. The following is a simple example of cash flow forecast.

A practice starts in business with a capital availability of £10 000. They have in addition approached the bank for a borrowing facility of £8 000. The bank has requested the first six months' trading forecast. Premises have been found and these will cost £250 per month inclusive of lighting, heating and cleaning. Equipment such as furniture will need to be purchased immediately, as will some stationery. This will need replenishing at regular intervals. It is intended to lease the cars and some fees will be payable to a solicitor. The total salaries bill is estimated to be around £5 000 per month. Fees for architectural work

	January	Feburary	March	April	May	June
Opening cash balance	0	2440	-3080	-8180	-6600	-2925
Capital introduction	10000	0	0	0	0	0
Fees received	0	0	500	7500	9000	500
Asset sales	0	0	0	0	200	0
Receipts	10000	0	500	7500	9200	500
Salaries	5000	5000	5000	5000	5000	5000
Equipment	1000	0	0	300	0	400
Stationery	350	0	0	150	0	0
Rent	250	250	250	250	250	250
Telephone/postage	10	20	100	20	25	125
Insurance	400	0	0	0	0	0
Cars	250	250	250	250	250	250
Legal/accountancy	300	0	0	0	0	0
Payments	7560	5520	5600	5920	5525	6025
Movement in cash	+2440	-5520	-5100	+1580	+3675	-5525
Closing cash balance	+2440	-3080	-8180	-6600	-2925	-8450
Borrowing facility	8000	8000	8000	8000	8000	8000
Additional needs	0	0	180	0	0	450

Figure 16.1 Example of cash flow forecast.

completed are a little slow in coming into the practice, and although these represent about £35 000, only £17 500 has been received to date. Some of the equipment purchased at the beginning will be replaced and this is shown as an asset sale in the month of May (Figure 16.1).

This set of cash outflows is typical of a starting up, when substantial sums are expended in advance of any fees being received. Provided that the practice is being run profitably this outflow will be reversed before too long. The practice will need to renegotiate its borrowing facility in the first six months of trading up to at least £8 500. Provided subsequent months indicate a constant cash recovery, then most banks would agree to such a top-up on the basis of this information.

16.5 *Depreciation*

Depreciation is the loss of value in an asset resulting from usage or age. Allowance for depreciation as an accounting practice is the stating of a figure which represents the lost value. The depreciation of the architect's assets is normally shown on the balance sheet and is a tax-deductible item. The amount to be included for depreciation can be calculated in several different ways (straight-line method, reducing-balance method, valuation method), all of which will provide a different set of figures from the same data. In practice there may be little relationship between the accounting amount for depreciation shown in the firm's books and the actual depreciation of the asset concerned. Allowing for depreciation is a simple enough matter when money values are more or less stable. In times of high inflation the true statement of profitability may be distorted, and the depreciation charged may be insufficient to replace the asset at the end of its life. Whatever method of calculating depreciation is chosen in calculating profit it must be remembered that the Inland Revenue have specific rules of their own.

16.6 *Profit and loss account*

The profit and loss account shows the results of trading over a certain period of time. It is prepared by transferring the balances of all revenue accounts remaining at the close of the financial year. It does not include capital or asset accounts which are itemized in the balance sheet. Income is the revenue derived from fees for the rendering of a service. The money received from the sale of a capital item will not appear in

Income		Expenditure	
Fees	28 500	Rent	4 000
		Salaries	20 000
		Insurances	2 000
		Fuel	1 000
		Profit before tax	1 500
	28 500		£28 500

Figure 16.2 Example of a simple profit and loss account.

the profit and loss account since this would wrongly inflate the profit, and a similar position governs expenditure. These items include the costs of operating the practice such as wages, insurance, fuel etc.

An excess of income over expenditure indicates a profit and the converse is therefore a loss. In order to measure the profitability of the individual sections of a practice, separate profit and loss accounts for each of the areas of work can be prepared, assuming that the fees and costs have been kept separate. The combination of each of these accounts will show an overall profit or loss.

The calculation of profit is one of the main objectives of the accounting function and the following are some of the reasons why the practice will need to show what its profits are:

- To compare them with the profits which they hoped to have made.
- To assist them to plan ahead.
- To help them to obtain a loan from the bank or other sources.
- To show to a prospective partner.
- To show to someone to whom they wish to sell the practice.
- For income tax purposes.

An example of a simple profit and loss account is shown in Figure 16.2.

16.7 Balance sheet

This is the most important statement which is prepared in connection with any business, whether it be a partnership or a company. All companies are required under the Companies Act 1985 to keep accounts and to file them annually with the Registrar of Companies so that they may be available for inspection by any interested party. This

Act requires companies to prepare a balance sheet, normally at the close of each financial year, which will show:

- All sums of money received and expended by the company.
- All purchases of goods by the company.
- The assets and liabilities of the company.

Professional practice partnerships should also present their accounts in this way for the sake of clarity. The accounts kept by the practice will only be regarded as accounts if they provide a true and fair view of the state of the business's affairs and explain its transactions. It should be borne in mind, however, that a balance sheet will reflect the peculiarities of the practice to which it relates. It may, therefore, be necessary to read between the lines in connection, for example, with the valuations put upon the assets. These could be valued at a nominal figure even though they may be in perfect working order, and consequently therefore have a considerably higher value in the market and to the firm itself. The whole question of the value of assets is therefore of great importance. A typical example of a balance sheet is shown in Figure 16.3.

A balance sheet is a statement of the firm's wealth. It also reveals the aggregate claims on that wealth by those lending funds to it, such as creditors and banks. The statement is in two halves, the left-hand side of which contains the assets and the right-hand side the liabilities. The two sides of this statement will, by definition, balance.

Assets		Liabilities	
Fixed assets		Capital	
Equivalent	23 650	Ordinary capital	28 000
Fixtures and fittings	8 250	General reserve	8 000
	31 900	Profit and loss account	4 000
Less depreciation	4 100		40 000
	27 800		
		Current liabilities	
Current assets		Trade creditors	1 500
Work in progress	4 300	Salaries	3 000
Debtors	14 800	Tax liability	9 000
Cash at bank	6 100		13 500
Cash in hand	500		
	25 700		
	£53 500		£53 500

Figure 16.3 Example of a typical balance sheet.

The various items which go together to make up a balance sheet are as follows.

16.7.1 Assets

The amounts shown on the left-hand side of the balance sheet are usually subdivided between fixed assets and current assets. The nature of the fixed assets will indicate whether or not they could be quickly released for cash and used elsewhere. The degree of flexibility in this investment is therefore very important. The depreciation included is for accounting purposes and may not therefore reflect the true value of this item. The term 'assets' covers the following:

- Intangible assets, which include goodwill, trademarks, licensing agreements usually at original cost, less any subsequent write-offs.
- Fixed assets, which include land and buildings, fixtures and fittings, equipment, motor vehicles, etc., shown at original cost (occasionally at a revaluation) less total depreciation written off to date.
- Current assets, which represent those items which can be quickly turned into cash, usually within a year. It includes cash, and trade debtors. It will also include payments made in advance.

16.7.2 Liabilities

These consist of money owing for goods supplied to the firm, and for expenses, and also loans made to the firm. It therefore includes capital of the various types, bank overdrafts, taxation provisions and trade creditors. Contingent liabilities do not form part of the total liabilities but will appear in the form of a note on the balance sheet as supplementary information.

16.7.3 Interpreting the balance sheet

The trade creditor balances which represent money owed for materials, etc., the trade debtors which represent money owing by customers for goods supplied, and work in progress, all help to reveal the trading position of the company. Generally the larger these relative amounts, the more business the company is doing. The debtors and creditors figures will usually represent the full amount without any allowance for discounts. Provision should also be made for the possibility of doubtful debts. The debtors figures should exceed the creditors figure if trading is good.

In order for any practice to function adequately it must be supplied with sufficient working capital. This is represented by the current assets. The working capital should preferably be obtained from within the business rather than from the bank, which may recall the loan at any time, and thus could cause difficulty or danger. Trade debtors may also be regarded as supporting the liquid cash position. Solvency is closely related to the cash position. A business becomes insolvent when the liabilities exceed the assets. The converse is not always true, since the assets may be fixed in the business and be of little value elsewhere. A safe test is to deduct the current liabilities from the current assets.

A deficiency in current assets indicates that a firm is likely to have difficulty in meeting its immediate liabilities and may be in danger of insolvency in that it cannot pay its debts. An excessively large amount of surplus current assets, especially in cash, will show that the firm is not usefully employing its capital. The excess will only be justified where the cash has been accumulated for some special purpose.

The figure of net worth indicates the capital employed in the business. It is necessary, however, to bear in mind the changing value of money in inflationary conditions. Static net worth will show that the practice is not growing. This could be due to a lack of profits. The net worth is therefore a combination of capital and taxation provisions. If the net fixed assets exceed the net worth, that is if they are partly financed by current liabilities, then the practice is likely to be in need of more permanent capital. Where the net fixed assets are reducing it is likely that these will represent inadequate replacement where suitable expansion of the plant is not taking place. In a flourishing business, ageing plant is financially undesirable, as well as having other practical disadvantages. Where the fixed assets are increasing, without a corresponding growth in profits, then it is probable that there has been excess investment which cannot be gainfully employed.

The assessment of a balance sheet must be made in the light of the facts available at the time, but examined in relationship to the other figures over a number of years. A single balance sheet can, however, reveal the factors described above.

16.7.4 Goodwill

Goodwill arises when one firm purchases another firm for more than the book value of its assets. It is an amount included on a balance sheet, which might include:

- A monopoly interest.
- Trade names and patents.
- Management expertise or a skilled workforce.
- Know-how.
- The cost of research and development.

In order to balance the accounts the accountant must take the difference between what was paid for the company and what the balance sheet of that company actually shows.

16.7.5 Ratio analysis

Comparisons can be made between the various items of information available to the practice from within the firm. They are known as ratios and can be divided into two categories: financial ratios give a means of expressing relationships between the income received by a business and its expenditure; operating ratios interpret the output of work.

If these ratios are extracted on a regular basis, management will have some indication as to the pattern of profitability and liquidity and may, therefore, be able to take the appropriate action necessary, for example, studying trends may avoid bankruptcy. Practices need regularly to monitor their own situations by examining their various business ratios. A positive approach is to calculate the required ratios against which the actual ratios can be compared. Managers should be especially interested in the ratios which are concerned with profitability or liquidity, the latter being those which show the ability of the firm to pay its current debts. Any changes in working capital must be observed at regular intervals. A sudden demand for payment by creditors may cause severe cash flow problems, even though adequate profit is being made. The following are two important ratios, but there are many others which are worth examining.

Current ratio

This is calculated as the ratio between the practice's current assets to its current liabilities. The difference between the two represents working capital, and is considered to be an indication of the ability of a firm to pay its debts. Although different businesses will vary, a ratio of 2:1 should be looked for here.

For example:

$$\text{Current ratio} = \frac{\text{current assets}}{\text{current liabilities}}$$

$$= \frac{67\,500}{24\,500} = 2.81$$

Acid test

Liquid assets represent the cash available together with the outstanding debts. But because of the nature of the construction industry, a practice having work in progress or completed cannot be said to have a current asset readily convertible to cash.

For example:

$$\text{Acid test} = \frac{\text{cash and debtors}}{\text{current liabilities}}$$

$$= \frac{16\,000}{24\,000} = 0.67$$

Accountants tend to look for a ratio of 1:1, if commitments are to be met without delay.

It is essential when examining these ratios to compare them with a budget ratio and also with previously calculated ratios in order to determine any trend.

A deeper understanding of a firm's business potential can often be gained by investigating ratios and trends in ratios from data which are readily available.

16.8 *Use of computers*

Accounting functions used to be very time-consuming and laborious until the arrival of the computer. Practices have been able to demonstrate the economics of using these machines for accounting purposes and they are now in everyday use. This means that the use of old-fashioned ledgers is now a thing of the past. The computer is well suited to deal with the regular and routine entries and calculations which are necessary in any type of firm, large or small.

The advantages of good financial software are that single entries into the computer can be allocated to several different accounts, and perhaps more importantly, up-to-date information can be retrieved quickly and efficiently. In fact it is very difficult to control the finances of perhaps all but the smallest firms today without the availability of such equipment. Accounting is a necessary and important function in any office, and it is vital to be meticulous, methodical and logical throughout. The use of spreadsheets for these tasks, which allow the manipulation of the data very easily, has made the process simpler and less arduous.

16.9 The accounts

The following are the more common accounts which will need to be kept by the practice.

- *The cash account.* This is a copy of the bank account computed from the cheque book and the paying-in slips. Periodically (once a month or so) the bank statement should be obtained and checked with the cash account, so that any discrepancy can be corrected.

- *The personal account.* This contains all the 'personal' accounts. A separate account is opened for each client, to which fees and expenses are debited and payments received credited. There are also accounts for those to whom the architect will owe money, e.g. stationers, printers and other firms from whom regular purchases are made. It could be divided into two accounts, one for those who are generally debtors and one for those who are generally creditors, but in an architect's practice the creditors are usually few in number whereas the client of every job in hand (and probably some finished!) is generally a debtor, so that their accounts heavily outnumber the creditors' accounts.

- *The private or impersonal account.* This account contains such items as rent, cleaning, furniture and equipment, telephone and salaries, which will all have separate accounts; there will also be a fees account and a capital account.

- *The petty cash account.* The petty cash records will be kept by the secretary or a junior assistant. The petty cash account is compiled from these records (Figure 16.4). It is one of the ledger accounts, but for convenience it is usually kept in an analysed form with a number of columns having such heads as 'stamps', 'stationery', 'sundries' (such as expenses not chargeable to clients, or odd purchases).
  An exception is made of expenses chargeable to clients, which it is advisable should be entered immediately in the client's account.

	Receipts		Payments	Stamps	Stationery	Travelling not chargeable	Cleaner	Sundries	Office equipment	Running balance	Posted
Year	120.000	Brot fwd	99.15	22.39	18.36	11.17	36.00	11.23	– –	20.85	–
Month 19		Envelopes	2.23		2.23					18.62	
21		Bus J.G.J. Hoxton	0.50			0.50				18.12	
21	50.00	Cash								68.12	
24		Fares Birmingham J.G.J.	26.16						8.05	41.96	F11 26.16
24		30 m tape	8.05							33.91	
25		Cleaning materials	3.50				3.50			30.41	
28		Stamp a/c	20.50	20.50						9.91	
28		Calculator batteries	2.00					2.00		7.91	
31	50.00	Cash								57.91	
31		Cleaning materials	3.15				3.15			54.76	
31		Fares and subsistence J.G.J. B'ham	17.48							37.28	F11 17.48
31		Paper	6.50		6.50					30.78	
	220.00		189.22	42.89	27.09	11.67	42.65	13.23	8.05		
					4 6		1 5	13.23	2 1		
								42.89			
								11.67			
								67.79			
								3 4			
Month 1	30.78	Balance									

Figure 16.4 Specimen petty cash account entries.

The 'Posted' column is for items to be posted immediately to a client's account and reference is given to the Personal (or Fees) ledger with the prefix F to distinguish such references from those to the Private ledger which would be without prefix. A running balance column showing balance after each entry is convenient but not essential. When totalled at the end of the quarter, check should be made as follows:

Receipts total minus payments total = last running balance figure.

Expense total add up horizontally = the total of 'Payments' columns.

The totals of Stamps, Travelling and Sundries are added together to be posted as one total £67.79. The totals posted are marked with the reference to the Private ledger. Value added tax where applicable must be separately accounted for.

- *Fees account.* In this are entered, as charged, the fees for each job, which at the same time are entered in the client's account to which expenses will already have been charged. It is, in fact, a subdivision of the fees account. Periodically, again say quarterly, the entries will be totalled and the total transferred to the fees account. In connection with this it is advisable to keep a list of jobs in hand, the fees for which have not been entered. This must be kept up to date by crossing out the name of the job when its fee is entered and adding the names of new jobs as they arise. This list will be a reminder when reviewing the position, either to send out accounts or to make a valuation of work not charged. If the job register suggested above is kept, this will serve the purpose.

- *Expenses book.* It is wise to keep an expenses book, in which can be noted down the principal's expenses in travelling, odd purchases, etc. These in turn can be credited periodically to a personal expenses account, at the same time being debited to the client's account, or, if not so chargeable, to stationery, sundries, or whatever might be appropriate. If a car is kept, a car mileage book can be kept and dealt with in the same way.

16.10 Vouchers

Related to the accounts are vouchers which record the detail of transactions. These comprise:

- *Receipts.* These should be filed as received in a file by themselves. Receipts referring to petty cash payments will be in a separate file kept with the petty cash book. Where assistants' travelling expenses, etc., are paid out of petty cash, the memos giving particulars will be kept with petty cash receipts or in a separate file.

- *Invoices.* These are received from creditors, such as printers and stationers, and should be put in a 'pending' folder until such time as the accounts are being entered up. The necessary double entry will be made, e.g. debiting a client and crediting the printer, or debiting 'stationery' and crediting the stationer's account. The invoices should then be filed, so that they can be turned up when reference is required. In a small business they will be kept in one file, but with a larger business there could be separate files for each firm or each category.

- *Bank statements.* These will be obtained from the bank from time to time as a check on the keeping of the cash account and filed in the folder usually supplied by the bank for the purpose.

● *Accounts rendered.* A copy of all accounts rendered should be kept in a file. These will give the detail of entries made in the fees account, which need only show the total fee.

16.11 *Keeping the accounts*

In a small office the accounting will be done by the principal, but in larger offices it may well justify a full-time accountant.

The following procedure is suggested:

● Bring cash account up to date from cheque book and paying-in book counterfoils.
● Make up petty cash account from vouchers, etc. Petty cash vouchers should be numbered and filed to correspond with the entries in the petty cash account.
● Go through the list of jobs in hand and enter any fees settled in the fees account, making the second entry in the client's account.
● Separate entries may be incorporated in the fees account to record VAT on outputs, but most firms will require an additional account to record VAT on inputs. The VAT account will be built up from monthly totals of the VAT columns in the accounts. In the case of inputs, the VAT will comprise the totals of the VAT figures from the fees and petty cash accounts. The firm's professional accountant or auditor can often advise on ways in which VAT information may be provided without too much duplication of labour by integrating the VAT records partly or wholly with the normal accounts.

16.12 *Making up annual accounts*

Once a year accounts must be totalled up and balanced. A profit and loss account and balance sheet must be prepared. It will probably be found that the final statement does not balance, but a search for the error might be a prolonged affair. It is best, therefore, to leave such error to be found on audit, when all the entries made are followed through and mathematics are checked. An omission to make an entry, or other cause of the error, will then be found.

16.13 *Audit*

It is advisable to have accounts audited by a qualified accountant. Accounts so certified carry more weight with the Inspector of Taxes, who will have to make assessment of tax payable, than the mere statement of the principal. The accountant is also available for advice if in difficulty with the income tax authorities and, if necessary, to carry on negotiations with them. Moreover, in the case of a partnership, the accountant is somebody impartial who can be entrusted with interpretation of the financial terms of the agreement.

Additional reading

Bassett, P.H. (1987) *Computerised Accounting*, NCC.
Berry, A. and Jarvis, R. (1991) *Accounting in a business context*, Chapman-Hall.
Blake, D. (1987) *Company Reports & Accounts.*
Clifton, H.D. (1990) *Business Data Systems*, Prentice Hall.
Dyson, J.R. (1987) *Accounting for non-accountants*, Pitman.
Fardon, M. and Cox, D. (1989) *Accounting*, Osbourne Books.
Marlow, A.J. (1989) *Computerising your accounts*, NCC Blackwell.
St. John Price, A. (1986) *Understanding your accounts: a guide to small business finance*, Kogan-Page.
Vale, P. (1987) *Financial Management Handbook.*

Chapter 17

Insurance

17.1 *Introduction*

This topic is included because it is important for every architect. Insurance is a contract between the insurer and the insured. Some kinds of insurance are more important for some architects than others. For example, the insurance of premises and public liability rests firmly with the partners or directors, but professional indemnity insurance affects every architect. What follows is of necessity a brief survey of the main kinds of insurance which an architect meets with during a professional career.

Insurance is complex and an experienced broker should always be consulted. There are, however, two important principles which should be understood by anyone taking out insurance:

- *Uberrimae fidei:* of the utmost good faith
- subrogation: standing in the place of another.

Uberrimae fidei

The basic principle is that the party seeking insurance must disclose all material facts whether the insurer specifically asks for them or not. Failure to make such disclosure can render the contract voidable. Thus an architect must reveal all circumstances in the past which might lead to a future claim when seeking professional indemnity insurance.

Subrogation

If an insurer pays out to a third party in respect of a claim against the insured, the insurer has the right to stand in the place of the insured for the purposes of recovering against any other person who may be liable in respect of the claim. A simple example will make this clear. Where a firm has professional indemnity insurance (see section 17.5 below), an employee may perform a negligent action which leads to the firm being sued for negligence by its client. If the insurer pays out in respect of the claim, it is entitled to stand in the place of the firm and take action against the employee to recover the full amount paid out. To avoid this distressing situation, most professional indemnity policies contain a waiver of subrogation in favour of the firm's employees. In other words, the insurer agrees not to exercise rights of subrogation against the particular employee whose negligent action lay at the root of the claim against the firm.

17.2 *Premises and contents*

Loss or damage of the office and contents is potentially disastrous for a practice. The first thing to decide is the beneficiaries under the policy. In the case of a partnership, all the partners may own the property jointly or one may own and lease to the rest. Alternatively, the premises may be leased from a landlord and the practice may be only one of a number of tenants in the same building.

It is essential that the policy should provide protection for the partners or directors and the possibility of the insurance company's exercising rights of subrogation should not be ignored. Thus, in the case of a tenant responsible for fire damage to the landlord's property, the landlord will be able to claim from the insurers, but they may subsequently take action to recover from the negligent tenant.

The basis of insurance will usually be 'full reinstatement': i.e. the insurers make no deductions for dilapidations. Care must be taken that sufficient cover is purchased and that the appropriate perils are included. If the premises are under insured, the result will be that in the case of loss, the insurers will only pay out a proportion of the amount claimed.

The contents of an architectural practice are particularly vulnerable to damage, consisting as they do largely of paper representing many hours of work. It is essential that a practice takes a proper inventory of the contents of the office and updates it regularly. So far as drawings are concerned, their value for insurance purposes must include the estimated cost of redrawing them after total destruction. Expensive pieces of equipment such as computers must receive special consideration, and if equipment is to be used outside the office, the insurance must cover such use.

17.3 *Public liability*

This insurance must be taken out and maintained to cover the liability of the practice to third parties for injury or death or damage to property as a result of the negligence of the partners or one of its employees. The insurance does not cover professional negligence (section 17.5). A large indemnity limit should be specified (£1 000 000 plus) and it should be upgraded at regular intervals, because if a court gives an award in excess of the insurance cover, the additional amount must be borne by the practice. Where the practice becomes involved in other activities, such as social events or car parking facilities, the insurance cover should be appropriately extended.

17.4 *Employer's liability*

A practice is required by law to take out insurance to provide an indemnity against its liabilities to its employees.[1] The indemnity should be unlimited. The policy is to cover death or injury and it includes sickness provided that:

- It arises in the course of employment, and
- The employer has legal liability.

Examples of such liability could be employer's breaches of the Factories Acts or Employer's Liability (Defective Equipment) Act 1969, unsafe systems of work, the negligent acts of other employees, or an employee's being attacked while going to the bank.

17.5 *Professional indemnity*

This is probably the most important area of insurance for all architects. Every practice should have an adequate level of insurance to cover the possible negligence of its staff. Although no architect likes to contemplate the possibility of facing a claim for professional negligence, few practices escape such a claim or the threat of such a claim at some period. The insurance is for the benefit of both practice and clients. It ensures that there is a fund to compensate a client if the architect is found to have been professionally negligent, and it also protects the partners of a practice against the chance that they are held liable in respect of a large sum which they would otherwise have to find from their own resources. Although one might hope that a client would not press a claim to the extent of making all the partners bankrupt, it does happen, and the good nature of a client facing a huge bill to correct the consequences of an architect's negligent design could be overstretched. The subject is complex and a specialist text on the subject should be studied.[2]

There are certain important points to bear in mind regarding professional indemnity insurance:

- Premiums are high.
- It is difficult to decide upon the amount of cover required, because the value of commissions actually being carried out is no indication of the likely maximum amount of any claim.
- Insurers prepared to provide the necessary cover are relatively few.
- The cover is only effective on a yearly basis: for example, in respect of matters notified during that year. Thus if cover is not maintained, perhaps because a practice has fallen on hard times, a claim made during that period cannot be referred to the insurance company even though cover may have been in place for ten years before.
- The policy normally covers the amount of any damages awarded against the insured together with the amount of legal costs up to the limit of indemnity noted in the policy. Note, however, that all policies carry excesses which may be substantial.
- Insurers usually claim the right to defend any claim. Alternatively they may decide to settle. Whichever course they take, it will be on the basis of sound business principles. This may not suit the architect. Policies should contain a clause which allows the insured to demand opinion from leading counsel, and the insurers are obliged to proceed accordingly.
- Once cover is in place, the insured must immediately notify the insurers of any circumstance which may give rise to a claim. Failure may lead to the insurers repudiating liability.

It is possible to extend the cover to deal with certain other matters such as pursuing a claim for infringement of copyright, or to provide indemnity in an action alleging libel or slander.

17.6 BUILD insurance

BUILD stands for 'building users insurance against latent defects'. It was the subject of a NEDO report in 1988 which recommended that this type of insurance should be available for buildings. At first, the insurance was not available in the UK although it was common in many European countries. The signs are that more insurers are interested in offering this type of insurance in this country. Some of its characteristics are as follows:

- It is non-cancellable for a period of ten years from practical completion.
- Cover is generally limited to structure, weathershield envelope and optional loss of rent.
- Risk assessment is carried out on behalf of the insurer by independent consultants. This may necessitate amendments to proposals in certain instances.
- Policy is taken out during the early design stages and a single premium paid.
- Benefit to the employer.
- Waiver of subrogation against architect, contractor, etc, can be purchased for an additional premium.

If this kind of insurance becomes general or even mandatory by law, the burden of liability on the architect and other professionals could be eased. However, there is little benefit unless subrogation is waived, and that is usually quite costly. It is also unlikely that an employer would be prepared to pay an extra premium for this purpose. Even where subrogation is waived, the cover provided is very limited.

17.7 *Other insurances*

Some other common forms of insurance which a practice may take out are:

- Partnership: to cover the situation which may arise if a partner retires or dies and the practice loses a large slice of capital in consequence. A partnership will usually also insure the lives of all partners in favour of the others.
- Pensions: for the benefit of the partners and staff.
- Medical insurance: a popular 'perk'.
- Insurance of company cars.
- Personal accident insurance.

References

(1) Employers' Liability (Compulsory Insurance) Act 1969.
(2) Cecil, R. (1991) *Professional Liability*, 3rd edn, Legal Studies & Services (Publishing) Ltd.

Chapter 18

The Architect as Employee

18.1 Acceptable job titles

The use of the title 'Architect', when applied to a person carrying on a business, is governed by the Architects Registration Acts 1931–1969.[1] Such a person must be registered and therefore, nowadays, qualified. The RIBA have issued a Practice Note[2] setting out job titles and descriptions which are acceptable and unacceptable. They are as follows.

Acceptable titles

- Chief architect.
- District architect.
- Principal architect.
- Project architect.

Acceptable descriptions

- Chartered architect.
- Experienced architect.
- Architect at B/C/D level of responsibility.

Each of these titles or descriptions adds something to the basic 'architect' so as to indicate the status or job. The professional status, however, is not in doubt.

Unacceptable titles

- Assistant architect.
- Senior assistant architect.
- Chief assistant architect.

Unacceptable descriptions

- Registered architect.
- Qualified architect.
- Fully qualified architect.

Each of these titles or descriptions detracts from the status of the architect. The descriptions suggest that it is possible to be termed 'architect' while at the same time being unregistered, partly or wholly unqualified. To qualify 'architect' by 'assistant' indicates that the unfortunate title holder is somehow less than an architect. Some titles are of course unlawful, such as where a job advertisement calls for the post of architect but the requirements are clearly for a person who need not be registered. Such phrases as 'architect at or about qualification standard' fall into this category. So do 'student architect' and 'trainee architect' as a matter of law.

18.2 Employment

18.2.1. Employed or self-employed?

The very first thing which an architect should be sure about is whether he or she is an employee. It is possible to work on an employed or self-employed basis. An employee enters into a *contract of service*; someone who is self-employed enters into a *contract for services*. The difference is very important:

- Employment law applies only to employees.
- Statutory rights apply only to employees.
- Duties at common law will be implied only in an employment situation.

It may seem obvious into which category a person falls, but this is not always the case. Often the situation is straightforward. An architect working for a client in return for a fee is self-employed, whereas most architects working in practices for a salary are employed. A self-employed person is sometimes referred to as an independent contractor. If the matter comes before the courts, they will look at the actual situation rather than the title.[3] Thus a person referred to as a 'consultant architect' may be held to be employed while a 'project architect' may in reality be self-employed. In order to resolve the issue in situations where there may be some doubt, the courts have devised some tests which can be applied. Briefly, they are as follows.

Control

If the employer has control over the architect's method of working, the architect is an employee. The greater the degree of control, the greater the likelihood that the architect is an employee. Although this is quite a good test where the work is of a manual nature, whether skilled or unskilled, it is less satisfactory in the professional context where even an employee must have a significant amount of freedom to exercise his or her profession. The test is relative, therefore, and the amount of control exercised over a particular architect must be compared with the usual degree of control exercised in architectural practice.

Integration

Architects who are integral parts of a business are likely to be employees. This test is probably more telling than the last so far as professional people are concerned. Thus it is easy to see the difference between an employed architect and one who freelances, self-employed, but perhaps works for a day or two a week for several practices, increasing or decreasing involvement to suit varying office workloads and the permanent staff member. Some self-employed architects work permanently for one office.

Multiple test

This is probably the best test. If the other tests are inconclusive, the questions to ask are: Does the architect work for an agreed salary? Is the degree of control such that there is a master and servant situation? Are the other provisions of the contract consistent with employment? For example, who is responsible for paying the architect's tax? Is there a company pension scheme to which the architect belongs? Who owns the drawing equipment which the architect uses?

There has been a growing tendency for architects to be employed on a self-employed basis. This is possibly because of the uncertain economic climate. An employer takes less risk by using self-employed persons, because they are not protected by statute like an employee.

There are advantages to being self-employed. Architects in this situation pay tax on a different system, usually in arrears, and there is greater scope for claiming expenses against tax. In addition, many architects like the freedom which self-employment brings. Of course, if an architect is self-employed, but nevertheless engaged permanently for one practice, the situation is mainly for the benefit of the office, with no commitment either side. Note also that the self-employed can be caught if they are negligent and the practice has to make a claim against the insurance policy. In such cases, the insurer does not waive rights of subrogation, as is usual in the case of employees, and the self-employed may face the prospect of a personal writ from the insurer.

18.2.2 Employment contract

A contract of employment may be written or oral. The only problem with an oral contract of employment is the problem with all oral contracts: the parties may have conflicting recollections of the terms. The contract can also be implied as the result of the conduct of the parties. Some firms, so it is said, still engage staff with a shake of the hand. There is nothing illegal in this, and if the firm is equally relaxed about all aspects of its relations with employees, it may be the ideal environment for some. In general, however, a written contract of employment is an advantage, because both sides then know for certain the basis of the relationship, at least in respect of the main issues. In the absence of express terms between employer and employee, the general law will imply that the employer:

- Has a duty to pay the employee.
- Has a duty to provide work: if without work, the employee would be unable to earn money.
- Has a duty to reimburse the employee for reasonably incurred expenses in carrying out duties.
- Has a duty to take care for the employee's safety.

and that the employee:

- Must provide personal (i.e. not delegated) service.
- Must obey the employer's lawful instructions.
- Must take reasonable care when about the employer's business.
- Must show good faith in revealing to the employer that which should be revealed and in safeguarding confidential information.

In addition there is much statutory law which governs the employer/employee relationship and which has now almost supplanted the common law for most purposes.

18.2.3 Written statement

The employer must give the employee a *written statement* of the principal contract terms not later than 13 weeks after commencement of employment. The statement, however, is not the contract and, if appropriate, the employee can contend that the statement attempts to modify the terms of employment. The fact that the employee may be asked to sign a written statement is not thought to indicate anything other than acknowledgement of receipt of the statement. Many employers are slow to issue the statement because there is no effective sanction. An industrial tribunal may make a decision on the points in dispute, but that is all. The statement must be given to the employee personally, but it need not be issued at all if all the points have been covered already in a written contract of employment. It is not sufficient, however, for the employer to pin the statement to a notice board or to refer to standard conditions.

The statements must contain the following:

- The identities of the employer and employee.
- The job title.
- The date of commencement of employment and whether a previous period of employment counts as part of the period of continuous employment for statutory purposes.
- Rate of pay and interval between payment.
- Hours of work.
- Holiday entitlement, including public holidays and the method of calculating holiday pay (see section 18.10 below).
- Rules regarding absence from work due to sickness or injury and any sick pay provision. There is no right to sick pay under the general law, but most employers make some provision. An employer is obliged to pay statutory sick pay for 28 weeks in any year, after which responsibility for payment of statutory sick pay lies with the Department of Social Security.
- Details of the pension scheme. The employee may be referred to another document.
- The period of notice required to bring the contract to an end. The statement may stipulate any period, but if it is less than the statutory minimum, the statutory minimum will apply. If no period

is stipulated, the statutory minimum does not apply and reasonable notice must be given (unless a fixed term contract is in force).

- Disciplinary rules and the grievance procedure. The procedures are not regulated by statute, but codes of practice have been produced by ACAS which, if adopted, tend to demonstrate to an industrial tribunal that the procedure was reasonable.

If the contract is silent about any of these points, a note to that effect must be put in the written statement. If there is any change, a further written statement must be furnished by the employer within one month of the change.

18.3 Job description

Job descriptions are often included in job advertisements. They may be brief in the extreme, of the 'Project Architect with flair for design' variety, or they may be extremely detailed. Although in general it might be assumed that architects know what they do, there is a tremendous range of functions in practice, depending on the kind of practice, the kind of work, and the position of the architect in relation to other members of the office. It is comparatively rare for a detailed job description to be included in a contract of employment for an architect.

The general rule is that the more senior the post, the less need there is for a job description. So the lowest-paid member of staff doing relatively unskilled work might have a very long job description setting out the varied tasks which might be requested of them. The highest-paid member or senior partner will have no job description because, at that level of responsibility, the person writes his or her own description day by day. The job, for such people, is whatever they make it.

The employment contract should contain some description of the general nature of the work. Professionals cannot expect their contracts to spell out every detail of their duties.[4] Those duties, however, will not be held to extend beyond the duties normally associated with the proper performance of the functions indicated. Thus an architect cannot refuse to do something on the basis that it is not in his or her contract of employment if it is consistent with an architect's normal duties. From the employer's point of view it is useful to include a general phrase requiring the employee to carry out other activities which are reasonably incidental to his or her principal job. Part of the

Type of work which can be handled	Knowledge and initiative	Influence on others	Responsibility
'A' level Perform simple jobs offering little or no alternative methods. Simple analysis of problems for which logical answers are readily obtainable.	No initiative required.	Able to understand and execute simple instructions. A minimum influence on the work of others.	Responsible for making minor decisions. All work closely supervised.
'B' level Perform work offering a limited number of alternative methods. Solve problems for which logical answers are not readily apparent and which will have some effect on the other aspects of the job.	Limited initiative required. Limited research into common technical literature required. Knowledge of the more common types of materials.	Able to understand and execute instructions covering a limited field. Able to give simple clear instructions.	Responsible for making decisions affecting his work only, which must be reported to his senior. Parts of his work closely supervised.
'C' level Perform work offering a variety of alternative methods. Solve problems for which answers are not apparent and which will have considerable effect on other aspects of the job.	Initiative is required. Considerable research into all technical literature required. General knowledge of all types of materials.	Able to understand and execute instructions, covering a wide field. Able to give instructions to allocate work among and to control the work of, up to 5 or 6 others working as a team and to co-ordinate their activities.	Responsible for making decisions for all the work of his team within the framework laid down. Receives general supervision.
'D' level Perform work offering an infinite variety of alternative methods. Solve problems for which considerable thought is required to produce logical answers, the solution to which will have a profound effect on the whole design.	Considerable initiative is required. Considerable basic research is required into fields not normally covered by normal technical literature. Wide detailed knowledge of all types of materials.	Able to initiate a plan of working and check progress, able to convert plan into a practical method of working and give the necessary instructions. Able to control and co-ordinate the work of a number of teams working independently.	Responsible for submitting and agreeing design policy with the principal within the framework laid down by the office. Receives administrative supervision only.

Figure 18.1 Grading table for architectural staff (from *The Architect and his Office;* courtesy RIBA Publications Ltd).

job description in the employment contract may be that an architect is required to work at another branch office at the discretion of any partner. Without such a clause, the architect cannot be compelled to move.

A simple form of job description was pioneered in the 1961 survey *The Architect and His Office*[5] (Figure 18.1). It graded all architectural staff in four grades: A, B, C, D. Each grade carried a brief description of the qualities required and the person's responsibility. Thus an architect seeing that a firm was advertising for a post grade C would have a good idea of the kind of person being sought. It also formed the basis of the salary structure. Some kind of job description is essential if the office carries out job evaluation (see section 18.6 below).

18.4 Hours of work

The hours which an architect is expected to work should be detailed in the contract of employment, although this is seldom the case. They must, however, be specified in the written statement (see section 18.2.3 above), but there are no statutory provisions about the actual hours. There really is no such thing as 'normal' office hours. In London, the usual start is 9.30 a.m; elsewhere 9.00 a.m. is common, the normal week being 35 and 37½ hours respectively.

It is very uncommon for any professional to keep strictly to the specified hours of work, and architects are no exception. Whatever the appointed hours of work, architects will tend to work longer. More about this later (see section 18.5 below). In many places, some form of flexible working hours is operated. There was resistance in some quarters, but it is the norm in local authorities and it is becoming acceptable elsewhere. In principle, an employee is required to work during a 'core' period from perhaps 10.00 a.m. to 3.00 p.m. each day together with other hours to choice or as agreed with the employer. The overriding rule is that the employee must put in an agreed minimum number of hours every week or month. There are obvious advantages for the employee and the practice is likely to become universal eventually. The contract should state the office policy regarding the accumulation of hours into additional days' leave.

18.5 Overtime

Attitudes to working overtime vary tremendously. Most architects will be expected to work overtime when there is a heavy workload or when there is a temporary crisis which demands attention. The way in which overtime is handled will depend on the particular office. Although, particularly in difficult times, it is better to be somewhat understaffed, it is not a good idea for anyone to work regular overtime. Everyone needs time to relax and recharge batteries, otherwise tiredness becomes normal and mistakes occur.

Some offices repay overtime by offering time off in lieu. This can be useful to the employee, but if all members of staff exercise the option, there may be times when the office is seriously understaffed. In addition, those architects who work most overtime usually find difficulty in finding a space in their workload to enable them to take normal holidays, let alone time off in lieu. No architect should allow this kind of situation to develop. Overtime should always be paid with time off in lieu as an alternative.

Some offices do not pay for overtime and still the staff work extra hours. This reflects well on the commitment of the staff and badly on the partners. Overtime payment should be on a higher scale than normal, to reflect the unsocial hours and the fact that it is over and above what an architect can reasonably be expected to work. Fair rates are usually taken to be one and a half times the normal hourly rate, to twice the normal hourly rate if the hours are especially late or during the weekend. It is not unknown for an office to pay only normal rates, however much overtime is worked. It has also been known for an office to stipulate that no overtime will be paid until the employee has worked in excess of a stated number of hours overtime on any one day.

Some architects will work overtime without requesting payment in order to gain advancement in the firm. Whether that is a good idea will depend on circumstances.

18.6 Salary

Starting salaries should be settled at the time of interview. What should also be settled, and this is sometimes overlooked, is the frequency and timing of salary reviews. Every employer is obliged by law[6] to issue full-time employees with an itemized statement of pay setting out the gross salary, details of all deductions and the net amount payable. Remuneration is the 'consideration' which the employer gives for the employee's service.

In addition to the basic salary, many firms operate a bonus or profit-sharing scheme. If the term 'bonus' is used, it is possible that the employer thinks of it as an occasional rather than a regular thing, something with which he can reward exceptional endeavour. In law, a contractual promise to pay a bonus as part payment for work done will be enforceable although the amount of the bonus will depend on the terms laid down. A profit-sharing scheme is probably the most satisfactory arrangement. What constitutes 'profit' should be clearly stated, and the sharing may take place on the basis of a points system: a greater number of points represents a greater share. Points may be allocated for length of service, salary, status, or in any other way deemed fair, or set in the contract of employment.

Job evaluation is a technique which is sometimes used to relate each post and its pay to every other post. There are two stages:

- Every post must be given a rank.
- Appropriate salaries must be attached to each post.

The system is said to have many advantages. It should produce a pay structure within the practice and an overall level of pay which is clearly recognized as being reasonable in itself and in comparison to external pay levels. In addition, the employees should feel secure from arbitrary changes in the pay structure, and the practice has a method of fixing rates of pay for new posts.

It is quite difficult to grade the work of professionals. Job evaluation is usually based on a points system which is most appropriate to manual work. Although there is no reason why such a system should not work when applied to professionals, a considerable amount of subtlety is required. It is the post and not the individual which is being graded. Points are normally given for such things as effort, skill, experience, qualifications and working conditions. It is open to a practice to establish its own criteria so long as they can be seen to be fair and reasonable when applied to all members of staff. A basic job decription is described in section 18.3 above.

18.7 Perks

This is an important part of the remuneration package. Indeed, in some instances it may be a significant factor in determining whether an architect takes one post in preference to another. The most highly prized perk is still a company car, particularly the more expensive kinds which architects may covert, but be unable to buy themselves. Firms have varying policies. In many practices it is still quite rare for an architect below the status of associate to be given a company car. An alternative is the 'pool' system whereby architects may have the use of a car, but must take whichever car is available on that particular day.

Stricter tax rules have meant that a company car is less of a good deal than it once was. As an alternative, a firm may require employees to provide their own cars for use on firm's business and give an annual or monthly running and depreciation allowance together with a realistic mileage payment. In such cases, the employer should also provide a generous interest-free loan facility. Problems can arise with this kind of provision. Employees who have major repairs to finance can find themselves in breach of contract if they are unable to afford the repair. If car use is essential, the car should be provided by the firm, either personally to the employee (as is common in other parts of the construction industry) or in a pool.

Second only to a car is a telephone. In the case of senior appointments, it is common for the employer to at least pay all rental charges and the cost of business calls. It is also becoming common for telephones to be provided in cars with a 'hands-free' facility. Whether such provision is universally a good idea only time will tell if the quality of reception and transmission improve.

Luncheon vouchers are fairly commonplace in London, rather less so elsewhere.

Some firms automatically enrol all employees in a medical insurance scheme. This can have obvious benefits for the employees and the great advantage for the employer is that hospital procedures can be carried out quickly and, in the case of non life-threatening conditions, to suit the employee's office commitments. These schemes usually exclude cover for any illness even remotely connected with a previous illness in the same employee. For example, an employee who has had investigations for stomach ulcer prior to enrolling on the scheme might well find that cover is excluded for any abdominal ailment. The actual extent of expense which will be reimbursed should be carefully checked. Such insurance counts as a benefit for tax purposes (see Chapter 17).

Parking is often a problem in centrally situated offices and a parking space is a valuable provision although it may be going too far to call it a perk. Many architectural practices have located in semi-rural areas to take advantage, among other things, of the easier parking situation.

18.8 Professional activities

All employees should be encouraged to take part in professional activities, but many firms are mean about such things and what should be regarded as commonplace has almost come to be regarded as a perk.

The degree of encouragement often depends upon the principal, and his or her mood on a particular day. The particular economic climate is also of prime importance. The following may be said to fall into the category of professional activities of varying degrees of importance.

Continuing professional development

Every employee should be allowed some time each year to go on courses, either in or out of the office. Employers vary considerably regarding whether they are prepared to continue paying salary during days off for this purpose. The imposition of compulsory CPD by the RIBA on its members is particularly significant in this regard (see Chapter 2, section 2.2).

Examinations

Students require time off to sit their Part III examinations. They also need time for study and attendance at short courses during the period immediately before examinations. Employers must allow attendance at examinations. They should allow attendance at appropriate short courses, but pure study time is probably best left to the student to organize.

Sabbaticals and study trips

Sabbatical leave is now less frequently an important constituent of some posts, although still encountered in education. It refreshes the mind and generates ideas. Above all, it plays an important part in the development of the employee. Study trips also assist the employee to develop a particular interest. It is rare for offices to allow such trips, except of course during the employee's own holiday period. Where an office does allow or even encourage such trips, the effect on salary payments should be clarified in advance.

Professional subscriptions

It is relatively unusual for an employer to reimburse an employee's subscription to a professional body. This kind of provision is generally regarded as a perk for architects of high status such as associates.

Journal subscriptions

It is even rarer for an employer to reimburse professional journal subscriptions, but virtually all offices subscribe to a range of journals for the benefit of staff as a whole.

Attendance at branch meetings

Architects should be as active in the local professional branch as their other commitments allow. It is a way of keeping up to date, not only in regard to technical matters, but also as far as professional matters are concerned. Most branches have a series of sub-committees and they are usually desperate for members. It is a useful way of getting to know other architects in the area and of finding out what is happening in other offices. Most of these meetings take place in the evenings, and therefore time off is not required. Where an employee is particularly active in the local branch, it makes sense for the office to allow time off to attend any special meetings during the day. Apart from other considerations, it is a useful piece of exposure for the practice and a means of keeping the practice tuned into what is happening elsewhere.

18.9 Expenses

Expenses are often linked to remuneration. That is wrong. Employees are not expected to make a profit out of expenses, but neither are they expected to make a loss. The intention should be that they are reimbursed; no more, no less.

The general law implies a term in every contract of employment that the employer will indemnify the employee against any expense reasonably incurred in the performance of duties. Within that statement, however, there is considerable scope for differences in application. Thus, although there is not strictly any necessity for details of expenses to be set out in the contract of employment, it is worth doing so that both parties are perfectly clear at the outset. The key word is 'reasonable'. An expense will be reasonably incurred if authorized or, if prior authority is not possible, if it is justified by the circumstances. This latter category causes most trouble and there is much to be said for giving guidelines, if not in the contract itself, as soon as possible thereafter.

The most common expense is travelling. The preferred mode of transport should be stipulated by the office: car, train, bus or taxi. Most probably, the type of transport authorized will depend upon the length of journey and whether or not a client is in the party. Where cars are involved, the mileage rate should be stated, as should the class where rail travel is involved. Taxis are normally reserved for transport between station and office or hotel and for emergencies.

The employee must be reimbursed if he or she incurs expense in entertaining clients. In some offices, only partners are permitted that sort of expense account. The company policy should be made clear.

The type of practice and the location of its work will determine how often an employee may be away from his or her office base on business. The rates of subsistence payments in such cases should be sufficient to ensure a fair standard of accommodation and meals.

It is essential for employees properly to record all expenses so that the practice can recover them from the client if appropriate. However, the fact that an office cannot recover certain expenses from the client should not preclude payment to the employee. Expense repayments should be prompt. Some firms get the free use of money by making employees wait several weeks before payment. Expense repayments should ideally be *on demand* and there is no good reason why not *in advance* if the anticipated expense is likely to be more than the employee wishes to advance from his or her own resources.

18.10 Leave

There is no automatic right to paid holidays either in statute or at common law. An employee's holiday entitlement will, therefore, be whatever is agreed with the employer. It must be included in the written statement (see section 18.2 above), but it is preferable to have the details recorded in the employment contract.

Holiday entitlement commonly includes all public or bank holidays together with 20 or 25 additional days to be taken during the holiday year. This normally runs from 1 January to 31 December or from 6 April to 5 April (the financial year). It is generally stipulated that the holiday days must be taken within the holiday year to which they relate. Some firms allow a few days to be carried over to the next 'year' or give payment in lieu.

Payment in lieu of holidays is not generally encouraged by employers, because it tends to encourage employees to forego holiday entitlement which every working person needs. It is better to allow a few days to overlap into the next period if pressure of work has prevented the taking of holidays at the appropriate time. Obviously, chaos would ensue if employees enjoyed untrammelled power to save their entitlement from one year to the next until perhaps they could take six months off to tour the world. Not that such an idea is bad in itself, but there are other ways of accomplishing that kind of ambition.

The taking of holidays should be tempered by the need to keep the office running smoothly.

It is good practice for an office to have all the rules regarding holidays, as other things, clearly set out. There are few things worse than the office which is full of unwritten (and therefore, constantly changing) rules. Many offices close down completely from Christmas to New Year. Employers should make clear whether this period is included or additional to the annual leave. Additional days are often added on to the annual holiday to reward long service with a firm.

In addition to holidays, there are other kinds of leave which may affect the employee architect. They are:

- Maternity leave.
- Compassionate leave.
- Leave for public duties.
- Unpaid leave
- Sick leave.

18.10.1 Maternity leave

This is subject to statutory regulations which change from time to time. Currently, the position is that, to qualify for maternity pay and the right to return to work:

- The reason for absence must be pregnancy; and
- The woman must be employed until the eleventh week before the expected delivery week; and
- She must have completed two years' continuous employment by the beginning of the eleventh week before confinement; and
- Not less than 21 days before absence, she must inform the employer that she will be absent due to pregnancy and state whether she wishes to return to work afterwards (she is not bound by this statement); and
- She must produce a medical certificate if required.

A woman is entitled to a total of 29 weeks' maternity leave. She must give 21 days' notice of intention to return to work, but she may postpone her return for a further four weeks on account of illness. The employer is entitled to request written notice of intention to return to work after 49 days from the confinement week. He may also postpone her return for four weeks if he cannot make appropriate arrangements in time.

18.10.2 Compassionate leave

No employee has the right to compassionate leave; it is entirely at the discretion of the employer. Many firms, however, lay down useful guidelines in their employment contracts and they will allow paid leave for such things as death, serious illness or accident to a close relative. In general, such leave is dealt with on an *ad hoc* basis depending on the particular circumstances. Some employers lay down a maximum compassionate leave allowance in any year. Such a provision is comparatively rare, however, because it can be considered by employees to be an entitlement which must be taken before the end of the year on sometimes flimsy grounds. Most firms are generous once they know that the need is genuine.

18.10.3 Leave for public duties

Legislation stipulates that certain persons holding official posts must be allowed time off from work to attend to their duties. A common example of this is the trades union official who is entitled to a reasonable time off with pay to attend to union affairs. In most other cases, however, time off must be granted, but it need not be with pay. Common examples are JPs, members of the local authority or other authority, members of tribunals and school governors. Although, because it is a statutory requirement, there is no necessity to include references to such leave in an employment contract, many firms include a statement on the position for the avoidance of doubt. Employers can be quite generous in continuing to pay employees, less only any attendance allowance, for carrying out official duties. This may also reflect the recognition that it does the firm no harm at all to have one or more of its employees in the public eye (see Chapter 19).

Specific trades union members are allowed to have reasonable leave for all trade union activities (except industrial action). Unlike trades union officials, however, ordinary members must take the time off without pay.

Although not public duties, there are two further situations in which an employer must allow time off with pay. The first is the case of an employee whose post becomes redundant. Reasonable time off with pay must be allowed for the purpose of seeking alternative employment. The second situation is when an employee becomes pregnant. She is entitled to reasonable time off with pay for antenatal care.

18.10.4 Unpaid leave

Apart from the situations already mentioned, which are regulated by statute, some employers allow staff to take unpaid leave from time to time. It is useful if the employer's policy is clearly stated in the employment contract, but very often it will be dealt with on an *ad hoc* basis. The employee does not have a right to take leave without pay, but such leave will often be granted for a special purpose.

18.10.5 Sick leave

Although the general law gives no right to sick pay, legislation fills the gap and most firms have quite detailed provisions of their own. If they are not in the contract of employment, they must be included in the written statement. The employer is obliged to pay statutory sick pay for a period of 28 weeks of sickness. Certain procedures must be carried out and it is usual to make compliance with the procedures a condition of employment. This is because strict adherence to the procedure is necessary if the employer is to be able to reclaim any sick pay under the entitlement from the DSS.

An employer will often undertake to pay an additional amount to bring the statutory sick pay up to an employee's usual salary. Such payment is sometimes linked to length of service and commonly consists of one or more months at full pay and an equal number of months at half pay. The more generous schemes provide for an employee to be paid six months' half salary if a period of illness occurs after a qualifying period of two years. Less than two years' service gives rise to a reduced entitlement. This kind of provision is more likely in larger offices where the absence of a member of staff for a prolonged period is not likely to be more than inconvenient. The chances of several architects taking several months off for sickness at the same time is so unlikely as to be suspicious.

Subject to what may be included in the employment contract, there is nothing to prevent an employer terminating employment on the grounds of prolonged absence due to sickness. Some employers set out the relevant criteria in the employment contract, but it is rare. Where criteria are set out, they often include the right of the employer to ask for an independent medical examination of the employee after absence from work for a specified period or at the employer's discretion.

18.11 *Disciplinary and grievance procedure*

Every office should have a disciplinary and grievance procedure. There is no particular statutory requirement, contrary to popular belief, regarding the exact form of the procedure. ACAS has produced codes of practice which firms may adopt. The general principles are:

- The procedure should be described in writing.
- The person who may operate the procedure should be specified.
- Possible action should be specified.
- Except in the case of gross misconduct, a first offence should not incur dismissal.
- The employee should be informed of the complaint and he or she is entitled to representation.
- There should be a warning procedure including at least one oral and one written warning followed by a sanction less than dismissal before dismissal actually takes place.
- There should be an appeal system.

The grievance procedure should state whom the employee should approach with a complaint and to whom appeal may be made.

The procedures may be contained in the office manual. Less commonly, they are spelled out in the employment contract. Some firms appear to be a trifle coy about this, as if admitting that a procedure exists is tantamount to encouraging disputes.

18.12 *Notice and dismissal*

Every employee must be aware of the period of notice required to end the employment contract. If the period is less than the statutory minimum, the statutory minimum will apply. Most firms give reasonably detailed terms governing the termination of employment, but such terms cannot override statutory provisions. The statutory periods of notice which must be given by the employer range from one week if the employee has been continuously employed for more than one month but less than two years and, thereafter, one week for every complete year worked up to a maximum of twelve weeks. The employee, on the other hand, has a statutory obligation to give one week's notice of termination. If the contract stipulates a greater period, the employee will be in breach of contract if he or she gives less.

There is confusion between unfair and wrongful dismissal. The terms are often used as if they were interchangeable. There are in fact four circumstances in which employment can be terminated:

- Wrongful dismissal.
- Unfair dismissal.
- Fair dismissal.
- Redundancy.

Wrongful dismissal is a breach of contract: for example, if insufficient notice is given. Damages are available at common law. Unfair dismissal, however, is enshrined in statute and it refers to the situation when the correct notice is given, there is no breach of contract, but the reason for the dismissal is considered by statute to be unfair. In this case, the employee's remedies are prescribed by statute also. Fair dismissal is when the correct notice is given, there is no other breach of contract and the reason for dismissal is considered to be fair. Redundancy comes into a special category which lays down the particular statutory rights of the employee in such a situation. Dismissal will not be wrongful or unfair if the employee is guilty of gross misconduct or is unable to carry out the work properly. Some contracts attempt to set out precisely what may fall into these categories to avoid disputes later, but those contracts are rare in architectural practice.

18.13 Spare-time practice

Many architects engage in spare-time practice during the period they are employees. It may be a means of obtaining extra cash or a means of starting up in practice with a client nucleus. The *RIBA Code of Professional Conduct* is very clear that such practice must be allowed (see Chapter 2, section 2.6) and the general law will imply that an employee may so practise unless there is a term in the contract expressly forbidding it.

The employer's attitude, however, may be less than enthusiastic, either directly forbidding spare time practice, in spite of the Code, or hedging it around with so many rules that it is not a practical proposition. Reasonable conditions are:

- The employee must inform the employer in advance.
- The clients must be informed that the employee is carrying out the work in a personal capacity.
- The clients must not be existing clients of the firm.

- Private work must not be carried out in office hours or making use of office equipment or materials unless prior permission has been obtained.
- The firm's interests must not be affected in any way.

Many firms encourage employees to introduce work into the firm. Again, it is preferable if the policy is clearly stated. Very small jobs may not be welcome. Employees introducing work will expect something more than the usual salary for their trouble. Some employers reward the employee by a special payment related to the final profit on that particular project. Provided that the method of calculating the payment is known to all, it is a sensible way to proceed, because it associates the employees with the firm, it links futures and paves the way for closer association in due time.

There is a great advantage to an employee in bringing all work into the office rather than carrying on spare-time practice. The employee will have the protection of the office professional indemnity insurance (see Chapter 17, section 17.4). Private work is carried out at the employee's risk. If the employee is negligent in his or her own work, the client will look to them for damages. In theory, such employees should carry their own insurance to cover their spare-time practice. The reality is that such cover is not easily affordable. All may be well during the time the architect is employed and is not considered worth suing by clients. The situation may be different if the employee later sets up in practice and earlier negligence results in a heavy claim for damages.

There are two matters which are closely associated with spare time practice: copyright and confidential information. In general, copyright in work prepared by an employee belongs to an employer.[7] Employees should be aware that permission must be obtained from an employer to produce copies of their drawings to take to interview for the purpose of securing other employment. Employees, of course, retain copyright in work which they produce during their spare time.

Confidentiality is a difficult area. Information which an employee may gain in employment was considered in *Faccenda Chicken Ltd v. Fowler* [1986][8] to fall into three categories:

- Information well known to people in the industry.
- Confidential information which becomes part of the employee's own skill and knowledge.
- Information of such confidentiality that it cannot be used lawfully to benefit anyone other than the employer.

Information in the third category can never be divulged by an employee even after leaving the employment. The second category of information cannot be protected when an employee leaves, but to reveal such information while still in the original employment would be a gross breach of trust and entitles the employer to damages. The problem lies in correctly identifying what information falls into which categories. It is probably for this reason that some firms purport to state the type of information which is considered to be highly confidential in the employment contract. An employee, of course, will be bound by such terms.

Some architects in employment, usually those with considerable responsibility and possibly access to information regarded by the practice as highly confidential, may have a restraint clause in their contracts. Such a term may try to restrict an employee from setting up in practice within a certain distance of the previous employer for a period of time. Terms in contracts which attempt to restrict future employment are basically void at common law as being in restraint of trade. Such terms may be valid and enforceable if:

- They are reasonable between the parties.
  - (a) The restriction must protect the employer's legally recognized interest: protection of trade secrets; and/or protection of business connections.
  - (b) The restriction must be no greater than necessary to so protect: in respect of the period of restriction; in respect of the geographical restriction.
- They are reasonable in the public interest; for example, they do not deprive the public of special skills which the employee may possess.

(Where a restriction is placed on ex-partners, the same principles generally apply, but it is generally considered reasonable to enforce stricter time periods and geographical areas.)

18.4 Discrimination

The reader may be surprised to learn that discrimination on the grounds of age, religion, politics or membership of a trades union is not directly unlawful.

An employer may not discriminate against a person on the grounds of that person's sex or marital status.[9] The Act has particular application to the recruitment of staff and to any benefits. Indirect discrimination is also unlawful: for example if criteria are laid down which favour one sex. An exception is made in the case of occupations where decency or physiology dictates that only a man or a woman can do the work.

Discrimination against a person on the grounds of race, colour or nationality is also outlawed.[10] Again, indirect discrimination is also forbidden and the Act applies equally to fellow employees. Exceptions to the provisions are allowed, for example, if a particular racial group would have difficulty in doing certain work or if certain work could only be performed by a certain group.

A woman may not be treated less favourably simply because of her sex.[11] Pay and conditions of service are covered. The Act of course does not apply where the reason for differences in pay are due to such things as differing job responsibilities.

References

(1) See also section 2.4.
(2) Approved by the RIBA Council in February 1974.
(3) *Ferguson* v. *John Dawson* [1976] 1 WLR 1213.
(4) *Sim* v. *Rotherham MBC* [1986] IRLR 391.
(5) *The Architect and His Office* (1962) RIBA Publications Ltd.
(6) Employment Act 1982.
(7) Copyright Designs and Patents Act 1988.
(8) [1986] 1 All ER 617.
(9) The Sex Discrimination Act 1975.
(10) The Race Relations Act 1976.
(11) The Equal Pay Act 1970.

Chapter 19

Attracting Work

19.1 Active marketing

The first thing for any architect to realize is that marketing any professional service is not like selling baked beans. An altogether different approach is necessary.[1] Not very long ago, the only acceptable way for an architect to attract work was through existing clients. Apart from a brass plate with letters of a prescribed size, there were few ways the architect could advertise the existence of the practice. The situation now is vastly changed, and a wide range of activities are allowed by the Code of Conduct (see Chapter 2, section 2.6).

Every practice must develop a unique marketing strategy for that firm. Very large practices may employ one or more full-time marketing people to keep the firm in the public eye and follow up particular opportunities. Most firms, however, must rely on the part-time efforts of their own staff. Some architects have the gift of attracting work. They can go to a party and come back with three new commissions. Such architects are worth their weight in gold and they need never do any architectural work themselves. They are rare, however. Specific marketing objectives must therefore be set to ensure that all the staff in a practice are pulling in the right direction.

There are some very simple straightforward things that every practice can do:

- Clients Advisory Service.
- Architects' notice boards.
- Lectures and articles.
- Direct approach.

19.1.1 Clients Advisory Service (CAS)

A practice can register with this service at the RIBA. Not only does CAS promote architects in a general way, it also responds to the many queries it receives from prospective clients seeking an architect for a particular project. Architects have an entry in the *Practice Directory* (which may be expanded for an additional fee). Practices are responsible for keeping the information held by CAS up to date, and when an enquiry is received, CAS furnishes a client with a list of three or four names of architects appropriate for the project outlined by the client. CAS operates through a network of regional RIBA offices where further information can be obtained.

19.1.2 Architects' notice boards

Most practices have standard notice boards which are erected in a prominent position on new development. If the development is of any size, the architect's board will be just one of many professionals' boards and there will be boards giving the particulars of the main contractor and sub-contractors. Remember that such boards require planning permission (see Chapter 9, section 9.4.5) and the architect is usually responsible for approving, if not actually designing, the layout of such boards. An architect now has the right to insist that the practice is credited with the design in permanent form on the outside of the finished building.[2] Although there may be isolated instances where the architect definitely does not wish to be remembered as the designer of a particular building, in most cases it is a valuable means of additional publicity.

19.1.3 Lectures and articles

Although it may be difficult for a one-man practice to find the time to give lectures or write articles, many practices contain members who can give short talks and others who can put together an interesting articles on aspects of architecture in general and the work of the practice in particular. Many organizations, such as civic and amenity societies, and chambers of commerce, have difficulty in finding speakers for lunch or evening meetings. There is nothing to prevent a practice from writing to such organizations offering a talk on architectural matters of interest. Although speaking in public can be daunting at first, practice makes perfect, and provided a speaker is prepared with notes (and possibly slides) the experience can be enjoyable for all parties. This is a good way of putting the firm's name in front of a wider public. An article is a more permanent record and likely to reach a wider audience provided it appears in an appropriate magazine or local paper.

19.1.4 Direct approach

Architects may now approach a client directly before there has been any initial enquiry by the prospective client. For example, an architect may hear that a company is expanding and looking for sites for additional factory production. There is nothing to stop the architect from writing to the company offering his or her services in finding a suitable site and designing the factory. Experience suggests that many commissions are obtained in this way.

19.2 Practice brochure

It has been suggested that a client will spend only seven seconds flicking through a brochure.[3] This does not tend to promote confidence that a practice brochure will do much to assist in getting work. A practice brochure is not normally produced for wholesale distribution. Pressing a brochure on an unwilling client is counter-productive.

The brochure should explain who's who in the firm, how long it has been established and the kind of work it carries out, preferably with illustrations. Special areas of expertise should be highlighted. Although the brochure should be well designed in layout and typeface, it should avoid being gimmicky. It should be easy for a prospective client to find their way through to the information required (remember the seven seconds: quite a long time actually). The brochure should be available in the waiting area of the practice office. It should be taken by a partner and left with a client after presentation. In other words, it should be used selectively.

A small practice cannot afford a large and expensively produced brochure, but there is no evidence that a modestly prepared, but informative document is any less effective. Indeed, some clients are wary of architectural firms projecting a high gloss image. The question in the client's mind is: 'Who is paying for this?'

19.3 Advertising

Advertising must be used with caution. Architects may now advertise their services (since 1986), but whether it is wise to do so depends on circumstances. There is still a general feeling that advertising is not a very professional thing to do. It may be that it is worthwhile for a small practice to advertise in the local newspaper or in a magazine devoted solely to the subject of the practice's principal expertise.

Looked at in a broad sense, advertising can be fruitful. That is the publicity a practice can get through the official opening ceremony of a prestigious building, or for assisting in fund raising for a charitable building. The practice can get a high profile by offering to organize foundation-laying or opening ceremonies, or by becoming involved in the design of the commemorative brochure. A relatively poor client might want some assistance in putting together a fund-raising leaflet and the practice could well donate the services of a member of staff to draw a suitable pen-and-ink perspective for the front. Advertising can also be carried out by setting up exhibitions at galas, meetings and locations such as libraries and museums provided the subject matter is local and topical.

19.4 Contacts

This is probably the best method of attracting work. In the most basic form, the architect looks to relatives to provide commissions and to provide introductions to other sources of work. This can be easily expanded to include friends and acquaintances. It is surprising how often one reads of old acquaintances achieving positions where they can be a useful source of work or further contacts. Those contacts are more a matter of luck than anything else, but the members of a practice can work to make contacts by joining clubs and organizations of a social, religious, sporting, civic or political nature. That is not to say that an architect should join a club for the sole purpose of getting work; there is nothing surer than that such an architect will not only get no work (his or her purpose will be obvious to all), but that there will be no other enjoyment either. Civic societies and conservation panels are a useful way of getting to know the local planning officers.

Some architects make a practice of frequenting a local pub where solicitors, accountants and insurance brokers gather and sometimes a new commission will be obtained in that way: not usually directly, but because when the solicitor is trying to think of an architect who can carry out a particular project on behalf of a client, the drinking companion may spring to mind.

19.5 Competitions

Competitions as a way of getting business should not be overlooked although it is not usually the first line of attack in this regard. Very often the winning of a competition can be the start of a successful career for a young architect. Whether an office will enter for a competition depends very much on the volume of work in the office and the enthusiasm of its members.

Members of the RIBA are prohibited from entering a competition which the RIBA has declared to be unacceptable. The RIBA has produced a guidance handbook to assist those intending to organize an architectural competition.[4]

There are various types of competition depending on the particular requirements of the promoters. In the first place, the competition may be single- or two-stage. In a single-stage competition the competitors are required to submit fairly complete small-scale drawings sufficient to describe their designs, but in a two-stage competition they are required to submit simple line drawings only in the first stage, indicating the broad outline of the scheme. From these entries, a short list is drawn up and the competitors on it are invited to submit a developed entry similar to the submissions in a single-stage competition. An obvious advantage of this method is that a relatively small number of entrants are expected to devote large amounts of time and effort. A variant is where the second stage consists of the competitors selected from the first stage together with a limited number of competitors specifically invited to submit schemes at the second stage. Persons invited to submit at the second stage only must be named in the conditions so that other competitors know the calibre of persons they have to beat.

Another type of competition is the 'ideas competition' which is intended to solve particular problems. This kind of competition is sometimes set by manufacturers or the professional press as well as by clients, in order to air specific issues or to encourage rising architectural talents.

Competitions may be open or limited. Open competitions are those which can be entered by any eligible architect. Sometimes clients will promote a limited competition and invite architects of established merit; or entrants may be limited to architects from within a particular geographic area. Architects who are invited to submit designs or who are successful in proceeding to a second stage receive an honorarium. All winners should receive an appropriate premium and the author of the design placed first should be appointed to carry out the work. The premium is then subsumed into the fee for the project.

The assessors must be approved by the President of the RIBA and they are debarred from competing; nor may an architect assessor take a commission to carry out the design in the event that no submitted entry is satisfactory.

19.6 Keeping clients

The very best way of building a practice is to keep every client who is attracted enough to commission work. There is nothing so comforting as repeat business. It shows that the client is really satisfied and it provides a solid base from which the practice can grow. Although such devices as regular mailshots, parties and regular correspondence on matters of interest help to show clients that their architect is concerned for their interests, the very best way of keeping clients is for the architect to give a first-class service.

References

(1) Sharp, D. (1991) *The Business of Architectural Practice*, 2nd edn, BSP Professional Books, Oxford.
(2) The Copyright, Designs and Patents Act 1988.
(3) *Architect's Journal*, 13 December 1989, p. 69.
(4) RIBA (1986) *Architectural Competitions: RIBA Code of Practice*.

Table of Cases

Index